A Preface to Conrad

Second Edition

Cedric Watts

Longman, London and New York

Longman Group UK Limited,
Longman House, Burnt Mill,
Harlow, Essex CM20 2JE, England
and Associated Companies throughout the world.

Published in the United States of America
by Longman Publishing, New York

First Edition © Longman Group Limited 1982
This Edition © Longman Group UK Limited 1993

First published 1982
Second Edition 1993

ISBN 0 582 08883 6

British Library Cataloguing-in-Publication Data

A catalogue record for this book is
available from the British Library

Library of Congress Cataloging-in-Publication Data

Watts, Cedric Thomas.
    A preface to Conrad / Cedric Watts. – 2nd ed.
        p.   cm. – (Preface books)
    Includes bibliographical references and index.
    ISBN 0-582-08883-6
    1. Conrad, Joseph, 1857–1924 – Criticism and interpretation.
    I. Title.
    PR6005.04Z924   1993
    823'.912 – dc20   92-24895
                                                               CIP

Set 90 in 10/11pt Baskerville
Printed in Hong Kong
WC/01

Contents

58404.

Contents

List of illustrations and maps

Foreword to the first edition

This authoritative volume sets forth both informed personal response and academic knowledge in the service of the student of the novels of Joseph Conrad. The views that this Polish novelist held constituted a unique aristocratic and artistic reading of human nature and its aims and philosophy: they have to some degree been heard from other Europeans or Americans in our century but before Conrad hardly at all in England. Cedric Watts, offering an account of his subject's beliefs and literary output, furnishes the reader at the same time with an introduction to much early twentieth-century thought and culture also.

The earlier sections that constitute Part One, whose rationale is explained on pp. 7–8, should be read as varied modes of access to Conrad's own writings. They govern the highly effective discussion of his art following in Part Two. Here, after a close commentary upon a number of passages from the novels in order to accustom the reader to the linguistic development and modernist overtones of a writer who came to English out of Polish and through French as his second language, follows a substantial essay on *Nostromo*. I know no more thorough and yet imaginative discussion of this novel than forms the crown of the whole Preface. How Conrad's varied experiences prepared him for writing that masterpiece is one of the principal purposes and accomplishments of Dr Watts's contribution to the series. This he does most helpfully after an extensive and intimate awareness of everything that Conrad left us, through which he speaks most powerfully to us today.

MAURICE HUSSEY
General Editor

Maurice Hussey died suddenly in June 1991. The Publishers and author would like to pay tribute to his wisdom, inspiration and friendship as Editor of Preface Books. He will be sadly missed.

Acknowledgements and editorial notes

Unless otherwise specified, quotations from Conrad's novels, tales, essays and autobiographical volumes are taken from the Collected Edition published by J.M. Dent & Sons, London, between 1946 and 1955. (This Collected Edition does not include all Conrad's works.)

In any quotation, a row of three points (. . .) indicates an ellipsis already present in the printed text, whereas a row of five points indicates an omission that I have made. When discussing *Nostromo*, I correct the novel's accentuation of Spanish names.

When preparing Part One of this book, I was helped by Jocelyn Baines' *Joseph Conrad: A Critical Biography*, Norman Sherry's *Conrad and His World* and Zdzisław Najder's *Joseph Conrad: A Chronicle*. In Parts One and Two I have drawn on my previous writings about Conrad, particularly *Conrad's 'Heart of Darkness': A Critical and Contextual Discussion*, *The Deceptive Text: An Introduction to Covert Plots* and *Joseph Conrad: A Literary Life*.

For advice and guidance, I am indebted to the late Maurice Hussey (the original General Editor of the series) and to R.A. Foakes, M.B. Hrynkiewicz-Moczulski, Barbara Koc, Susan Salters and Alan Sinfield. To Hans van Marle I owe special gratitude for his generously unstinting help in many matters concerning Conrad's life and works. Preparation of the second edition of my *Preface to Conrad* has enabled me, accordingly, to make various revisions; and I apologise to these advisors for any blemishes which, in spite of careful checking, may mar the new text. I thank all those reviewers, colleagues and students who made encouraging comments on the first edition and whose suggestions have helped me to bring the second edition up to date. I have added substantial new material to Chapters 7, 8 and 9, and to the Reference Section. Numerous minor changes have been made to the other parts of the book.

The author and Publishers are indebted to the following for permission to quote copyright material:

Cambridge University Press and the Estate of Joseph Conrad for extracts from Conrad's correspondence; the author's agent for an extract from *A Sort of Life* by Graham Greene (The Bodley Head, 1971). © 1971 Verdant SA.

Acknowledgements and editorial notes

For permission to reproduce photographs and illustrations, we are grateful to the following:

BBC Hulton Picture Library, frontispiece and page 39; the British Library, London, page 69; Lilly Library, Indiana University, Bloomington, page 98; The Mansell Collection, page 17; National Maritime Museum, London, page 23; The New York Public Library, Astor, Lenox and Tilden Foundations and the Trustees of the Joseph Conrad Estate, page 97; Mrs Eva Reichmann, page 45 (photograph from the Bodleian Library, Oxford); The Rosenbach Museum and Library, Philadelphia, pages 142–3. Cedric Watts holds the copyright of the photograph on page 34 and the maps on pages 174 and 175.

Abbreviations

With a few clearly-indicated exceptions, the quotations from Conrad's novels, tales, essays and autobiographical works are from the Collected Edition published by J.M. Dent & Sons (London, 1946–55).

AF	Joseph Conrad, *Almayer's Folly* (London: Dent, 1947).
Baines	Jocelyn Baines, *Joseph Conrad: A Critical Biography* (London: Weidenfeld and Nicolson, 1960).
BB	Joseph Conrad, *Letters to William Blackwood and David S. Meldrum*, ed. William Blackburn (Durham, N.C.: Duke University Press, 1958).
CL	*The Collected Letters of Joseph Conrad*, ed. Frederick R. Karl and Laurence Davies (Cambridge: Cambridge University Press. Vol. I, 1983; Vol. II, 1986; Vol. III, 1988; Vol. IV, 1990).
CN	Albert Guerard, *Conrad the Novelist* (Cambridge, Mass.: Harvard University Press, 1958).
CP	Avrom Fleishman, *Conrad's Politics* (Baltimore, Maryland: Johns Hopkins Press, 1967).
CWW	Norman Sherry, *Conrad's Western World* (London: Cambridge University Press, 1971).
EG	*Letters from Conrad, 1895 to 1924*, ed. Edward Garnett (London: Nonesuch Press, 1928).
HD	'Heart of Darkness' in *'Youth', 'Heart of Darkness' and 'The End of the Tether': Three Stories* (London: Dent, 1946).
KRZ	*Joseph Conrad: Centennial Essays*, ed. Ludwik Krzyżanowski (New York: Polish Institute of Arts and Sciences, 1960).
LCG	*Joseph Conrad's Letters to R.B. Cunninghame Graham*, ed. Cedric Watts (London: Cambridge University Press, 1969).
LE	*Joseph Conrad: Last Essays* (London: Dent, 1955).
LL	*Joseph Conrad: Life & Letters*, ed. G. Jean-Aubry, 2 vols (London: Heinemann, 1927).
N	Joseph Conrad: *Nostromo* (London: Dent, 1947).
Najder	*Conrad's Polish Background*, ed. Zdzisław Najder (London: Oxford University Press, 1964).
NLL	Joseph Conrad, *Notes on Life and Letters* (London: Dent, 1949).
NN	Joseph Conrad, *The Nigger of the 'Narcissus'* (London: Dent, 1950).

PR	Joseph Conrad, *A Personal Record* (London: Dent, 1946).
R	Joseph Conrad, *The Rescue* (London: Dent, 1949).
SL	Joseph Conrad, *The Shadow-Line* (London: Dent, 1950).
TH	Joseph Conrad, *Tales of Hearsay* (London: Dent, 1955).
TLAS	Joseph Conrad, *'Twixt Land and Sea: Three Tales* (London: Dent, 1947).
TU	Joseph Conrad, *Tales of Unrest* (London: Dent, 1947).
UWE	Joseph Conrad, *Under Western Eyes* (London: Dent, 1947).
V	Joseph Conrad, *Victory* (London: Dent, 1948).
Y	Joseph Conrad, *'Youth', 'Heart of Darkness' and 'The End of the Tether': Three Stories* (London: Dent, 1946).

The only legitimate basis of creative work lies in the courageous recognition of all the irreconcilable antagonisms that make our life so enigmatic, so burdensome, so fascinating, so dangerous – so full of hope.

(Joseph Conrad: letter to the *New York Times*, 2 August 1901)

Part One
The Writer and his Setting

Chronological table

| --- | --- |
1853	Crimean War begins.
1856 Marriage of Apollo Korzeniowski to Ewelina Bobrowska at Oratów in partitioned Poland.	Crimean War ends. Freud born.
1857 Birth of their son, Józef Teodor Konrad Korzeniowski (later to be known as Joseph Conrad).	Flaubert, *Madame Bovary.* Baudelaire, *Fleurs du mal.*
1859 Family moves to Żytomierz.	Dickens, *A Tale of Two Cities.* Darwin, *Origin of Species.*
1860–61	Dickens, *Great Expectations.*
1861 Apollo arrested in Warsaw for patriotic conspiracy.	
1862 Conrad's parents exiled to Vologda, Russia; he accompanies them.	Turgenev, *Fathers and Sons.*
1863 Family moves to Chernikhov.	Polish uprising.
1865 Death of Conrad's mother.	Birth of Kipling.
1866 Stays with uncle at Nowochwastów.	Dostoyevsky, *Crime and Punishment.*
1869 Death of Apollo Korzeniowski.	Tolstoy, *War and Peace.*

1870	Taught by Adam Pulman in Kraków.	Dickens dies. Lenin born.
1871	Also taught by Izydor Kopernicki.	Dostoyevsky, *The Devils*.
1872	Resolves to go to sea.	George Eliot, *Middlemarch*.
1874	Leaves Poland for Marseille to become a seaman.	Hardy, *Far from the Madding Crowd*.
1875	Sails Atlantic in *Mont-Blanc*.	Thomas Mann born.
1876	Serves as steward of *Saint-Antoine*.	Death of George Sand.
1877	Possibly involved in smuggling arms.	Tolstoy, *Anna Karenina*.
1878	Suicide attempt. Later enters British Merchant Navy.	Afghan War. Congress of Berlin.
1879	Serves on *Duke of Sutherland*.	Ibsen, *A Doll's House*.
1880	Sails to Australia in *Loch Etive*.	Dostoyevsky, *Brothers Karamazov*.
1881	Second mate of *Palestine*.	Death of Dostoyevsky and Carlyle.
1882	Storm-damaged *Palestine* repaired.	Birth of James Joyce and Virginia Woolf.
1883	Shipwrecked when *Palestine* sinks.	Marx dies. Mussolini born.
1885	Sails to Calcutta in *Tilkhurst*.	Birth of D.H. Lawrence.
1886	Takes British nationality; qualifies as captain.	Cunninghame Graham becomes MP.

3

1887	Sails to Java in *Highland Forest*.	'Bloody Sunday': Graham arrested.
1888	Master of ship *Otago*.	Birth of T.S. Eliot.
1889	Settles in London, writing *Almayer's Folly*.	Hitler born.
1890	Works in Belgian Congo.	Ibsen, *Hedda Gabler*.
1891	Officer of *Torrens* (until 1893).	Hardy, *Tess of the d'Urbervilles*.
1894	*Almayer's Folly* accepted by Unwin.	Stevenson dies.
1895	*Almayer's Folly* published. Meets Jessie George.	Crane, *The Red Badge of Courage*.
1896	*An Outcast of the Islands*. Marries Jessie George.	William Morris dies; Scott Fitzgerald born.
1897	*The Nigger of the 'Narcissus'*. Corresponds with Cunninghame Graham.	Queen Victoria's Diamond Jubilee.
1898	*Tales of Unrest*. Collaboration with Ford Madox Hueffer. Birth of son (Borys).	War between Spain and United States.
1899	'Heart of Darkness' serialised. Serialisation of *Lord Jim* begins.	Boer War (until 1902).
1900	*Lord Jim* (book). J.B. Pinker becomes Conrad's agent.	Wilde, Crane and Nietzsche die.
1901	*The Inheritors* (co-author Hueffer)	Death of Queen Victoria.
1902	*Youth* volume.	Gorky, *The Lower Depths*.

1903	*Typhoon* volume. *Romance* (co-author Hueffer).	Panama secedes from Colombia. James, *The Ambassadors.*
1904	*Nostromo* (serial and book).	Russo-Japanese War (until 1905).
1905	*One Day More* (play) fails.	Wells, *Kipps.*
1906	*The Mirror of the Sea* (with Hueffer). Birth of second son (John).	Ibsen dies. Samuel Beckett born.
1907	*The Secret Agent.*	Birth of W.H. Auden.
1908	*A Set of Six* (tales).	Bennett, *Old Wives' Tale.*
1909	Quarrels with Hueffer.	Death of Swinburne.
1910	'The Secret Sharer'. Conrad has breakdown after completing *Under Western Eyes.*	Freud becomes internationally famous around this time.
1911	*Under Western Eyes* published.	William Golding born.
1912	*A Personal Record. 'Twixt Land and Sea* (tales). *Chance* serialised.	First Balkan War. Sinking of *Titanic.*
1913	Meets Bertrand Russell.	Second Balkan War.
1914–18		First World War.
1914	Book of *Chance* has large sales.	
1915	*Within the Tides* (tales); *Victory.*	Lawrence, *The Rainbow.*
1916	*The Shadow-Line* serialised.	Henry James dies.
1917	*The Shadow-Line* (book).	Russian Revolution.

5

1918	Borys Conrad wounded in war.	Armistice. Polish Republic restored.
1919	*The Arrow of Gold.*	Treaty of Versailles.
1920	*The Rescue* published, twenty-four years after its commencement.	Poles rout Russian invaders. League of Nations created.
1921	*Notes on Life and Letters.*	Irish Free State created.
1922	*The Secret Agent* (play) fails.	Eliot, *The Waste Land*; Joyce, *Ulysses.*
1923	Visits United States to acclamation. *The Rover.*	Yeats wins Nobel Prize.
1924	Declines knighthood. Dies of heart attack; buried at Canterbury.	Ramsay MacDonald becomes Prime Minister.
1925	*Tales of Hearsay*; *Suspense.*	Eliot, *Poems 1909–25.*
1926	*Last Essays.*	Kafka, *The Castle.*
1927	*Joseph Conrad: Life & Letters.*	Woolf, *To the Lighthouse.*

1 Biographical background

The double man

Since August 1924, Conrad's body has been dissolving beneath the granite chippings in a public cemetery at Canterbury. 'As to the soul', he once remarked, 'You and I, cher ami, are too honest to talk of what we know nothing about.' His imagination, however, can be said to be more alive than ever before, as more and more readers have come to enjoy and respect his works; and one of the main reasons for this continuing vitality is that he was a double man.

'Homo duplex has in my case more than one meaning', he wrote to a Polish friend. 'Homo duplex': the double man. The phrase will serve as a theme for this book. As an approach to Conrad's complexity, it is helpful to imagine that if any god presides over Conrad's best work, it is the god Janus. Janus is the two-headed god: he looks in opposite ways at the same time; he presides over paradox; and he is the patron of janiform texts.

Let us imagine that we could travel back in time to call on Conrad in 1903, when he was writing *Nostromo*. We would see a middle-aged man of less than average height; square-shouldered, short-necked, almost stocky in build; dark hair neatly brushed back, a dark beard tidily trimmed; high cheek-bones, with penetrating eyes somewhat hooded at the corners by drooping lids. Expecting visitors, he has taken care to dress in formal gentlemanly style: a smart suit, waistcoat, stiffly starched collar and cuffs, a monocle. His manner would be elaborately courteous, yet at the same time reserved and watchful; outwardly composed, yet sensitive, touchy: a tactless political or literary reference could draw a cold stare of rage or a snarl of exasperation. He could be capable, too, if we won his trust, of impetuous, passionate agreement, seizing our hands in his to make his point, speaking rapidly in a fluent English with a marked Polish accent (so that 'these' and 'those' became 'deeza' and 'dohza'), misplacing stresses and substituting French phrases when the English did not come rapidly enough; but happy to reminisce about his many years of voyaging.

Already some meanings of his phrase 'homo duplex' would suggest themselves. Conrad was a patriotic Pole who became a British citizen. He was 'a Polish nobleman cased in British tar'. He was a seaman who laboriously rose to the peak of his career as a captain in the Merchant Navy, yet abandoned that career to try his luck as a creative writer. His manner retained both an aristocratic air of command and the neurotic intensity of a ruthlessly dedicated artist. To his Uncle Tadeusz, he was a mixture of dreamer and practical man; to Cunninghame Graham, his mind seemed 'a strange compact of the conflicting qualities'; and, to Edward Garnett, he seemed 'so masculinely keen yet so femininely sensitive'.

A survey of his career from its Polish origins will help us to understanding the duplicity of his nature and the janiformity of his works.

Poland

'. . . . . We had once more to murmur "*Væ Victis*" and count the cost in sorrow. Not that we were ever very good at calculating, either, in prosperity or in adversity. That's a lesson we could never learn, to the great exasperation of our enemies who have bestowed upon us the epithet of Incorrigible . . .'

The speaker was of Polish nationality, that nationality not so much alive as surviving, which persists in thinking, breathing, speaking, hoping, and suffering in its grave, railed in by a million of bayonets and triple-sealed with the seals of three great empires . . . . .

Patriotism [is] a somewhat discredited sentiment, because the delicacy of our humanitarians regards it as a relic of barbarism.

(Joseph Conrad: 'Prince Roman'; *TH*, p. 29)

Poland was and is a strongly patriotic country: its people pride themselves on the nation's liberal traditions, its cultural riches, and their heroism down the ages in defence of their homeland. To the Western imagination, there is something romantic, tragic and also quixotic about Poland. Romantic, for it is the birthplace of Chopin and of celebrated defiant patriots like Prince Roman Sanguszko, the poet Mickiewicz and the warrior Kościuszko; quixotic and tragic, because its patriotism has burnt all the more brightly for its oppression by stronger, more powerful neighbours.

In the 1970s, during a visit to Poland, I spoke to a lady who had lived through the Second World War and who spoke of the time when Poland might be a free nation once more. 'And when will that be?', I asked. 'Who knows?', she replied; 'We outlived the German barbarians, and we shall outlive the Russian barbarians too.' A scholar told me the apocryphal story of a noted atheist who had recently been seen, apparently at prayer, in one of the Roman Catholic churches. When a neighbour said, 'What are *you* doing here?', the man replied fiercely: 'I may be an atheist, but I am also a Pole.' On another occasion there, a student reminded me in an undertone that for many years after the war, in spite of Conrad's popularity, certain of his works were unavailable in Polish – notably *Under Western Eyes* and 'Autocracy and War', which had prophesied that the Russian Revolution would be followed by further tyranny. Every so often, as I walked down the main streets of Warsaw, I could see candles glimmering by plaques on the walls; and the plaques commemorated the patriots who had been executed there or who had died fighting at those places during the wartime uprisings.

If Conrad could have revisited Poland then, in the 1970s, he would have found wearisomely familiar the fact that Poland was part of the Russian empire; but he would also have found encouragingly familiar the stubborn spirit of independence and the hunger for individual and national freedom which remained alive among many of its people. His essays 'The Crime of Partition' and 'Autocracy and War' (both in *Notes on Life and Letters*) celebrate that spirit and condemn sardonically the nation's oppressors – a condemnation that subsequent and prior events so fully vindicated. In 1989, thanks in large part to Lech Wałęsa and the Solidarity movement, that spirit triumphed; and Poland became not only the first Eastern European nation to break free from Marxist imperialism but also the catalyst in a process which enabled democratic liberty to burgeon in numerous formerly subjugated states.

In the late eighteenth century, Poland was one of the more liberal of the European nations, having an elective monarchy and a loosely federal administration. But in 1772, at the instigation of Frederick the Great, one-third of Poland was seized and divided by Prussia, Austria and Russia. A second 'Partition' followed in 1793; Russia seized more land. Then Tadeusz Kościuszko, who had once fought for the American Army in the War of Independence, organised an insurrection: under his leadership the Poles rose against the Russians and defeated them at Racławice; but eventually the insurrection was crushed and Kościuszko captured. In the Third Partition (1795), the whole of the country was engulfed by the three autocracies: Poland vanished from the map of Europe, though its patriots kept up resistance and led revolts in 1830 and 1863. After German defeat in the First World War, and in the wake of the Russian Revolution, an independent Poland was re-established in 1918.

The Polish Republic, however, was short-lived. In 1919 Conrad had astutely prophesied of Germany and Russia: 'The old partners in "the Crime" [of Partition] are not likely to forgive their victim its inconvenient and almost shocking obstinacy in keeping alive' (*NLL*, p. 121). Twenty years later, following the signing of the

9

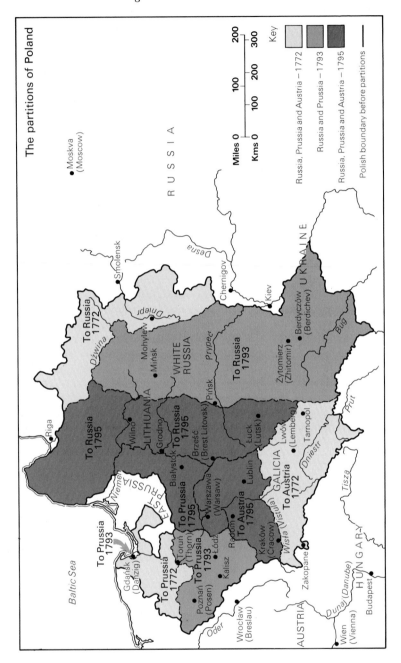

The partitions of Poland

Molotov–Ribbentrop Pact, whereby the USSR conspired with Hitler's Germany, the Germans carried out their *Blitzkrieg* against Poland with tanks, stukas and paratroops. The ill-equipped Polish troops fought bravely but in vain: poignant spotty newsreels of the time show Polish cavalry charging – and being mown down by – the invaders' tanks; and, while the Germans thus engulfed most of Poland from the west, the Russian army, in compliance with the pact with Hitler, seized territory in the east. Many of the Poles, exiled but undefeated, made their way to England, where, in the RAF, the Navy and the Army, they continued their struggle, fighting and dying at Tobruk, Monte Cassino, Arnhem and elsewhere. In conquered Warsaw there were heroic but doomed revolts: the Ghetto uprising, by the Jews against their exterminators in 1943, and the general uprising of 1944, when for two months, contesting every street, every block of houses, the men and women of the Polish resistance withstood the might of German tanks, dive-bombers and heavy artillery. By the end of that second uprising, during which the Russian Army had cynically halted on the outskirts of Warsaw, much of the city was in ruins, its palaces and churches reduced to rubble. Hitler ordered its total destruction, and with dynamite and fire the troops systematically obliterated street after street. Again, a Conradian prophecy was fulfilled, for in 1905 the author had declared:

> Germany . . . . . is a powerful and voracious organisation, full of unscrupulous self-confidence . . . . . The era of wars so eloquently denounced by the old Republicans as the peculiar blood guilt of dynastic ambitions is by no means over yet. They will be fought out differently, with lesser frequency, with an increased bitterness and the savage tooth-and-claw obstinacy of a struggle for existence . . . . .
>
> Civilization has done its little best by our sensibilities for whose growth it is responsible. It has managed to remove the sights and sounds of battlefields away from our doorsteps. But it cannot be expected to achieve the feat always and under every variety of circumstance. Some day it must fail, and we shall have then a wealth of appallingly unpleasant sensations brought home to us with painful intimacy.

Left: *Among writers of fiction, Conrad was the most incisive commentator on imperialism. This map suggests one of the reasons for his preoccupation. 'As an act of mere conquest the best excuse for the partition lay simply in the fact that it happened to be possible; there was the plunder and there was the opportunity to get hold of it.' (NLL, p.115.)*

..... Germany's attitude proves that no peace for the earth can be found in the expansion of material interests .....

(*NLL*, pp. 104–5, 110, 113)

On the defeat of Germany, Poland became part of the empire of the USSR, controlled by a Communist government subservient to Moscow and unfettered by such inconveniences as democratic elections. Nevertheless, massive reconstruction took place: with the aid of old prints, maps and photographs, Warsaw was slowly rebuilt. Even the Old City, with its alleys and market-square and steeply-roofed houses, was restored as an exact visual replica of the ancient centre the Nazis had destroyed; even the Royal Palace was reconstructed stone by stone – a monument to political inconsistency and Polish indomitability.

A man who had fought with the resistance told me that during the war, Conrad's novel *Lord Jim* was regarded almost as a Bible, a moral support, by some of the Polish combatants. J. J. Szczepański, too, recalled: 'For us ..... Conrad was topical as never before. His books turned into collections of practical maxims for men fighting alone and in darkness.' For many Poles, as for some Conradian heroes, the choice lay between a doomed struggle which entailed moral victory, or acquiescence which entailed moral failure. After the war, Conrad was officially disapproved by the régime: Jan Kott and other Marxist critics attacked his work for being negative, reactionary, defeatist. Kott declared:

> Conradian fidelity to oneself is the fidelity of slaves, for a slave is he who obeys the lord whom he despises, and cares only about his inner rectitude.

In the 1970s, however, with the official translation into Polish of his collected works, the régime seemed to have bestowed its blessing; but there were tell-tale omissions. These omissions were 'The Crime of Partition', 'Autocracy and War', 'A Note on the Polish Problem', the 'Author's Note' to *Under Western Eyes*, part of the 'Author's Note' to *Notes on Life and Letters*, and 'The Censor of Plays'. Among those writings, Conrad claims that post-revolutionary Russia will be as tyrannical as Tsarist Russia and that censorship is a contemptible weapon of tyranny. By censoring his claims, the Marxist authorities neatly verified them. As the Polish people regained their liberty, Conrad's works at last became fully available again. And throughout the nation's long struggles for freedom, Conrad's father, Apollo Korzeniowski, had remained alive in memory as a patriot.

Apollo Korzeniowski was a member of the land-owning gentry. He had little aptitude for practical, business matters, though he worked for a time as an estate manager; his real interests were literature and Polish politics. He wrote comedies and mystically patriotic poems, and translated works by Shakespeare, Dickens, Victor Hugo and Alfred de Vigny. In 1856 he married Ewelina (or Ewa, pronounced Āva) Bobrowska, a young woman of another prosperous land-owning family; and their only child, Józef Teodor Konrad Nałęcz Korzeniowski, was born in December of the following year. To commemorate his son's baptism, Apollo composed a poem which is dated 'in the 85th year of Russian tyranny' and which ends thus:

> My child, my son – tell yourself that you are without land, without love, without homeland, without humanity – so long as Poland, our Mother, is enslaved.

There is no doubt that the Christian name 'Konrad' (by which the boy's father referred to him, and which, anglicised, was to serve as the novelist's pseudonym) was chosen for its patriotic literary associations. In Adam Mickiewicz's drama *Dziady* (*Forefathers' Eve*, 1832), the hero changes his name, formerly Gustavus, when he awakens to a mystical sense of his power to free Poland from Muscovite tyranny: he declares in Latin, 'Gustavus obiit . . . . . Hic natus est Conradus' – 'Gustavus is dead . . . . . Here Conrad is born.' Furthermore, in Mickiewicz's poem of historic legend, *Konrad Wallenrod* (1828), the eponymous hero, though leader of the Teutonic crusaders, proves to be a Lithuanian who had cunningly gained that leadership in order to direct the German army into an utterly disastrous campaign against Lithuania. The poem thus expresses an idea which would later so frequently permeate Conrad's fiction: the seeming paradox that loyalty may entail treachery. Here loyalty to one's homeland is seen by Wallenrod as justifying treachery to one's trusting followers; the patriotic end justifies the ruthlessly duplicitous means.

In Warsaw, Apollo became one of the leaders of the 'Reds', the more extreme of the two main patriotic parties: it advocated the liberation of the serfs as well as national independence. On his initiative was formed the underground committee which was eventually to launch the bloodily suppressed insurrection of 1863. But in 1861 Apollo was arrested and imprisoned; both he and Ewa were sentenced to exile for their subversive activities, and the four-year-old Conrad accompanied them on the bitter journey to the dreary Russian province of Vologda. This period of exile sapped Ewa's health: after her return, ailing with advanced tuberculosis, she died in 1865 at the age of thirty-two.

Understandably, Apollo became a brooding, melancholy figure, possessed by a rather morbid religiosity. He wrote:

I have kept my eyes fixed on the Cross and by that means fortified my fainting soul and reeling brain. The sacred days of agony have passed, and I resume my ordinary life, a little more broken but with breath still in me, still alive. But the little orphan is always at my side, and I never forget my anxiety for him . . . . . He grows up as though in a monastic cell. For the *memento mori* we have the grave of our dear one.

(*LL*, I, p. 16)

Even before then, at the age of five, that 'little orphan' had acquired a proudly self-conscious sense of social and political destiny, to judge from Conrad's earliest extant piece of writing, an inscription on the back of a photograph:

To my beloved Grandma who helped me send cakes to my poor Daddy in prison – grandson, Pole, Catholic, nobleman – 6 July 1863 – Konrad.

(Najder, p. 8)

After Ewa's death, Apollo attempted to undertake Conrad's education himself, teaching him some French, for example; and Conrad came to know his father's work as a translator into Polish of Hugo's *Les Travailleurs de la mer* and of Shakespeare's *Two Gentlemen of Verona*. But eventually the dispirited father, stricken with tuberculosis as Ewa had been, was prostrate, confined to a sick-room, attended by nuns. Many years later, Conrad recalled the atmosphere:

The air around me was all piety, resignation, and silence.
I don't know what would have become of me if I had not been a reading boy. My prep finished I would have had nothing to do but sit and watch the awful stillness of the sick room flow out through the closed door and coldly enfold my scared heart. I suppose that in a futile childish way I would have gone crazy. But I was a reading boy.

(*NLL*, p. 168)

On 26 May 1869 Apollo died, and Conrad became thus an eleven-year-old orphan. He followed his father's coffin in the funeral procession through the streets of Kraków – a procession that was also a huge nationalist demonstration.

What I saw with my own eyes was the public funeral, the cleared streets, the hushed crowds; but I understood perfectly well that this was a manifestation of the national spirit seizing a worthy occasion. That bareheaded mass of work people, youths of the University, women at the windows, school-boys on the pavement, could have known nothing positive about him except the fame of his fidelity to the one guiding emotion in their hearts.

(*PR*, p. viii)

Already, then, by the age of eleven, Conrad knew bitterly well many of the themes which were later to be so prominent in his writings. The themes of loneliness; of tragic death; of Polish nationalism; of self-sacrifice for a noble cause; of beleaguered solidarity. And he could also have sensed some paradoxes, too: that loyalty may entail subversion or betrayal; that there may be conflicts between the claims of honour, the claims of the law and the claims of affection; and that works of literature may awaken us to reality, yet also offer us an escape and refuge from it. He knew the power of words over flesh and blood: their power to heal or kill.

Conrad's uncle, Tadeusz Bobrowski, became his guardian. Bobrowski was wealthy, astute, and unfailingly conscientious in his guardianship, which virtually extended until his death a quarter of a century later. In letter upon letter, even long after Conrad had left Poland, he gave detailed advice and exhortations, always trying to steer Conrad towards the path of diligent work and practical attainment, and away from introspection, inconsistency and speculative schemes. Initially, he provided Conrad with a tutor and enrolled the boy in a Kraków school. Gradually the young Conrad became stubbornly determined to go to sea; and in 1872 the pupil and the tutor, Adam Pulman, journeyed on a long tour of Switzerland, during which Pulman was charged with the task of dissuading Conrad from his ambition to become a sailor. The climax of the argument, as Conrad recalled it many years later, was strangely oblique:

We sat down by the side of the road to continue the argument begun half a mile or so before. I am certain it was an argument because I remember perfectly how my tutor argued and how without the power of reply I listened with my eyes fixed obstinately on the ground. A stir on the road made me look up – and then I saw my unforgettable Englishman . . . . . He marched rapidly towards the east (attended by a hang-dog Swiss guide) with the mien of an ardent and fearless traveller . . . . . His calves exposed to the public gaze and to the tonic air of high altitudes, dazzled the beholder by the splendour of their marble-like condition and their rich tones of young ivory. He was the leader of a small caravan. The light of a headlong, exalted satisfaction with the world of men and the scenery of mountains illumined his clean-cut, very red face, his short, silver-white whiskers, his innocently eager and triumphant eyes. In passing he cast a glance of kindly curiosity and a friendly gleam of big, shiny teeth towards the man and the boy sitting like dusty tramps by the roadside, with a modest knapsack lying at their feet. His white calves twinkled sturdily, the uncouth Swiss guide with a surly mouth stalked like an unwilling bear at his elbow; a small train of three mules followed in single file the lead of this inspiring enthusiast . . . . .

The enthusiastic old Englishman had passed – and the argument went on. What reward could I expect from such a life at the end of my years, either in ambition, honour or conscience? An unanswerable question. But I felt no longer crushed. Then our eyes met and a genuine emotion was visible in his as well as in mine. The end came all at once. He picked up the knapsack suddenly and got on to his feet.

'You are an incorrigible, hopeless Don Quixote. That's what you are.'

(*PR*, pp. 40–1, 43–4)

In this passage from *A Personal Record* (1912), Conrad is recalling events of long ago; his memory, like anyone else's, is fallible; and, like any imaginative writer, he is imparting to his recollections a dramatic heightening and an increase in thematic order. It is admirably vivid writing, with a gently ironic humour and an eye for the quietly absurd or mildly ridiculous, and with a characteristic deviousness in the narrative sequence. The argument over Conrad's apparently quixotic determination to go to sea is clinched not so much by logic as by the incursion of an English reincarnation of Don Quixote – almost as though a tutelary deity in disguise had crossed the scene. And indeed there *was* something quixotically arbitrary or irrational about Conrad's choice of career. His country lacked a navy; there were no naval connections in his family; and, in those days of sailing ships, when vessels were commonly lost at sea in storms and gales, to choose a career which promised hard knocks and mortal risks could well seem foolhardy. There is nothing uncommon, however, about a youthful desire to travel the world and see exotic places; and Conrad had probably been influenced by his youthful reading, which included the maritime adventure tales by Captain Marryat and Fenimore Cooper, as well as travel books such as McClintock's *Voyage of the 'Fox'*. Poland could have seemed psychologically oppressive after his bitter childhood experiences. Furthermore, as he was legally a Russian citizen and the son of a political convict, Conrad was liable to conscription in the Russian Army for up to twenty-five years. There is no certain explanation of his ambition; and, as he himself remarked, 'The part of the inexplicable should be allowed for in appraising the conduct of men in a world where no explanation is final' (*PR*, p. 35). Whatever the

Conrad as a young man, around the time of his departure for Marseille.

reason, in October 1874 his uncle and his weeping grandmother saw the sixteen-year-old Conrad board the train, alone, for Marseille: the start of a journey to the Mediterranean, and thence to the oceans of the world; to England, and, after many years, to a plot of earth at Canterbury.

Marseille

After the sombre, death-haunted years in Poland came the utter contrast of southern France with its long hot summers and the crowded colourful streets. Conrad's four years in Marseille were probably the most varied and adventurous of his whole career, though death hovered even in this lively Arcadia. Marseille in the 1870s was both a bustling, thriving port and a cosmopolitan city, with its theatres, operas and salons, its fashionable or bohemian restaurants, its brothels and waterfront taverns. Conrad received a generous financial allowance from his uncle, but he repeatedly overspent it wildly on a very full social life. It was here, almost certainly, that he came to know the plays of Scribe and Sardou, the operas of Meyerbeer and Offenbach; his later writings indicate that he had an intense love-affair, and at his age it would be surprising if he had

17

not; and he evidently made friends easily, being popular with aristocrats and artists, sea-captains and pilots.

> The very first whole day I ever spent on salt water was by invitation, in a big half-decked pilot-boat, cruising under close reefs on the lookout, in misty, blowing weather, for the sails of ships and the smoke of steamers rising out there, beyond the slim and tall Planier lighthouse cutting the line of the windswept horizon with a white perpendicular stroke. They were hospitable souls, these sturdy Provençal seamen . . . . . Their sea-tanned faces, whiskered or shaved, lean or full, with the intent wrinkled sea-eyes of the pilot-breed, and here and there a thin gold loop at the lobe of a hairy ear, bent over my sea-infancy . . . . . And I have been invited to sit in more than one tall, dark house of the old town at their hospitable board, had the *bouillabaisse* ladled out into a thick plate by their high-voiced, broad-browed wives, talked to their daughters – thick-set girls, with pure profiles, glorious masses of black hair arranged with complicated art, dark eyes, and dazzlingly white teeth.
>
> (*PR*, pp. 123–4)

Conrad's love of the sea stood him in good stead with these pilots, and in course of time he was in demand as a pilot himself; and his aristocratic 'drawing-room manner' gave him entry to the salons of the wealthy and fashionable – of Monsieur Delestang, for example, 'a frozen, mummified Royalist', and Delestang's imperious wife, who reminded Conrad of Dickens' Lady Dedlock. Bohemian companions included Frétigny the sculptor, who later appeared as Prax in *The Arrow of Gold*, and Clovis Hugues, a left-wing journalist and poet who had shot and killed an opponent in a duel. Many of the experiences of these years were to find their way – sometimes deceptively transformed – into the pages not only of the late novel, *The Arrow of Gold*, but also of the autobiographical *The Mirror of the Sea* and *A Personal Record*, while sunny Provence and the Mediterranean provided the location for *The Rover*.

It is certain that during this period Conrad made his first oceanic voyages on sailing-ships: at first as a passenger, then as an apprentice or 'boy', then as a steward. He voyaged to the West Indies in the *Mont-Blanc* ('She leaked fully, generously, over-flowingly, all over – like a basket', he remarked later) and subsequently in the *Saint-Antoine*. During the *Saint-Antoine* period he had his sole glimpse of South America, probably going ashore briefly in Venezuela; and it is quite possible that, as he later hinted, he was engaged in smuggling arms, perhaps to insurgents in Colombia. The first mate was Dominic (or Dominique) Cervoni, bold, broad-chested and vain: 'His thick black moustaches, curled every morning with hot tongs by the barber at the corner of the quay, seemed to hide a perpetual smile': a character later to be reincarnated as the fictional Nostromo and as the Dominic of *The Arrow of Gold*. In *The Mirror of the Sea*, Conrad says that he had joined Dominic Cervoni in a syndicate which smuggled arms from Marseille along the coast to Spanish Carlists, the Royalists who supported the Pretender, Don Carlos. According to Conrad, the syndicate was betrayed to the authorities by Dominic's nephew, César; their vessel, the *Tremolino*, was pursued by coastguards; the crew wrecked her to elude the pursuers, and during the crisis Dominic hurled his nephew (who happened to be weighted with stolen gold) to death in the sea. As common sense rightly warns us, this last past of the yarn is pure invention: César lived on to a ripe old age and was not, it appears, related to Dominic; but there is ample evidence that Conrad was indeed involved in a smuggling venture that ended disastrously during a run of bad luck which, we now know, culminated in his attempt at suicide.

His long-suffering Uncle Tadeusz wrote to a Polish friend:

> I was absolutely certain that he was already somewhere in the Antipodes, when suddenly, amidst all the business at the Kiev Fair in 1878, I received a telegram: 'Conrad blessé envoyez argent – arrivez.' ['Conrad wounded send money – come.']
>
> (Najder, p. 176)

Conrad's troubles had begun when he had found that as an alien he was barred by law from French ships; nor did he have a consular permit for service at the port.

> While still in possession of the 3,000 fr[ancs] sent to him for the voyage, he met his former Captain, Mr Duteil, who persuaded him to participate in some enterprise on the coasts of Spain – some kind of contraband! He invested 1,000 fr. in it and made over 400 which pleased them greatly so that on the second occasion he put in all he had – and lost the lot.

Heavily in debt, he borrowed a further 800 francs from a friend, went to Villefranche to try to join an American squadron, but failed; and finally in desperation gambled the money away at Monte Carlo.

> Having managed his affairs so excellently he returns to Marseilles and one fine evening invites his friend the creditor to tea, and before his arrival attempts to take his life with a revolver. (Let this detail remain between us, as I have been telling everyone that he was wounded in a duel . . . . .) The bullet goes durch und

durch [straight through] near his heart without damaging any vital organ.

Bobrowski paid the debts, 'influenced by considerations of our national honour' as well as by familial loyalty, while Conrad recovered from the deep wound in the chest.

> My study of the Individual has convinced me that he is not a bad boy, only one who is extremely sensitive, conceited, reserved, and in addition excitable. In short I found in him all the defects of the Nałęcz family. He is able and eloquent . . . . . very popular with his captains and also with the sailors . . . . . In his ideas and discussions he is ardent and original . . . . . and is an imperialist. De gustibus non est disputandum [it is pointless to argue about tastes] . . . . .
>
> (Najder, pp. 176–8)

Finally, Bobrowski agreed that Conrad should join the British Merchant Navy ('where there are no such formalities as in France'); so that, four years after leaving Poland, the young voyager arrived at Lowestoft on the coal freighter *Mavis*.

England and the Merchant Navy

In his letters to his nephew, Uncle Tadeusz repeatedly offered warnings that Conrad was a double man, an inheritor of a janiform personality. On the father's side, Tadeusz claimed, he had inherited an unstable temperament, changeable, imaginative, impatient, impractical; while, on the mother's side, he had inherited powers of patient diligence and steady application. Conrad's career as a seaman would illustrate this dual-nature. He never stayed on any vessel for long, sometimes because of quarrels with his captains, sometimes for no evident reason (and to the disappointment of the owners); yet, on the other hand, his zealous endeavours took him to the pinnacle of a naval career by the age of thirty.

His beginnings in England could not have been more humble. He obtained a berth in a small coaster, the barquentine *Skimmer of the Sea* (also known as *Skimmer of the Seas*), which, belying her romantic name, carried coal from Newcastle to Lowestoft; and Conrad's wage was recorded as one shilling per month, when even the ship's boy received twenty-five shillings. Two and a half years after Conrad left her, she foundered at sea, drowning some of his former shipmates; and in one of his letters he was to look back nostalgically:

> 'Skimmer of the Seas' what a pretty name! But she is gone and took a whole lot of good fellows away with her into the other world! Comme c'est vieux tout ça! [How long ago it all seems!]

In that craft I began to learn English from East Coast chaps each built as though to last for ever, and coloured like a Christmas card. Tan and pink – gold hair and blue eyes with that Northern straight-away-there look! Twenty two years ago!

(*LCG*, pp. 74–5)

After *Skimmer*, he soon found a berth as an ordinary seaman in the wool clipper *Duke of Sutherland*, which plied between London and Sydney; and, during the subsequent sixteen years, with numerous voyages on ships ranging from elegant three-masters to rusty tramp-steamers, he rose in rank – third mate, second mate, skipper. Repeatedly in the great ocean-going sailing-ships he made the run between England, Bombay and Australia; gradually, struggling with the wayward English language, he learned the rules of seamanship and passed the successive inquisitorial examinations; and, in 1886, he not only gained his master's certificate but also took British nationality. Tadeusz Bobrowski was delighted by the double achievement: he had long urged his nephew to relinquish Russian citizenship and become 'a free citizen of a free country'. Ford Madox Ford, subsequently Conrad's literary collaborator, emphasises Britain's reputation in Europe as a land of liberty:

> During the last century if you went down to Tilbury Dock you would see families of Jewish-Poland emigrants landing. As soon as they landed they fell on their hands and knees and kissed the soil of the land of Freedom . . . . . England of Conrad's early vision: an immense power standing for liberty and hospitality for refugees; vigilant over a pax Britannica that embraced the world.
>
> (*Joseph Conrad*, 1924, pp. 57–8)

If Conrad had ever found himself amid a crowd of soil-kissing immigrants at Tilbury Dock he would probably have picked his way through the crowd, wearing an expression of patrician distaste at such emotionalism; but there is no doubt that Ford's note of enthusiasm for Britain accorded well enough with Conrad's feelings. Culturally, Conrad's upbringing had been anglophile; as recently as the 1850s, the British at Crimea had fought the Poles' most hated oppressors, the Russians; and intermittently Conrad the writer was to offer warm tributes to that 'liberty, which can only be found under the English flag'. And it was in the service of the 'pax Britannica that embraced the world' that Conrad repeatedly voyaged across the globe: to Bombay, Singapore or Melbourne. This was the last great era of sail, of the full-rigged iron sailing ships like the *Tilkhurst* that carried jute from Calcutta to Dundee (Conrad was her second mate in 1886; she endured until 1923), and of majestic clippers like the *Torrens* that carried wool from Adelaide to London.

21

He came to know the foaming seas and hot sunsets, the storms and calms which later he was to celebrate in his books; he came to know Bombay, Singapore, Celebes and Borneo, regions which provide settings for *Lord Jim* and the early novels; and he became familiar with those borderline areas of human experience where the civilised meets the primitive and the familiar meets the alien. He also gained an intimate knowledge of work – monotonous, exhausting work as a crewman; of the worries of responsibility as a mate or captain; the fears of storm and fog at sea; or even the fear of fear.

Of the risks and frustrations that Conrad encountered, the *Palestine* voyage (on which he was second mate) provides some of the best examples. The *Palestine*, an old and decrepit barque with an appropriate captain, left Newcastle for Bangkok with a cargo of coal, but after three hundred miles she lost her sails in a gale, sprang a leak, and returned to England for repairs, which took eight months. At the second attempt, the vessel voyaged from September to March, reaching the Bangka Strait off Sumatra, before disaster struck. In the words of the Court of Inquiry:

> Smoke was discovered issuing from the coals . . . . . Water was thrown over them until the smoke abated, the boats were lowered, water placed in them. On the thirteenth some coals were thrown overboard, about four tons, and more water poured down the hold. On the fourteenth, the hatches being on but not battened down, the decks blew up fore and aft as far as the poop . . . . . About 11 p.m. the vessel was a mass of fire, and all hands got into the boats, three in number.
>
> (Official report)

That was in March 1883. More than fifteen years later, in the tale 'Youth', Conrad's narrator recalls the explosion, thus:

> I seemed somehow to be in the air. I heard all round me like a pent-up breath released – as if a thousand giants simultaneously had said Phoo! – and felt a dull concussion which made my ribs ache suddenly. No doubt about it – I was in the air, and my body was describing a short parabola . . . . . I did not know then that I had no hair, no eyebrows, no eyelashes, that my young moustache was burnt off, that my face was black . . . . .
>
> (*Y*, pp. 22–3)

And later, as the narrator looks back at the wreck from the lifeboats:

> Between the darkness of earth and heaven she was burning fiercely upon a disc of purple sea shot by the blood-red play of gleams; upon a disc of water glittering and sinister. A high, clear flame, an immense and lonely flame, ascended from the ocean,

The Torrens, *1892.*
On this ship, Conrad, serving as her first mate, met John Galsworthy and Edward Sanderson, who were travelling as passengers. He paid tribute to the vessel in Last Essays *(pp. 22–3): 'The* Torrens *had a fame which attracted the right kind of sailor, ... for, apart from her more brilliant qualities, such as her speed and her celebrated good looks . . . . ., she was regarded as a "comfortable ship" in a strictly professional sense . . . . .'*

and from its summit the black smoke poured continuously at the sky. She burned furiously; mournful and imposing like a funeral pile kindled in the night, surrounded by the sea, watched over by the stars. A magnificent death had come like a grace, like a gift, like a reward to that old ship at the end of her laborious days.

(*Y*, pp. 34–5)

On these voyages he encountered so many of the people, vessels and locations that were to appear in the subsequent works of fiction. The *Palestine* reappeared in 'Youth' as the *Judea*; the captain and first mate retain their original names and, it appears, their original temperaments. Conrad came to learn about A.P. Williams, the seaman involved in scandal who tried to make good, and who became one of the models for Lord Jim. (Williams and the other European officers had abandoned a crowded pilgrim-ship, the *Jeddah*, when they thought it was about to sink, leaving the pilgrims to their fate. On reaching shore they announced that the ship had foundered – but the next day she was towed into harbour with the thousand pilgrims safely on board.) On a voyage to the Berau River in Borneo, Conrad met Charles Olmeijer, the egoistic trader whose fictional counterpart was the Almayer of *Almayer's Folly*. Then there was William Lingard, a formidable sea-rover who had fought pirates and knew the coastal waters better than any other European – the genitor of the Tom Lingard of *Almayer's Folly*, *An Outcast of the Islands* and *The Rescue*. At Singapore there was Captain Ellis, the laconic Master–Attendant of the harbour, who was to make brief appearances in two novels and a long tale, 'The End of the Tether'. And it was at Bangkok in 1888 that Conrad took charge of his first command – the beautiful *Otago*, a 367-ton three-masted thoroughbred: 'a harmonious creature in the lines of her fine body, in the proportioned tallness of her spars'. There was disease (dysentery and cholera) among her crew, and his first voyage, from Bangkok to Singapore, took three weeks instead of the usual three days, for she was often becalmed; but out of Conrad's frustrations and anxieties would eventually be born one of his finest novels, *The Shadow-Line*.

It was while he was captain of the *Otago* that on a visit to Mauritius he fell in love with a pretty young woman called Eugénie Renouf, and actually announced to her brother that he hoped to marry her – only to discover that she was already engaged. He retreated rapidly to the sanctuary of his cabin. In Australia in March 1889 he resigned his command and returned as a steamship passenger to England, to furnished rooms at Bessborough Gardens, near Vauxhall Bridge in London; and it was in that riverside setting that at the age of thirty-one, with time on his hands while seeking another command, he 'on an autumn day with an opaline atmosphere' began his first novel, *Almayer's Folly*. The manuscript was to accompany him on his travels for the next five years: a wad to be brooded over, forgotten for a while, then pulled out for additions and revisions. With Conrad the papers survived even the heart of 'darkest Africa'.

The Congo and its aftermath

In 'Geography and Some Explorers' (1924), Conrad wrote of his schooldays:

> One day, putting my finger on a spot in the very middle of the then white heart of Africa, I declared that some day I would go there. My chums' chaffing was perfectly justifiable . . . . . Yet it is a fact that, about eighteen years afterwards, a wretched little stern-wheel steamboat I commanded lay moored to the bank of an African river . . . . . The subdued thundering mutter of the Stanley Falls hung in the heavy night air of the last navigable reach of the Upper Congo . . . . . and I said to myself with awe, 'This is the very spot of my boyish boast.'
>
> (*LE*, pp. 16–17)

In 1890 Conrad had gained employment with the Société Anonyme Belge pour le Commerce du Haut-Congo, the company largely responsible for exploiting the resources of the Belgian Congo – that vast tract of central Africa which was the private property of King Leopold II. Conrad expected to be given command of one of the steam-boats that plied up and down the River Congo, because one of the company's captains, Freiesleben, had been killed by local inhabitants during a petty quarrel. Part of Conrad's African journey was overland, through dense bush, his European companion sick and the native bearers mutinous; part was upstream in the frail *Roi des Belges*, a wood-burning paddle-steamer that reminded him of a sardine-can or a Huntley & Palmer biscuit-tin; and, after a journey of well over a thousand miles, he reached the township at Stanley Falls, the settlement closest to the heart of the continent. But there, he recalled later, his mood was one not of achievement but of disillusionment:

> A great melancholy descended on me. Yes, this was the very spot. But there was no shadowy friend to stand by my side in the night of the enormous wilderness, no great haunting memory, but only the unholy recollection of a prosaic newspaper 'stunt' and the distasteful knowledge of the vilest scramble for loot that ever

disfigured the history of human conscience and geographical exploration.

(LE, p. 17)

That 'stunt' was the much-publicised 'discovery' of Livingstone, the missionary, by Stanley, the journalist; and Conrad was rightly sceptical of its value, since Livingstone had never actually been lost. The 'vilest scramble for loot' was, of course, the Belgian exploitation of the Congo. Even in his few months in this wilderness, Conrad saw ample evidence of the brutal ways in which the supposed emissaries of European civilisation were plundering the land of rubber and ivory by treating its inhabitants as expendable slave-labour. Conrad noted in his diary:

> Met an off^{er} of the State inspecting. A few minutes afterwards saw at a camp^{g} place the dead body of a Backongo. Shot? Horrid smell . . . . .
>
> Saw another dead body lying by the path in an attitude of meditative repose . . . . .
>
> On the road to-day passed a skeleton tied up to a post. Also white man's grave – no name – heap of stones in the form of a cross.

(LE, pp. 163, 165, 169)

Such horrors, and their implicit comments on the arrogance and hypocrisy of imperialism, were to be incentives to the writing of his most mordant tale, 'An Outpost of Progress', and his most complex novella, 'Heart of Darkness'.

Conrad was invalided home to London, having been stricken with dysentery and malaria: malarial gout and feverish ailments were to recur for the rest of his life. After convalescing at Geneva, he took a desk job, helping to manage a warehouse in London; and he maintained an ample correspondence with his 'aunt' (really the wife of a distant relative), Marguerite Poradowska. She lived at Brussels and was establishing her reputation as a novelist, and she certainly encouraged Conrad to persevere with his literary ambitions. Conrad's letters to her established a pattern that was to recur in others to various later acquaintances, for his epistles are often jeremiads: eloquent, rhythmic, sonorous lamentations about the futility of life and the hopelessness of his situation. Even a letter of consolation becomes almost gloatingly pessimistic:

> Man must drag the ball and chain of his individuality to the very end. It is the [price] one pays for the infernal and divine privilege of thought; consequently, it is only the elect who are convicts in this life – the glorious company of those who understand and who lament, but who tread the earth amid a multitude of ghosts with

maniacal gestures, with idiotic grimaces. Which do you prefer –
idiot or convict?

(CL, I, pp. 162–3)

In 1891 Conrad sailed as first mate in the *Torrens*, one of the most
famous and beautiful of the clippers, on the first of two voyages to
Australia and back. Long afterwards, in 'The *Torrens*: A Personal
Tribute', Conrad wrote:

> The *Torrens* had a fame which attracted the right kind of sailor
> . . . . . for apart from her more brilliant qualities, such as her
> speed and her celebrated good looks (which by themselves go a
> long way with a sailor), she was regarded as a 'comfortable ship'
> in a strictly professional sense, which means that she was known
> to handle easily and to be a good sea boat in heavy weather . . . . .
> I can testify that, on every point of sailing, the way that ship had
> of letting big seas slip under her did one's heart good to watch.

(LE, pp. 22–3)

On the final journey, one of the passengers was E.H. Jacques, a
young Cambridge man who was the first reader of the manuscript
of *Almayer's Folly*.

> 'Is it worth finishing?' . . . . .
> 'Distinctly,' he answered in his sedate veiled voice, and then
> coughed a little.
> 'Were you interested?' I inquired further, almost in a whisper.
> 'Very much!' . . . . .
> 'Now let me ask you one more thing: Is the story quite clear to
> you as it stands?'
> He raised his dark, gentle eyes to my face and seemed
> surprised.
> 'Yes! Perfectly.'

(PR, pp. 17–18)

Jacques, who was dying of tuberculosis, did not live to see the end
of the story; but, by prophetic coincidence, another of the *Torrens'*
passengers was the young John Galsworthy, who listened avidly to
the mate's yarns of 'ships and storms, of Polish revolution, of
youthful Carlist gun-running adventure', and who subsequently
maintained a friendly correspondence with Conrad through the
years when both men achieved fame.

In 1894 there came a lull in Conrad's maritime career when,
having joined another ship, the *Adowa*, as first mate, the voyage was
cancelled. He learned that his uncle Tadeusz ('the wisest, the
firmest, the most indulgent of guardians') had died. In this period
of waiting and melancholy, he continued the slow work on *Almayer's*

Folly, and at last, on 24 April, he was able to write to Marguerite Poradowska: 'J'ai la douleur de Vous faire part de la mort de M. Kaspar Almayer qui a eu lieu ce matin a 3ʰ' ('I regret to inform you of the death of Mr Kaspar Almayer, which occurred this morning at 3 o'clock'). He wrapped the manuscript in two pieces of cardboard and some brown paper, enclosed twelve penny stamps in case of rejection, and sent the book to the publishing house of T. Fisher Unwin.

The second career: Conrad the novelist

Early writings

In October 1894 Fisher Unwin accepted *Almayer's Folly* for publication in the following year, paying Conrad just £20 for the copyright. For this acceptance the publisher's two readers were responsible. One was W.H. Chesson, who was immediately impressed by the book's 'magical melancholy' – 'its note of haunted loneliness called me into isolation, while I read it in the clamorous heart of London'; the other was Edward Garnett, who, equally impressed, was to be an enthusiastic, loyal and keenly intelligent correspondent and publicist of Conrad for many years to come. Garnett – tall, bespectacled, floppy-haired, careless over matters of dress, forgetful of fly-buttons, but passionately vigilant to maintain high literary standards – was probably the most brilliant reader ever to be employed by a publisher. He was male midwife to the literary offspring of W.H. Hudson, Cunninghame Graham, John Galsworthy, W.H. Davies, and later of D.H. Lawrence, Dorothy Richardson, T.E. Lawrence, Henry Green and H.E. Bates. Though 'poor as a church mouse', he readily lent money to authors who were sometimes slow to repay. The respect and affection with which he was regarded is well shown in his subsequent fictional characterisation as Lea in *The Inheritors*, a novel written jointly by Conrad and Ford Madox Hueffer:

> Lea had helped me a good deal in the old days – he had helped everybody, for that matter. You would probably find traces of Lea's influence in the beginnings of every writer of about my decade; of everybody who ever did anything decent, and of some who never got beyond the stage of burgeoning decently. He had given me the material help that a publisher's reader could give, until his professional reputation was endangered, and he had given me the more valuable help that so few can give . . . . . He was sprawling angularly on a cane lounge, surrounded by whole rubbish heaps of manuscript . . . . . And on the floor, on the

chairs, on the sideboard, on the unmade bed, the profusion of manuscripts.

(*The Inheritors*, Dent, 1923, pp. 46, 47–8)

Garnett was eager to meet the unknown author of *Almayer's Folly*: 'The strangeness of the tropical atmosphere, and the poetic "realism" of this romantic narrative excited my curiosity about the author, who I fancied might have eastern blood in his veins' (EG, p. vi). And at their first meeting, it was Conrad's janiformity, his duplicity of character, that struck the twenty-six-year-old Garnett:

> My memory is of seeing a dark-haired man, short but extremely graceful in his nervous gestures, with brilliant eyes, now narrowed and penetrating, now soft and warm, with a manner alert yet caressing, whose speech was ingratiating, guarded, and brusque turn by turn. I had never seen before a man so masculinely keen yet so femininely sensitive.

(EG, p. vii)

There is no doubt that in recommending the acceptance of *Almayer's Folly*, Chesson and Garnett were influenced first and foremost by its literary merits rather than by considerations of its commercial profitability. Certainly the book had some of the ingredients of popular fiction. It had an exotic eastern location – the jungles and riverbanks of Borneo. It told a tale of long-sought treasure, of smuggling, and of the elopement of a Eurasian woman with a brave Balinese prince. But it was also an uncompromisingly original work, difficult in the convolutions and ellipses of its narrative, subversive in its scepticism and cynicism, complex in its interweaving of political and anthropological material with the fortunes of individuals in the foreground: a novel that would have to be read twice before its main ironies would be fully perceived. And it was a novel which, for all its cumbrously literary descriptions, remained plangent and strange in its emphasis on human isolation, on the inadequacy of communication between people, and on the cracks in the shields of illusion forged by men to ward off hard realities.

Almayer's Folly was widely reviewed, though the reviews were mixed. A few critics were dismissive or derisory ('Borneo is a fine field for the study of monkeys, not men'); most spoke of the book with respect modulating to enthusiasm; and some hailed the arrival of a writer of genius. A large number of the reviews emphasised its originality and power (the diffuseness notwithstanding) and the author's skill in establishing an exotic atmosphere. Conrad was frequently compared with Kipling; and, even when the review concluded that he was Kipling's inferior, the comparison remained encouraging, given that in the mid-1890s many British reviewers regarded Kipling as the leading contemporary writer. The *Spectator* prophesied that 'Joseph Conrad . . . . . might become the Kipling of the Malay Archipelago', while the *Manchester Guardian* later claimed that he was 'as masculine as Kipling, but without that parade of masculinity which Kipling loves'.

Conrad, who followed the reviews closely, had good grounds for feeling proud of his achievement. After twenty arduous years at sea, he had dared to embark on a career which financially was even riskier: that of a full-time novelist; and a novelist, moreover, in an alien and difficult language: English. 'I had to work like a coal-miner in his pit quarrying all my English sentences out of a black night', he said. His inheritance (eventually of about £1,600) from Bobrowski's estate may explain the timing of the decision. In any case, maritime commissions appropriate to his qualifications were increasingly elusive, as recently-built ships were larger and more efficient, so that fewer seamen were needed. The reception of *Almayer's Folly* helped to confirm him in the new course. Though there would be a phase in 1898 when he attempted to return to sea, he was to remain a writer until his death in 1924. 'But I *won't* live in an attic', he had told Garnett at their first meeting; and his life-style was never poor: he lived the life of a country squire or upper-middle-class gentleman, and moved through a succession of ever larger houses. In 1896 he married Jessie George, a buxom young typist who would become the mother of two sons; and the early Conrad households generally had a servant or two to help her with the menial work. For decades Conrad lived beyond his means, dependent on the generosity of appreciative publishers such as William Blackwood, on loans from various friends, on massive advances (after 1900) from his trusting literary agent, J.B. Pinker, and, between 1902 and 1917, on state grants provided by the British taxpayer. In his old age, following the commercial success of *Chance* (published as a book in 1914), he became prosperous; but until then he was repeatedly in a state of anguish and sometimes near-madness resulting from the strain of trying to write uncompromisingly while yet racing against time in order to gain more money or to repay in pages the cash that he had already received and spent. Again and again he spoke of his current engagement with a manuscript as a hideous ordeal, his mind blank, the words elusive; repeatedly his completion of a novel was marked by physical and mental break-down, a combination of gout, exhaustion, depression and mild derangement. Had he known of the repeated ordeals that lay ahead, it is doubtful that he would ever have embarked on *Almayer's Folly*.

In 1896, however, appeared its sequel, *An Outcast of the Islands*, using the same exotic location and some of the same characters as the previous novel. This work further consolidated his critical reputation. Although there were complaints about the baseness portrayed ('Never did so mean a skunk figure as the hero of a novel') and again about the 'besetting sin of wordiness', comparisons with Kipling – and with Stevenson, another highly rated novelist – continued to imply that Conrad's work, though flawed, challenged comparison with the very best of the era.

Then came several false starts. Conrad embarked on *The Sisters*, of which only the opening was ever completed: the story of a sensitive young Slav, an artist who comes to live in Paris. The second start was on *The Rescuer*, a novel which gave Conrad such extreme and agonising difficulty that he took more than twenty years to complete it: eventually, as *The Rescue*, it was serialised in 1919. And in 1896–7 he published in magazines the highly uneven quartet of stories ('Karain', 'The Lagoon', 'The Idiots' and 'An Outpost of Progress') which, with the 'left-handed production', 'The Return', comprises *Tales of Unrest*.

The major phase

Conrad's major phase as a writer extends from 1897 to 1911. It includes *The Nigger of the 'Narcissus'*, 'Youth', 'Heart of Darkness', *Lord Jim*, 'Typhoon', *Nostromo*, *The Secret Agent*, 'The Secret Sharer', *Under Western Eyes* and 'A Smile of Fortune'. This is a period of astonishing richness and majesty. 'Heart of Darkness' or *Nostromo* alone would have sufficed to give Conrad an enduring reputation as a major writer; but when to them are added the diverse strengths of the other tales and novels in that list, the effect is to emphasise his stature as one of the dozen greatest fiction-writers in English.

It is a familiar irony of literary history that during this major phase Conrad's financial struggles were as bitter as ever; but there is no doubt that an increasing majority of reviewers sensed and respected (even if they could not fully define or comprehend) the stature of Conrad the writer. Edward Garnett noted that *The Nigger of the 'Narcissus'* received 'a general blast of eulogy from a dozen impressive sources'; and in the review columns Garnett himself seized every opportunity to proclaim Conrad's brilliance. The author's fame was spreading widely, partly by the prior publication of his works in magazines and journals. Conrad was frequently paid twice, thrice or more for the same material: even the convoluted novel *Nostromo* appeared as a serial in a popular periodical, *T.P.'s Weekly*, and all the other works mentioned in the previous paragraph appeared in magazines before being published in book form. Conrad had turned to writing at a time that was a golden age for aspiring writers. The vast expansion of education in the nineteenth century had created a huge literate public, and numerous magazines and new publishing houses sought to exploit this market. Technological advances in printing and paper-production helped this process by reducing unit-costs. International copyright agreements (notably the Chace Act between Britain and the United States in 1891) ensured payments to authors for work published abroad.

During his major phase, Conrad came into contact with many of the most brilliant writers and personalities of the day. R.B. Cunninghame Graham, the aristocratic socialist and adventurer, became a close friend; John Galsworthy maintained a fraternal correspondence; and there was a brief, touching friendship with Stephen Crane, the promising but short-lived author of *The Red Badge of Courage*. Conrad met H.G. Wells, who had enthusiastically reviewed *Almayer's Folly* and *An Outcast*; Kipling sent a flattering letter; and Ford Madox Hueffer became a friend and collaborator, subsequently establishing an enduring reputation of his own with *The Good Soldier*. Other contacts were with George Bernard Shaw, who irritated Conrad intensely, and with the magisterial Henry James, whom Conrad addressed in somewhat bleating tones as 'Cher Maître'. Most of these writers lived or stayed in the south to south-east corner of England: Kipling at Rottingdean (later at Burwash) in Sussex; Hueffer, Crane, Garnett and subsequently Conrad himself at the Pent (Pent Farm), near Hythe; James at Rye, Wells at Sandgate; and all, thanks to the splendid railway services, were within easy commuting distance of London, where Hudson lived, where Cunninghame Graham had a flat, and Garnett held literary luncheons at the Mont Blanc restaurant. The sense of friendly rivalry with various uncompromisingly innovatory figures in this group must repeatedly have incited Conrad to reject the second-rate or derivative in his own writing and to strive for vivid precision of utterance.

Meanwhile, Conrad was becoming as domesticated as was possible for so highly-strung and temperamental a person. His proposal of marriage to Jessie had been abrupt and awkward: 'Look here, my dear, we had better get married and out of this. Look at the weather'; and he had assured her mother 'that he hadn't very long to live and further that there would be no family'. In spite of the latter assurance, the plump Jessie produced two sons – Borys in 1898 and John in 1906. She claimed that when Borys was born, Conrad was wandering vaguely in the kitchen garden, and, hearing the child cry, he shouted to Rose (the maid): 'Send that child away at once; it will disturb Mrs Conrad!' 'It's your own child, sir', the patient maid replied. On rail journeys with his wife and the baby, Conrad pretended to be a stranger to them if other travellers were in the carriage; 'I hate babies', he told Garnett. Nevertheless he was to be an affectionate (if often sternly awe-inspiring) father to both boys and a generally loyal husband to Jessie. She, in turn, strove to organise the household so as to guard his privacy and enable him to work as steadily as possible, though her memoirs make quite evident the ripples of resentment and bitterness that she felt when her struggles lacked appreciation or recognition. There is no doubt that to his resourceful but rather naïve young wife, Conrad must often have been an alarming husband. When guests came to dinner, he would absent-mindedly roll pieces of bread into pellets and flick them about the room – 'I have seen them fly into the soup-plates and glasses of our guests. The more excited or irritated he got, the quicker flew the missiles, and those in the line of fire would look apprehensively at their host.' On another occasion, Conrad, suspecting that there was an intruder in the garden, seized his rifle and rushed down the path to the little building (a privy) in which the 'intruder' was concealed. Brandishing the rifle, he boldly burst into the place, shouting 'Come out you – Damn you', and found himself facing his startled mother-in-law.

Such social embarrassments were the outer signs of Conrad's long lonely ordeals in his study, wrestling to create a fictional Patusan or Costaguana. He was to say of the writing of *Nostromo*, for example:

> I hesitated, as if warned by the instinct of self-preservation from venturing on a distant and toilsome journey into a land full of intrigues and revolutions. But it had to be done.
>
> It took the best part of the years 1903–4 to do; with many intervals of renewed hesitation, lest I should lose myself in the ever-enlarging vistas opening before me as I progressed deeper in my knowledge of the country . . . . . On my return I found (speaking somewhat in the style of Captain Gulliver) my family all well, my wife heartily glad to learn that the fuss was all over, and our small boy considerably grown during my absence.
>
> (*N*, p. x)

Cunninghame Graham noted that Conrad 'almost needed a Caesarian operation of the soul before he was delivered of his masterpieces'; and often the delivery was marked by physical and mental collapse. When Conrad had completed *Under Western Eyes*, Jessie wrote:

> The novel is finished, but the penalaty [*sic*] has to be paid. Months of nervous strain have ended in a complete nervous breakdown . . . . . There is the M.S. complete but uncorrected and his fierce refusal to let even I touch it. It lays on a table at the foot of the bed and he lives mixed up in the scenes and holds converse with the characters.
>
> (*BB*, p. 192)

R.B. Cunninghame Graham.

Yet, after such deranging efforts, the material rewards could be ludicrously small: by 1909, when Conrad was fifty-one, his debts totalled £2,250, at a time when the average annual earnings of a doctor were less than £400. He wrote: 'My immortal works (13 in all) have brought me last year something under five pounds in royalties' (though this was after the repayment of various sums to Pinker). Understandably, he expressed bitter contempt for the popular, prosperous novelists of the day – Grant Allen, Marie Correlli and Hall Caine, for instance:

> All three are very popular with the public – and they are also puffed in the press. There are no lasting qualities in their work. The thought is commonplace and the style (?) without any distinction. They are popular because they express the common thought, and the common man is delighted to find himself in accord with people he supposed distinguished.
>
> (Najder, p. 228)

In spite of this patrician hauteur, he made various calculated attempts to win the popularity of that wider public. One was by the writing – or rather dictation – of *The Mirror of the Sea*, a book of ruminative (and sometimes waffling) reminiscences: 'I've discovered that I can dictate that sort of bosh without effort at the rate of 3000 words in four hours. Fact. The only thing now is to sell it to a paper and then make a book of the rubbish.' Another, related way of accelerating the flow of marketable material was collaboration with his eager admirer, Ford Madox Hueffer (who later changed his name to Ford Madox Ford). The main fruits of this collaboration were *The Inheritors* (1901), *Romance* (1903) and 'The Nature of a Crime' (1909). Hueffer also appears to have primed some parts of *The Mirror*; he provided the bases of the tales 'Amy Foster' and 'To-morrow'; his hints helped to engender *The Secret Agent*; and several pages of *Nostromo* are in his handwriting, though there he may only have served as amanuensis. Although Hueffer later revealed distinctive talents as a novelist, collaboration did little justice to the abilities of either man: Conrad called it 'our partnership – in crime'. *The Inheritors* (a mixture of science fiction, political allegory and topical *roman à clef*) will certainly bear some reconsideration; but 'The Nature of a Crime' is a negligible tale, while *Romance* is a trite and prolix venture into the Stevenson market of glamorous adventure narratives set in the picturesque past. Literary collaborations may be more productive of quarrels than of masterpieces, and by 1909 Conrad was complaining that Ford's conduct (as editor of the *English Review*) was 'impossible' – 'He's a megalomaniac who imagines he is managing the Universe.'

Transition: 1911–19

This was in two senses a period of transition. First, some of the novels and tales of this period are impressive, while others show signs of a decline in Conrad's powers; and, second, there was to be a rapid improvement in his income.

In order, the publications of this phase are: *A Personal Record* (originally *Some Reminiscences*), 1912, by far the more interesting of his two books of autobiographical reflections; *'Twixt Land and Sea*, 1912 (three tales, including 'The Secret Sharer'); *Chance*, serialised in the *New York Herald* in 1912 and published as a book early in 1914; *Victory*, 1915; *Within the Tides* (four of his more trivial tales), 1915; and *The Shadow-Line*, 1917.

The short stories in the collections are remarkably uneven in quality, ranging from 'The Secret Sharer', a vivid and enigmatic tale which has elicited a wealth of commentary, to 'The Inn of the Two Witches', a melodramatic piece reminiscent of Wilkie Collins' 'A Terribly Strange Bed'. Of the novels in this period, most critics concur in regarding *The Shadow-Line* as the best: a vivid study of the stresses on a young captain whose first command is a disease-haunted and becalmed sailing-ship. *Victory* is much more problematic for the critics, some seeing it as one of the Conradian masterpieces, others seeing it as a flawed and tainted work. The publication which most deeply affected Conrad's fortunes was, of course, *Chance*. Until then, Conrad's debt to J.B. Pinker remained great, and grants from the British taxpayer provided charitable aid. In 1902 (when the average earnings of an adult male were about £60 a year), the Royal Literary Fund had given him £300: in 1904, the 'Royal Bounty Special Service Fund' donated £500; in 1908, there had been a further donation of £200 from the Royal Literary Fund. Eventually, in 1910, he was awarded a Civil List Pension of £100 per annum: a pension which continued until 1917, when Conrad felt at last sufficiently solvent to renounce it.

Chance's success in the market may initially seem hard to explain. This is not one of Conrad's better novels; nor is it obviously 'popular' in its method, for the narrative is unfolded with elaborate deviousness. The *New York Herald*, however, had given prominent and astute publicity to the serialisation of the novel. Repeatedly the magazine stressed that this great novelist had written this work especially for the *New York Herald* and its *female* readers. Women had long constituted a majority of the fiction-reading public (as they still do today); previously, Conrad's fiction had seemed particularly masculine in its orientation. The publicity campaign modified Conrad's public image. When the American edition of the book appeared, its jacket showed centrally an attractive young woman with a naval officer at her side, implying that the text would be a love-story. That book was also zealously publicised: a Conrad enthusiast in a key position was Alfred Knopf, who persuaded his employer F.N. Doubleday to promote the novel lavishly; and Knopf elicited quotable tributes to the author from many cultural celebrities. Conrad was shrewd when he told Pinker: 'It's the sort of stuff that *may* have a chance with the public. All of it about a girl and with a steady run of references to women in general all along . . . . . It ought to go down.' Given the feminist upsurge in the period 1905–14, there was obvious topicality in the running discussion of woman's nature and in the satiric depiction of the lesbian Mrs Fyne; and the main love-story's dénouement was, by Conradian standards, unusually happy, with the inhibited hero and heroine eventually experiencing their long-delayed sexual embrace. One commentator has suggested that the success of *Chance* shows simply that Conrad's reputation was ripe and ready at last: ripe for general celebrity, ready for popular interest to burgeon. Many of the earlier volumes were soon reprinted in big print-runs, and preparations were made for collected editions of Conrad's works.

Even when in debt, Conrad had never stinted himself: he had dressed like a dandy or rural squire, owned a succession of expensive early motor cars, and rented increasingly large houses; but now, at last, his income was more than adequate for his life-style. His agent was able to obtain advances for *Victory* of £1,000 for the serial rights (*Munsey's Magazine*) and £850 for the book. This money helped Conrad to take his family on a visit to Poland in 1914; but the sentimental journey to Kraków and Zakopane was disrupted by the outbreak of the First World War, and it was with extreme difficulty that the family eluded internment, returning to England via Italy. Ironically, it was a war that Conrad had long prophesied; and his own son Borys served as a soldier at the front, and was gassed and shell-shocked. After the Armistice, Conrad was pessimistic about the prospects of the newly established League of Nations, but at least could take consolation from the re-establishment of the Polish State – a reborn republic.

Decline

In the closing years of his life, Conrad's main publications were *The Arrow of Gold* (1919), *The Rescue* (1920), *Notes on Life and Letters* (1921, a collection of essays and occasional pieces) and *The Rover* (1923). Posthumously published volumes were *Suspense* (never completed), *Tales of Hearsay* and *Last Essays*. All four novels of this late phase are disappointing; the narrative too often meanders, as though Conrad has lost his creative energy; and the farther in the past they are set (*The Rover* and *Suspense* dealing with the Napoleonic era), the more he seems to be turning his back on the problems of the present and the perennial which he had rendered with such rich intensity in 'Heart of Darkness' and *Nostromo*.

As his writing lost its bite, however, public adulation increased. Serialisations earned huge fees; collectors sought his manuscripts; and film rights brought thousands of pounds to the man who said: 'The Movie is just a silly stunt for silly people.' In 1919 he moved into Oswalds, a large and elegant Georgian house at Bishopsbourne, near Canterbury. On a visit to the United States, where he gave a talk, he was lionised: 'To be aimed at by forty cameras held by forty men that look as if they came in droves is a nerve-shattering experience', he wrote to his wife. He evidently enthralled his American audience by a reading of the death of Lena, the heroine of *Victory*. His Polish accent was still thick, rendering 'good' as 'goot', 'blood' as 'bloot'; but the hearers were moved – Conrad noticed 'audible snuffling'. In England, a further accolade was the offer of a knighthood from the Labour Prime Minister, Ramsay MacDonald; an offer that Conrad courteously and diplomatically declined: 'As a man whose early years were closely associated in hard toil and unforgotten friendships with British working men, I am especially touched on this offer being made to me during your Premiership' (*CP*, p. 47).

When Jacob Epstein, the sculptor, visited Oswalds in 1924 to make a bust of the author, he found Conrad 'crippled with rheumatism, crotchety, nervous, and ill. He said to me, "I am played out".' In July, Conrad suffered a heart attack: 'I begin to feel like a cornered rat', he remarked. Another attack followed, on 2 August; and at 8.30 the next morning he fell dead to the floor.

His funeral took place in Canterbury during the week of the annual cricket festival: the streets and shopfronts were decorated with gay bunting. After the service at the Roman Catholic church of St Thomas's, the body was buried under a stone which bore the words he had chosen as epigraph for *The Rover*:

Sleep after toyle, port after stormie seas,
Ease after warre, death after life, does greatly please.

By a further irony, these are the words uttered in Spenser's *Faerie Queene* by 'a man of hell, that cals himself Despaire'. Though Conrad was buried with Catholic obsequies, the paradoxical inscription is a reminder of the radical scepticism which gave so much power to his writings; and furthermore, by reminding us of old Peyrol, the hero of *The Rover*, who lives and dies by his work as a seaman, the words appropriately recall the dual career of Conrad,

Conrad in old age, near the time of his visit to the USA.

the seaman turned writer, who was still toiling at his literary work at the time of his death.

Subsequent reputation

Around the end of Conrad's life there were some significantly discordant notes amid the general crescendo of praise. E.M. Forster, reviewing *Notes on Life and Letters*, voiced the complaint (which subsequently became famous) that 'the secret casket of his genius contains a vapour rather than a jewel'. Leonard Woolf made much the same point when, echoing 'Heart of Darkness', he remarked of *Suspense*: 'I had the feeling which one gets on cracking a fine, shining, new walnut . . . . . only to find that it has nothing inside it. Most of the later Conrads give one this feeling.' And the *Spectator* said in 1925: 'We begin to see that he was an impressive rather than a likeable writer . . . . . He had stories to tell. And oddly enough he had nothing to say.' However, though such sceptical notes were sounded, Conrad's prestige remained generally high with critics and commentators during the 1920s; and, by means of the cinema, with its films of *Victory* (1919 and 1930), *Lord Jim* (1925), *Nostromo* (1926), *Romance* (1927) and *The Rescue* (1929), his fame was reaching a larger audience than he could have imagined possible when he embarked on his literary career. In the 1930s, as later generations of writers (Lawrence, Joyce, Huxley and Auden among them) moved into the foreground of discussion, there was a slackening of interest in him: the novelist Elizabeth Bowen remarked: 'Conrad is in abeyance. We are not clear yet how to rank him; there is an uncertain pause.'

If any single publication signalled the end of that 'uncertain pause', it was F.R. Leavis' *The Great Tradition: George Eliot, Henry James, Joseph Conrad* (1948), which ranked Conrad 'among the very greatest novelists in the language – or any language'. Thereafter the great and still-continuing surge of critical interest swelled, with many of the subsequent commentators taking as their starting-point the bold discriminations made in Leavis' account. Of course, the vast post-war expansion of higher education in many lands meant that the majority of significant literary figures soon became, inevitably, the centres of expanding industries of research and commentary. But, in the case of Conrad, the scale of the renewed attention has been particularly impressive. In addition to numerous critical and biographical studies, there have been several lengthy bibliographies; computers have produced concordances to a wide range of the novels and tales; work is proceeding on a scholarly Anglo-American edition of the entire canon; Pléiade in France and Mursia in Italy have published new translations; and Conrad is now served internationally by the Joseph Conrad Societies of the United States, UK, France, Italy, Scandinavia and Poland. The thrice-yearly periodical *Conradiana* is published in Texas; twice a year *The Conradian* is published in London. There have been post-war adaptations for the cinema of *An Outcast of the Islands*, 'The Secret Sharer', 'The Return', *Lord Jim* and 'The Duel' (filmed as *The Duellists*, and followed by Gordon Williams' 'novel of the movie'); and films of *The Shadow-Line* and 'Amy Foster' have been made for television. Of these, *An Outcast of the Islands* (directed by Carol Reed), *The Shadow-Line* (Andrzej Wajda) and *The Duellists* (Ridley Scott) have been the relatively successful adaptations, though all took quite gross liberties with the text, and (since cameras are dumb and seduced by surfaces) it is difficult to conceive of a close cinematic equivalent to a Conradian masterpiece. One critic, John Simon, has offered the following cynical rule for the dramatisation of fiction: 'If it is worth doing, it can't be done; if it can be done, it isn't worth doing.' Coppola's *Apocalypse Now* (1979) almost solved the problem by being a film *on* rather than *of* a Conradian text: a spectacular transposition of much of 'Heart of Darkness' from the Congo of *c.* 1890 to the Vietnam War *c.* 1970: a selective magnification of the surrealistic and ruthlessly prophetic aspects of the original. (It generated *Hearts of Darkness*, a film about the making of the film.) In recent decades, even operas have sprung from Conrad's pages: the novel *Victory* and the tale 'To-morrow' have been transformed into operas by Richard Rodney Bennett and Tadeusz Baird respectively.

Conrad has been admired by, and has influenced in various ways, an important sequence of writers ranging from T.S. Eliot to the Kenyan novelist, Ngugi wa Thiong'o; and that legacy will be the subject of a later section. One important critical development in the closing decades of the twentieth century was the burgeoning of radical approaches (particularly by 'Third World' and feminist writers) which gave prominence to previously neglected aspects of Conrad's works. Another development was the academic shift of interest from purely literary studies to cultural and media studies; and Conrad's fiction, by its interest in cultural comparisons and by its infiltration of the realms of the cinema, television, opera and videos, gained new and widespread attention.

2   Cultural background

The tensions

> There is no morality, no knowledge and no hope.
>> (Conrad to Cunninghame Graham, 31 Jan. 1898)

> It must not be supposed that I claim for the artist in fiction the freedom of moral Nihilism. I would require from him many acts of faith of which the first would be the cherishing of an undying hope . . . . .
>> (Conrad: 'Books' in *Notes on Life and Letters*)

> Those who read me know my conviction that the world, the temporal world, rests on a few very simple ideas; so simple that they must be as old as the hills. It rests notably, among others, on the idea of Fidelity.
>> (Conrad: 'A Familiar Preface' to *A Personal Record*)

> We live, as we dream – alone.
>> (Marlow in Conrad's 'Heart of Darkness')

A list of the salient features of Conrad's work would include pessimism, a pessimism capable of modulating deeply towards cynicism or even nihilism, yet coupled with some very ancient and traditional moral affirmations; and it would include an extreme pyrrhonism, a scepticism so thorough as to cast sceptical doubt even on the value of scepticism. As the four epigraphs remind us again, Conrad is a janiform writer: morally he may seem radically paradoxical or self-contradictory. In *Criticism and Ideology*, Terry Eagleton emphasises the 'disjuncture between fact and value, ideal and reality, matter and spirit, Nature and consciousness which pervades Conrad's work'.

Conrad's writing voices a combination of nineteenth-century and twentieth-century preoccupations; he stands at the intersection of the late Victorian and the early Modernist cultural phases; he is both romantic and anti-romantic, both conservative and subversive. Morally and politically, psychologically and philosophically, he can be a probing and challenging writer; yet he can also, in some areas, be embarrassingly conventional. Albert Guerard, in *Conrad the*

Novelist, offers a useful list of some of the main paradoxes or duplicities that we encounter in Conrad's works:

> A declared fear of the corrosive and faith-destroying intellect – doubled by [i.e. coupled with] a profound and ironic skepticism;
>
> A declared belief that ethical matters are simple – doubled by an extraordinary sense of ethical complexities . . . . .;
>
> A declared distrust of generous idealism – doubled by a pronounced idealism . . . . .;
>
> A declared commitment to authoritarian sea-tradition – doubled by a pronounced individualism . . . . .;
>
> A declared and extreme political conservativism [*sic*], at once aristocratic and pragmatist – doubled by great sympathy for the poor and disinherited of the earth . . . . .;
>
> A declared fidelity to law as above the individual – doubled by a strong sense of fidelity to the individual . . . . .;
>
> Briefly: a deep commitment to order in society and in the self – doubled by incorrigible sympathy for the outlaw, whether existing in society or the self.

(CN, pp. 57–8)

And these tensions are implicit in exciting stories, full of graphic incident, with characters who engage our sympathies and antipathies, in locations which extend richly before the imaginative eye. To see Conrad's art as one of self-cancellation, of ideological stalemate or 'fatal disjuncture' (as Terry Eagleton does in *Criticism and Ideology*), is to neglect the creative vitality that exposes the reductiveness of so much non-fictional ideological discourse. Conrad's ability to endure as a writer is strongly related to his janiformity, for that enables his works both to reflect and to question contrasting cultural preoccupations. Like anyone else, Conrad was influenced by the climate of ideas of his day; yet, like any major writer, he responded with a greater articulacy of intelligence and imagination to those ideas than most people would have done. A consideration of that background, under various headings, may help to explain him; it will not explain him away.

My method in the ensuing sections is the obvious one of saying 'What and why?' – 'What are the salient features of Conrad's work, and why are they there? What are the circumstances which permitted or encouraged their development?' The discussion of Conrad's pessimism leads to consideration of biographical and broader cultural factors; similarly, discussion of his political views entails consideration not only of his Polish background but also of the imperialistic fervour of the late nineteenth century. Scientific ideas had a multitude of philosophical and literary consequences: the sense of determinism induced by the prestige of the empirical method helped to engender a literary race of 'superfluous men' and inclined Conrad (like various other writers) to reflect that perhaps the central choice in life lay between passive rationality (the Hamlet-like) and irrational activity (the Quixotic). Other sections discuss some effects of evolutionary ideas on religion, politics and psychology, and their consequences for Conrad. Finally, I narrow the discussion to a survey of literary texts which probably or certainly influenced Conrad's writings; and that section appropriately precedes the final main part of this book, the account of 'The Art of Conrad' itself.

Conrad's pessimism

Conrad's works place heavy emphasis on death and isolation, on inadequate understanding between people, and on the bitterness of experience. In his first novel, the disillusioned protagonist suffers a drug-addict's suicidal death; in the second, the protagonist is shot; in *The Nigger of the 'Narcissus'*, James Wait dies betrayed, while patriarchal Singleton comes to recognise his own impending death; in 'Heart of Darkness', Kurtz dies, while Marlow gains bitter knowledge; in *Lord Jim*, Jim is killed by a leader of the natives he had tried to help; in *Nostromo*, Nostromo is shot, Decoud commits suicide, and Mrs Gould faces disillusionment; in *The Secret Agent*, Winnie stabs her husband and subsequently drowns herself. Even in his later works, which tend to be less bleak and uncompromising, death enjoys wide privileges: in *Chance*, Captain Anthony drowns; in *Victory*, Lena is shot and Heyst commits suicide in a burning building; and, in *The Rover*, old Peyrol sacrifices his life on a fatal voyage. In the shorter works, murder and (more frequently) suicide are just as common. Often the deaths come as a *coup de grâce* to people who have been misunderstood, frustrated or disillusioned. The isolation Conrad depicts is not merely the physical isolation of individuals or groups on ships surrounded by sea or in outposts surrounded by jungle; more tellingly, it is the covert loneliness that occurs within crowds or within marriages when seeming mutuality has been rotted inwardly by egotism. There are very few happy marriages in Conrad's pages (the comfortable domesticity of Hermann and his wife in 'Falk' is mocked by the narrator for its *petit-bourgeois* cosy conventionality); and on the joys of parenthood, on happy family reunions, on sociable celebrations, he has conspicuously little to say: loss, separation and the conflict of desires engage his imagination.

If we look ahead to Conrad from Dickens, we see that the warmths, genialities and festivities to which Dickens attunes us are absent from Conrad; and he excludes, too, those tender moments of mutuality which for George Eliot are local triumphs of humanity.

Somewhere in the Pacific. *This cartoon of Conrad by Max Beerbohm is the frontispiece to Beerbohm's* A Survey *(1921).*

Conrad, observing the emblems of death and evil, remarks: 'Quelle charmante plage! On se fait l'illusion qu'ici on pourrait être toujours presque gai.' ('What a charming beach! One has the illusion that here one could for ever be almost cheerful.')

Again, if we look back from D.H. Lawrence (who said 'I can't forgive Conrad for being so sad and for giving in'), we see that Conrad lacks Lawrence's sense of nature's miraculously potent vitality and of the individual's rich emotional and instinctual depths. Conrad has his own specialisations, his own eloquences, his own kinds of measured affirmation; but it is clear that his outlook is generally bleaker and more defensive than that of most other novelists. Memorable moments in his pages suggest the vulnerable littleness of the individual amid some great and ominous environment: the captain in *The Shadow-Line*, beset by an all-obliterating night; Decoud in *Nostromo*, marooned on a tiny island amidst the empty immensity of sea and sky; or Marlow in 'Heart of Darkness', surrounded by vast tangles of jungle which seem poised to annihilate intruding men.

Such symbolically charged contrasts between the lonely individual in the foreground and the neutral or threatening vastness of the background may remind us of Thomas Hardy's work. Conrad is more cosmopolitan than Hardy, not only in locations and characterisation, but also in thematic range: Conrad has a larger and more complex network of political, philosophical and psychological observations. Their pessimisms have different emphases: Hardy has a bitter sense of the ways in which destiny tortures the innocent and sensitive; Conrad has a more Augustan sense of the general vanity of human wishes. Yet there are clearly some common features in their pessimism which point to causes extending beyond private experience to the general background. In both writers, there is a strong sense that the heavens, once thought to be benevolent to humans, are empty or even hostile. In both, there is a keen post-Darwinian sense that man and his struggles are but part of a 'Nature, red in tooth and claw'. In both, there is a strong element of anti-rational primitivism: the feeling that 'Where ignorance is bliss / 'Tis folly to be wise.' And, in both, we often hear the plangent tones of the disillusioned romantic.

Any consideration of the sources of Conrad's pessimism should be prefaced by a reminder that Conrad is an artist with free will, with freedom of choice: a causal sequence is not a determining sequence. There are times when a pessimistic emphasis can be seen as tactical, as an attempt to offer a dissenting voice to a discussion in which, in the world at large, optimistic tones have sounded too frequently. Nevertheless, our biographical survey of Conrad's career up to the time when he started to produce his novels gives many reasons for his finding the tones of pessimism so seductive. They include his upbringing in a beleaguered Poland; the early deaths of his mother and father; and those long years at sea when he was first a Pole among Frenchmen and next a Pole among Englishmen. Even with marriage, his haunting sense of isolation was slow to fade, as is suggested by the tale 'Amy Foster'. In that tale, a Slavic emigrant who has been shipwrecked off the English coast comes ashore and, after cruel tribulations, marries a naïve young country-woman; but he is deserted by her when he is suffering a feverish illness: he calls for water, but in his native language, and she, frightened by the strange sounds, runs away. He dies, having been 'cast out by the sea to perish in the supreme disaster of loneliness and despair'. This tale may derive partly from Conrad's recollec-tions of the time during his honeymoon when he was ill with fever. In her memoirs, his widow Jessie was to write:

> For a whole long week the fever ran high and for most of the time J.C. was delirious. To see him lying in the white canopied bed, dark-faced, with gleaming teeth and shining eyes, was sufficiently impressive, but to hear him muttering to himself in a strange tongue (he thinks he must have been speaking Polish), to be unable to penetrate the clouded mind or catch one intelligible word, was for a young inexperienced girl truly awful . . . . . The sense of there being nobody at hand to help overpowered and silenced me.
>
> (*Personal Recollections*, 1924, pp. 25–7)

However, although the circumstances of his early life and sub-sequent voyages may well have predisposed Conrad towards a pessimistic sense of isolation, there were general cultural factors which operated to reinforce this sense. We have noted some connections with Hardy's writing, and we may recall, too, the pessimism of so much major poetry between the mid-nineteenth century and the early twentieth, from Tennyson's *In Memoriam* and Matthew Arnold's 'Dover Beach' to T.S. Eliot's *The Waste Land*. One obvious reason for this pessimism was the decline of religious belief (partly as a consequence of the rising prestige of science) and the resultant growth of the sense of loss and disinheritance.

Religious matters

In the Victorian age, while the influence of religion strongly pervaded the middle classes, scepticism spread among the intelli-gentsia. The decline of religious belief can generate a keen and pervasive sense of loss. If one is taught to believe that the existence of God makes moral sense of the universe and gives a happy ending (regeneration in Paradise) to all virtuous lives on earth, then the dwindling of faith may entail a grim awareness that the universe is no longer a homeland for humanity but a ruthlessly amoral territory on which humans, with their ideals, sensitivities and aspirations, are intruders. Conrad had a keen sense of this – of man decoyed into an alien and perhaps meaningless creation. 'C'est comme une forêt où personne ne connaît la route': 'It's like a forest in which nobody knows the way', he told Cunninghame Graham. 'Faith is a myth and beliefs shift like mists on the shore'; and even spring could seem a cruel fraud:

> There is twilight and soft clouds and daffodils – and a great weariness . . . . . Spring? We are an[n]ually lured by false hopes. Spring! Che coglioneria! [What nonsense!] Another illusion for the undoing of mankind.
>
> (*LCG*, pp. 82–3)

Not surprisingly, then, the novels and tales sound that recurrent theme of the seeming sanctuary which proves to be a baited trap.

Though his marriage took place in a registrar's office, Conrad maintained some connections with the Catholic Church (his son Borys was a Roman Catholic who attended a Catholic preparatory school, for instance); and he once told his younger son, John, that he ('like all true seamen') was a believer. Religious rhetoric and supernatural motifs can be found in some of his literary works. In his correspondence, his opinions veer from sceptical scorn to pious hopes, modulating towards the outlook of the correspondent addressed. Nevertheless, his scepticism is resilient and extensive. One of his recurrent attitudes to Christianity resembles not an agnostic's nostalgia for certitude (a common Victorian attitude) but rather an Augustan's distaste for fanaticism. He read with pleasure the work of the Augustan satirist, Swift, and compared himself with Swift's Gulliver. At Christmas 1902, Conrad told the irreligious Edward Garnett:

> It's strange how I always, from the age of fourteen, disliked the Christian religion, its doctrines, ceremonies and festivals . . . . . Nobody – not a single Bishop of them – believes in it. The business in the stable isn't convincing; whereas my atmosphere (vide reviews) can be positively breathed.
>
> (EG, pp. 188–9)

And later:

> Christianity . . . . . is distasteful to me. I am not blind to its services but the absurd oriental fable from which it starts irritates me.
>
> (EG, p. 265).

Conrad could also complain that Christianity's moral standards were (*a*) too high and (*b*) too low.

> (*a*) Great, improving, softening, compassionate it may be but it has lent itself with amazing facility to cruel distortion and is the

only religion which, with its impossible standards, has brought
an infinity of anguish to innumerable souls – on this earth.

(EG, p. 265)

(*b*) The doctrine (or the theory) of atonement through suffering
. . . . . is quite simply a sordid abomination when preached by
civilized people. It is a doctrine that on the one hand leads
straight to the Inquisition and on the other shows the possibilities
of bargaining with the Almighty . . . . . Each act of life is final
. . . . . I am strong enough to judge my conscience instead of
being its slave.

(*CL*, I, p. 95)

It was to his friend Cunninghame Graham, who himself asserted
at a public meeting that 'God was a man of the very best intentions
who died young', that Conrad wrote: 'There is no morality, no
knowledge, and no hope.' Dostoyevsky had claimed: 'If God is
dead, everything is permitted'; and, for those who lose belief in
God's reality, ethical relativism – the sense that morality is merely
a matter of convention which varies from place to place, without
there being any objective enduring test of right and wrong – presses
particularly strongly. In 'Dover Beach', Matthew Arnold spoke of
the present as a time of doubt and confusion,

> Swept with confused alarms of struggle and flight,
> Where ignorant armies clash by night;

Tennyson reflected in *In Memoriam* that if there were no afterlife, the
Creation, however beautiful, would seem the work of

> some wild Poet, when he works
> Without a conscience or an aim;

and Conrad, with dry irony, remarks:

> I have come to suspect that the aim of creation cannot be ethical at
> all. I would fondly believe that its object is purely spectacular . . . . .
> (*A Personal Record*, p. 92)

His Marlow (*Y*, p. 150) refers to life as 'that mysterious arrangement
of merciless logic for a futile purpose'.

Numerous factors contributed to the growth of scepticism in the
nineteenth century. One was the prestige of science in general,
which was yielding impressive results by following procedures that
ignored, or even defied, religious tradition. The prestige of physics
and technology led people to think of the universe as a vast
mechanism and of man himself not as the image of God with an
immortal soul but as a mechanism endowed with consciousness.

T.H. Huxley, the evolutionist, said 'We are conscious automata'; and the young Bertrand Russell confided to his journal in 1888: 'I do wish I believed in the life eternal, for it makes me quite miserable to think man is merely a kind of machine endowed, unhappily for himself, with consciousness.' Furthermore, the spread of evolutionary ideas made the Book of Genesis seem manifestly a fable, and, by indicating man's continuity with the animal kingdom, offered a humiliating affront to human dignity. Even before the publication of Darwin's *The Origin of Species*, the implications of the evolutionary theories in such works as Lyell's *Principles of Geology* had shocked Tennyson into sombre reflection:

> Are God and Nature then at strife,
>> That Nature lends such evil dreams?
>> So careful of the type she seems,
> So careless of the single life . . . . .
>
> 'So careful of the type?' but no.
>> From scarpèd cliff and quarried stone
>> She cries, 'A thousand types are gone;
> I care for nothing, all shall go.
>
> 'Thou makest thine appeal to me.
>> I bring to life, I bring to death;
>> The spirit does but mean the breath:
> I know no more.' And he, shall he,
>
> Man, her last work, who seem'd so fair,
>> Such splendid purpose in his eyes,
>> Who roll'd the psalm to wintry skies,
> Who built him fanes of fruitless prayer,
>
> Who trusted God was love indeed
>> And love Creation's final law –
>> Tho' Nature, red in tooth and claw
> With ravine, shriek'd against his creed –
>
> Who lov'd, who suffer'd countless ills,
>> Who battled for the True, the Just,
>> Be blown about the desert dust,
> Or seal'd within the iron hills?

A further blow to human dignity came with the popularisation of Lord Kelvin's second law of thermodynamics. This was the law of entropy, which emphasised that in course of time there would be a levelling of all the temperature differences in the universe; so that the sun, instead of pouring out its energy indefinitely, would eventually cool and die in the heavens, and man would suffer a chilly death on earth.

'What makes mankind tragic,' said Conrad, 'is not that they are the victims of nature, it is that they are conscious of it' (*LCG*, p. 70). Given the bleakness of the vistas opened by scientific discovery, it is not surprising that many writers entertained the idea (paradoxically, since they *were* writers) that ignorance might after all be bliss. As we shall see later, the anti-rational primitivism which burgeoned in the late nineteenth century and which has its fullest literary efflorescence in the twentieth, in the works of D.H. Lawrence, is of great importance in Conrad's writings. In the meantime, we now turn to some political matters.

Poland and Conrad's political outlook

We would expect Conrad, the son of a renowned patriot, to have inherited his father's defiant love of Poland; and indeed this patriotism can be found explicitly and implicitly in many of his works. Most obviously, there are political essays bearing directly on the subject: 'Autocracy and War' and 'The Crime of Partition' (*NLL*). Then there is the late tale, 'Prince Roman' (*TH*), in which Conrad recalls how, as a child, he was privileged to meet the deaf, aged prince who had once been sentenced for life to the Siberian mines as his punishment for fighting the Russians in the uprising of 1831 – fighting for that country

> which demands to be loved as no other country has ever been loved, with the mournful affection one bears to the unforgotten dead and with the unextinguishable fire of a hopeless passion which only a living, breathing, warm ideal can kindle . . . . .
> (*TH*, p. 51)

Then there are the poignant reminiscences in *A Personal Record*, and the accounts of later visits, 'First News' and 'Poland Revisited' (*NLL*). In 1916 Conrad actually called at the Foreign Office in London with a memorandum, later adapted as 'A Note on the Polish Problem' (*NLL*), advocating the establishment, after the war, of a protectorate of allied powers to nurse Poland to independence. (In fact she regained complete independence in 1918, and promptly was at war with her old enemy, Russia, whose invading armies were routed in 1920; but her democratic system crumbled: Marshal Piłsudski held power from 1926 to 1935, and after his death a military junta ruled the nation until the Second World War.)

One of the most interesting tensions in Conrad's nature is that between patriotic loyalty to his homeland and the need to gain and maintain his independence. He may well have felt some guilt at having left his native land as a youth, and at working in English, as a British citizen, under the anglicised name of Joseph Conrad – the surname Korzeniowski having been so often garbled by linguistically slothful Englishmen. Poles themselves debated the ethics of his action. In the Polish weekly *Kraj*, in March 1899, Wincenty Lutosławski said that men of talent had the right to emigrate from an oppressed Poland; and he cited Conrad's novels when explaining that their works, even if in a foreign language, could still 'preserve the national spirit'. This view was bitterly contested by Eliza Orzeszkowa, herself a well-known novelist, who wrote in a subsequent article:

> Creative ability is the very crown of the plant, the very top of the tower, the very heart of the heart of the nation. And to take away from one's nation this flower, this top, this heart and to give it to the Anglo-Saxons who are not even lacking in bird's milk, for the only reason that they pay better for it – one cannot even think of it without shame . . . . . Over the novels of Mr Conrad Korzeniowski no Polish girl will shed an altruistic tear . . . . .
>
> (KRZ, p. 114)

Conrad heard of this debate; and there is a passage in *A Personal Record* (p. 35) which seems intended as a defence against such accusations. He is referring to his decision to leave Poland for the sea:

> Alas! I have the conviction that there are men of unstained rectitude who are ready to murmur scornfully the word desertion. Thus the taste of innocent adventure may be made bitter to the palate. The part of the inexplicable should be allowed for in appraising the conduct of men in a world where no explanation is final. No charge of faithlessness ought to be lightly uttered.

Thus it is clear that Conrad was sensitive to the idea that he could be regarded as having deserted his country; yet, had he stayed at home, he could (as we have noted) have been conscripted into the Russian army – no honour for a Pole. It is not surprising, then, that his literary works should reveal so strong a thematic preoccupation with loyalty and betrayal, and particularly with ambiguous situations in which loyalty to one code or group entails betrayal of another. Some Poles have been inclined to see a personal political allegory in *Lord Jim*. Jim leaps from what he believes to be a sinking ship (the *Patna*), later experiences shame and disgrace as a consequence of this act, and strives to redeem himself by his toils in a far-off land. Gustav Morf, in *The Polish Heritage of Joseph Conrad*, speculated that Conrad was thus sublimating his feelings of guilt at leaving Poland, the name *Patna* standing for *Polska* (another suggestion is *Patria*).

Allegorical interpretations of Conrad's works, and particularly interpretations which treat them as autobiographical confessionals or psychological self-therapies, are often reductive. As Conrad the guilty is pushed to the fore, Conrad the truth-teller, the perceptive observer of many lives, the artist capable of generalising astutely, tends to be pushed to the rear. However, a preoccupation with the ambiguities of loyalty and betrayal is certainly one of *Lord Jim*'s most important features: as when the villainous Gentleman Brown implies complicity with Jim, who finds that his loyalties are divided between his indigenous followers and his white race, and between a practical but ruthless ethic and a chivalrous but risky one.

There are other ways in which Conrad's Polish background attuned him to such ethical ambiguities. His father, Apollo, by being loyal to Poland, became 'an enemy of the state', a subversive, law-breaking figure in the eyes of the Russian authorities. Loyalty to a nation could entail disloyalty to its rulers. And furthermore, Apollo's nationalism, which resulted in trial and exile, led to sufferings not only for himself but for his wife and young son, who was so soon orphaned. Thus Conrad could discern ways in which loyalty to nation might entail disloyalty to family – or at least entail a sacrifice of familial happiness on the altar of a patriotic ideal. We may recall that in *Nostromo*, Charles Gould sacrifices his wife's happiness to his increasingly inflexible devotion to the ideal of developing the silver-mine; in *Under Western Eyes*, Haldin's devotion to the revolutionary cause results in his death and also thereby in the death of his heartbroken mother; and, in *Lord Jim*, Jim's determination to offer himself as a sacrifice to the natives who feel he has betrayed them entails his desertion of his most loyal friends, the woman Jewel and the servant Tamb'Itam. Conrad once wrote of himself: 'His life . . . . . presented itself to his conscience as a series of betrayals.'

His multiple perspectives, his readiness to use both the under-dog's and the upper-dog's viewpoints, helped to make Conrad an exceptionally incisive, mature and subtle political novelist. Born into the Polish gentry, with nobles and wealthy landowners (whose workmen spoke Ukrainian) among his relatives and contacts, Conrad would know how it felt to be among the élite of a given society. Yet since the Poles were politically subjugated by Prussia, Austria and Russia, he also knew how it felt to be the under-dog in an imperialist situation. During his sea-life, his voyages took him to some of the outposts of empire – Bombay, Singapore, Sydney; and, when domiciled in England, he could experience directly the jingoistic enthusiasms within a nation at the zenith of imperialism: for in the late nineteenth century Britain commanded the greatest empire the world had ever known, an empire circling the globe, an empire 'on which the sun never sets'. Thus Conrad, who (like so many Poles) was an anglophile, respecting British traditions of regard for individual liberties, could share some imperialistic enthusiasms; and in the closing pages of *The Nigger of the 'Narcissus'* he writes of Great Britain, the 'ship mother of fleets and nations', with a patriotic fervour which would have delighted a Rudyard Kipling, an Edmund Bentley or a W.E. Henley. Indeed, *The Nigger* was first published in Henley's *New Review*, which partly accounts for that fervour. Nevertheless, since he had known at first hand the ruthlessness of Russian imperialism (and later the iniquities of Belgian imperialism), he was capable of asking astute questions about the supposed justification of the imperial ethos, questions which too few in the late nineteenth century were willing to ask; and his 'Heart of Darkness' is the most brilliant fictional account of the rapacity and brutality which sometimes flourished in the name of imperial progress.

Given the sufferings of his nation and his family at the hands of the Russian overlords, one would expect a bitterness against Russia to be prominent in Conrad's writings, and in certain works this is the case. In 'Autocracy and War' he expresses a contempt which might be more persuasive if it were less sweeping:

> Russia . . . . . is not an empty void, she is a yawning chasm open between East and West; a bottomless abyss that has swallowed up every hope of mercy, every aspiration towards personal dignity, towards freedom, towards knowledge, every ennobling desire of the heart, every redeeming whisper of conscience.
>
> (*NLL*, p. 100)

In this essay of 1905 he also makes the astute prophecy – a prophecy that was, of course, fulfilled in 1917 and the subsequent decades – that though a Russian revolution will come, her people are so immured to slavery that the overthrow of Tsarism will simply inaugurate a further tyranny:

> In whatever form of upheaval Autocratic Russia is to find her end, it can never be a revolution fruitful of moral consequences to mankind. It cannot be anything else but a rising of slaves . . . . . It is safe to say tyranny, assuming a thousand protean shapes, will remain clinging to her struggles for a long time before her blind multitudes succeed at last in trampling her out of existence under their millions of bare feet.
>
> (Ibid., pp. 102–3)

(The rhetoric may remind us of the indignation of a later exile from Russian rule, Alexander Solzhenitsyn.) Three years after the Russian revolution had taken place, Conrad declared in the 'Author's Note' to *Under Western Eyes*:

> These people [the revolutionaries] are unable to see that all they can effect is merely a change of names. The oppressors and the oppressed are all Russians together; and the world is brought once more face to face with the truth of the saying that the tiger cannot change his stripes nor the leopard his spots.

Conrad's inherited bitterness against Russia makes the more notable his endeavours, in various fictional works, to register the complexity of Russian experience and outlooks. It is true that in *The Secret Agent* the arch-villain is the sinister Russian diplomat, Mr Vladimir; but in 'Heart of Darkness' the altruistic (if gullible) admirer of Kurtz is also a Russian, while 'The Warrior's Soul' (*TH*) describes the pity which Tsarist officers felt for the exhausted troops of Napoleon's retreating Grand Army. Most notably: in *Under Western Eyes* Conrad discriminates finely among both the defenders of Tsarist autocracy and the revolutionary groups: on each side he shows relative turpitude and relative nobility; he observes that the ordinary people may be downtrodden by the régime – or casually killed by a revolutionary's bomb; and he even observes that the extremities of Russian experience may give to life there an intensity compared with which the life of a Swiss citizen may be tame, and the life of a British citizen may be emotionally muted and inhibited. This rendering of complexities suggests that Conrad's nature is most fully present in his best works of fiction: there we come closer to the true Conrad than in letters or non-fictional writing – closer even than we would come if we were to interview him in person. The disciplines of good fiction are truth-seeking disciplines; and at its best Conrad's preoccupation with ambiguity and paradox is a sign neither of uncertainty nor of ideological fence-sitting, but, on the contrary, of an uncompromising commitment to the actual complexities of human experience.

Imperialism

Politically, Conrad is janiform. He is in some respects very conservative; yet he has also a keen radicalism of temperament which can lead him to observations which seem socialistic or even anarchistic.

In one early letter (commenting on the General Election of 1885, in which the Conservatives had suffered setbacks), he writes:

> The International Socialist Association are triumphant, and every disreputable ragamuffin in Europe feels that the day of universal brotherhood, despoliation and disorder is coming apace, and

nurses day-dreams of well-plenished pockets amongst the ruin of all that is respectable, venerable and holy. The great British Empire went over the edge, and yet on to the inclined plane of social progress and radical reform.

. . . . . England was the only barrier to the pressure of infernal doctrines born in continental back-slums. Now, there is nothing!
. . . . .

Socialism must inevitably end in Caesarism . . . . .

The whole herd of idiotic humanity are moving in that direction at the bidding of unscrupulous rascals and a few sincere, but dangerous, lunatics.

(*LL*, I, p. 84; *CL*, I, pp. 16–17)

Given that this election, with its newly extended electorate, actually resulted in a Conservative government (albeit in a minority to the Liberal opposition), Conrad's response may seem a little hysterical; but during the nineteenth century numerous British writers had feared that democratic pressures might result in 'mobocracy' and violent chaos. Dickens conveyed the fear vividly; so too did Ruskin, Carlyle, Elizabeth Gaskell, George Eliot and Matthew Arnold. One reason is obvious. The memory of the French Revolution lingered like a nightmare: the Revolution with its idealistic slogans, its frenzies of bigotry, its waves of carnage and bloody futility. When Conrad said 'Socialism must inevitably end in Caesarism', he might have been recalling various lessons of history: that the republicanism of ancient Rome gave way to the rule of the Caesars; that after the English Civil War, victory for the parliamentarians led to the tyranny of Cromwell; and that the French revolutionaries' rhetoric of 'liberty, equality and fraternity' ushered in the autocracy of Napoleon – whom Conrad termed 'a sort of vulture preying over the body of a Europe' (*NLL*, p. 86).

Nevertheless, as we have noted, Conrad's closest literary friendship was to be with the brilliant pioneer socialist, R.B. Cunninghame Graham, a man notorious for his militant advocacy of extreme left-wing policies. To him Conrad wrote in 1898:

You with your ideals of sincerity, courage and truth are strangely out of place in this epoch of material preoccupations. What does it bring? What's the profit? What do we get by it? These questions are at the root of every moral, intellectual or political movement. Into the noblest cause men manage to put something of their baseness; and sometimes when I think of You here, quietly[,] You seem to me tragic with your courage, with your beliefs and your hopes. Every cause is tainted: and you reject this one, espouse that other one as if one were evil and the other good while the same evil you hate is in both, but disguised in different

words. I am more in sympathy with you than words can express
yet if I had a grain of belief left in me I would believe you
misguided. You are misguided by the desire of the impossible –
and I envy you. Alas! What you want to reform are not
institutions – it is human nature. Your faith will never move that
mountain. Not that I think mankind intrinsically bad. It is only
silly and cowardly.

(LCG, p. 68)

In a further letter to Cunninghame Graham he was even more
cynical:

> Fraternity means nothing unless the Cain–Abel business . . . . .
> Man is a wicked animal. His wickedness has to be organised
> . . . . . Society is essentially criminal – otherwise it would not
> exist. It's egoism which preserves everything – absolutely every-
> thing – everything that we hate, everything that we love. And
> everything holds together. This is why I respect extreme anarch-
> ists. – 'I wish for general extermination' – Very well. It is just;
> and what's more, it's clear.

(LCG, p. 117. I have translated Conrad's French.)

What is obvious in these varied and not entirely consistent
pronouncements is the distrust of human nature: the sense that
society, at best, holds in check the ever-present tendencies to
disruption. If the temperamental conservative is one who takes a
very pessimistic view of human nature, then for much of the time
Conrad was such a conservative. However, we should remember
that his father was not only a scion of the gentry, but also a leader
of the 'Reds' amongst the Polish patriots: he hoped that the Russians
might be cast out as a result of a popular uprising which would
unite high and low. So although Conrad's distrust of human nature
can be related to a very ancient sceptical tradition whose represen-
tatives include Lucretius, Hobbes, Mandeville, Voltaire and Schopenhauer, one complication is that sympathy with the under-dog
which can sometimes be found among aristocrats – particularly
when, as Polish aristocrats, they become political under-dogs themselves. *Noblesse oblige*: rank imposes obligations.

Conrad's father had denounced profiteering 'chapmen, mer-
chants, beermongers'. For obvious historical reasons, scions of the
land-owning gentry often feel threatened by the business-minded
middle class. As a feudal–agrarian economy gives way to a mercan-
tile–industrial economy, economic and political power tends to pass
from the land-owning interests to business interests. It is, therefore,
not entirely unusual for noblemen to espouse popular causes,
seeking alliance with the socially low against the middle classes

(Cunninghame Graham, as a land-owning aristocrat with a heavily mortgaged estate, is a good example), or to offer criticisms of the middle-class outlook which resemble those offered by socialists. Like Cunninghame Graham, Conrad had a keen eye for the ways in which impressive phrases and slogans might mask the ruthless acquisitiveness of individuals or of nations. 'Holy Russia' he had experienced in childhood as unholy tyranny. In 'Heart of Darkness' he was to write, with laconic audacity: 'The conquest of the earth, which mostly means the taking it away from those who have a different complexion or slightly flatter noses than ourselves, is not a pretty thing when you look into it too much' (*Y*, pp. 50–1). And he had a shrewd awareness of the ways in which democracy under capitalism may approach pseudo-democracy, since the man who pays the piper calls the tune:

> Industrialism and commercialism – wearing high-sounding names in many languages (*Welt-politik* may serve for one instance) . . . . . – stand ready, almost eager, to appeal to the sword as soon as the globe of the earth has shrunk beneath our growing numbers by another ell or so. And democracy, which has elected to pin its faith to the supremacy of material interests, will have to fight their battles to the bitter end . . . . .
>
> ('Autocracy and War', *NLL*, p. 107)

(This was virtually a prophecy of the First World War.) In the same essay of 1905 Conrad notes that in Africa, 'territorial spheres of influence' have been marked out 'to keep the competitors for the privilege of improving the nigger (as a buying machine) from flying prematurely at each other's throats'. His use of the term 'nigger' may make present readers flinch; but his sardonically reductive view of imperialism is a reminder that Conrad had seen at first hand the exploitative system in the Belgian Congo; and, in the tropics, he had often known 'frontier situations' which raise the question of what, if anything, really distinguishes the supposedly civilised from the supposedly primitive; and he had developed a keen sense of disparities between word and fact, slogan and deed.

From a survey of Conrad's works we can infer how he would probably have ranked various imperial nations in order of demerit. Beginning with the least corrupt and descending to the most corrupt, the order would be: Great Britain; France; Spain; Japan; Austria; Holland; the United States; Belgium; Prussia; Russia. Prussia and Russia are at the bottom of the list, mainly because of their treatment of the subjugated Poles. The Belgians are close to the bottom because of their predatory activities in the Congo. The Americans occupy a low position because Conrad (at least until his later years) was inclined to see North American society as the arch-capitalist society, dominated by the quest for the silver dollar. Furthermore, in the 1890s the United States had emerged as a newly aggressive imperial power by going to war against Spain over possession of Cuba and the Philippines; and, though the Americans were the victors, Conrad (like many British and European observers) was inclined to sympathise with Spain, on the grounds that while this old nation was now shorn of her former grandeur, at least she could boast cultural riches exceeding those of the United States.

> But, perhaps, the race is doomed? It would be a pity. It would narrow life, it would destroy a whole side of it which had its morality and was always picturesque and at times inspiring. The others may well shout Fiax lux! [Let there be light!] It will be only the reflected light of a silver dollar and no sanctimonious pretence will make it resemble the real sunshine.
>
> (*LCG*, p. 84)

Of Dutch imperialism Conrad took a mixed but somewhat hostile view, to judge from *Almayer's Folly*, 'Karain' and 'Freya of the Seven Isles'. Austria's place in the list is fairly high, because although she was one of the partitioning powers in Poland, her rule had often been relatively easy-going and tolerant. Conrad's respect for the Japanese stemmed mainly from the fact that they had defeated the Russians in 1905 and were allies of Britain in the early years of the century. France has a high position, partly because Poland was culturally a francophile nation (whose exiles often settled in Paris) and partly because Poles had joined the Napoleonic army to assail Russia: indeed, Conrad's great-uncle Nicholas had himself been one of the survivors of the retreat from Moscow (starving, he had eaten dog). And Britain has her position at the top of the table largely because of her liberal traditions of concern for the liberty of the individual: the traditions of free speech, the jury system in law-courts, habeas corpus, the parliamentary electoral system, and the principle of sanctuary for foreign refugees. Furthermore – notwithstanding many barbarities inflicted by her in Ireland and elsewhere – Britain's imperialism seemed to Conrad relatively paternalist and less ruthlessly exploitative than that of other nations.

In his letters, Conrad referred to that 'liberty, which can only be found under the English flag'. Some of his sea-tales are clearly inflected so as to flatter a British readership. The voyage of the real ship *Narcissus* had terminated not in London but at Dunkirk; by changing the place of landfall to England, the novel *The Nigger of the 'Narcissus'* sets the scene for a patriotic paean. Again, the tale 'Youth' bases its account of the *Judea* on the disastrous voyage of the *Palestine*, and Marlow (the inner narrator) salutes the heroic and conscientious labour of the English crew: 'I don't say positively that the crew of a French or German merchantman wouldn't have done it, but I doubt whether it would have been done in the same way.' In reality, the hard-working crew of the *Palestine* consisted of a black seaman from St Kitts, a Belgian, an Irishman, two men and a boy from Devon, and a Norwegian; while the officers were an Englishman, an Irishman and (of course) a Pole. The tale, by specifying a courageous British crew, illustrates the process of patriotic myth-making. Conrad characteristically tended to idealise the traditional and professional morality of the British Merchant Navy.

Nevertheless, though Conrad could speak like a proud British patriot on many occasions, he still held the view that imperialism in itself was always suspect and that the world would be a better place if there were no imperialism at all. In his very first novel, *Almayer's Folly*, he had dared to imply that what the imperial nations do on a big scale, with their gunboat diplomacy and their international rivalry for 'spheres of influence', is essentially no different from what the 'uncivilised' people do on a small scale in their jungle settlements. In that novel, the Dutch are in rivalry with the British for control of Borneo; the Arabs compete with the Malays for the control of Almayer's trading district; and Almayer himself competes with a Balinese, Dain, for possession of his Eurasian daughter. And she, Nina, who has lived among both Malays and Europeans, reflects bitterly that whatever the race, nationality, colour or creed, all men seem alike in their egoistic questing for material profit. In 'Heart of Darkness', Marlow emphasises that Kurtz, who becomes corrupt in the African wilderness, is the product of all Europe – including England. 'All Europe contributed to the making of Kurtz.'

The boldness and originality of Conrad's criticisms of imperialism are enhanced when we recall that the 1890s, when *Almayer's Folly* and 'Heart of Darkness' appeared, were the great heyday of imperialism, as trade rivalry grew between the various industrialised nations; and it was certainly a time when most British people – whatever their social class – were jingoists; indeed, a popular music-hall song of the day (by G.W. Hunt) was the origin of the term 'jingoism':

> We don't want to fight; but, by Jingo, if we do,
> We've got the ships, we've got the men, we've got the
> money too.

'An Outpost of Progress', that scathing attack on colonialism in Africa, was published in the international magazine *Cosmopolis* for June and July 1897 – the year of Queen Victoria's Diamond Jubilee. In the June issue of the magazine, Sir Richard Temple's article 'The Reign of Queen Victoria' is a eulogy of the growth of British economic power, military strength and territory; while, in 'The Globe and the Island', the regular political commentator, Henry Norman, praises British gunboat diplomacy in Africa. The July number of the magazine, in which Conrad's Kayerts shoots the unarmed Carlier and hangs himself from a cross, contains a commentary on the Jubilee celebrations in which Norman remarks:

> Britain is imperialistic now. The 'Little Englander' has wisely decided to efface himself. The political party which should talk of reducing the navy or snubbing the Colonies would have a short shrift. We are Imperialists first, and Liberals or Tories afterwards. I said this, for my own part, years ago, when the sentiment was not quite so popular. Now it has happily become a commonplace. The Jubilee is its culminating expression . . . . .

The issue of *Blackwood's Magazine* for March 1899 contained an article entitled 'An Unwritten Chapter of History: The Struggle for Borgu', of which the following remarks are typical:

> The little bush-fighting that was done against Lapai and elsewhere proved the superiority of the hard bullet over that used in the Sniders. The soft bullet is apt to break up when volleys are fired into bush where natives are hiding; but the Lee-Metford projectiles went through the cover so completely that the hidden party always ran before our men could get close . . . . .;

and this article accompanies the episode of 'Heart of Darkness' in which the 'pilgrims' empty their futile rifles into the bush, and in which Kurtz scrawls 'Exterminate all the brutes!'

Conrad's pessimistic sense that human nature is largely corruptible and fallible leads him to the humanitarian insight that since the 'civilised' people are not likely to be much better (if at all) than the so-called 'inferior races', we might as well leave remote nations alone. His anti-rational primitivism sometimes leads him to imply that the 'primitive' people may in fact be healthier, more vital and better attuned to their environment than are the restless Europeans. This is implied, for example, in Marlow's description, in 'Heart of Darkness', of the Africans paddling their canoe powerfully through the surf:

> 'They shouted, sang; their bodies streamed with perspiration; they had faces like grotesque masks – these chaps; but they had bone, muscle, a wild vitality, an intense energy of movement, that was as natural and true as the surf along their coast. They wanted no excuse for being there.'
>
> (*Y*, p. 61)

In ironic contrast to such vitality is the absurd automatism of the French warship shelling a continent (*Y*, pp. 61–2) and the moribund apathy of the Africans who have been used as slave-labour and abandoned to the grove of death by the Europeans (*Y*, pp. 66–7).

Conrad is particularly acute in his sense that aggression on the part of individuals *and* of nations may stem not from strength but from weakness, insecurity, fear and immaturity. In 'Autocracy and War', he eloquently declares:

> The intellectual stage of mankind being as yet in its infancy, and States, like most individuals, having but a feeble and imperfect consciousness of the worth and force of the inner life, the need of making their existence manifest to themselves is determined in the direction of physical activity. The idea of ceasing to grow in territory, in strength, in wealth, in influence – in anything but wisdom and self-knowledge [–] is odious to them as the omen of the end. Action, in which is to be found the illusion of a mastered destiny, can alone satisfy our uneasy vanity and lay to rest the haunting fear of the future . . . . . It will be long before we have learned that in the great darkness before us there is nothing that we need fear. Let us act lest we perish – is the cry. And the only action open to a State can be of no other than aggressive nature.
>
> (*NLL*, pp. 108–9)

The claims are bold, simple, polemical and plausible. His linkage of the immaturity of a state to the immaturity of an individual may remind us that one source of the power of Conrad's novels is that they offer simultaneously public and private histories: they are at once political, psychological and moral analyses of life. Here Conrad argues that just as the mature individual does not go punching and elbowing his way about the world but leads a more quiet, contemplative and cultured life, the mature nation does not concern itself with imperialistic aggression and expansion but cultivates its own human, cultural resources. (Conrad may partly be recalling the fact that the national life of subjugated Poland found expression in a flourishing artistic heritage.) Conrad's ideal may invite some critical reflections, however. Historically, an era of imperial expansion often provides the economic preconditions of flourishing culture: the Athenian empire generated the civilisation of Athens in the fifth century BC, and the later Roman splendours were financed by exploited subject-territories. Nevertheless, his ideal is nobly pacific and remains cogent.

There is a further aspect of imperialism which is of particular importance in Conrad's work. Conrad was greatly interested in 'one-man imperialism' – in the small, personal realms established by adventurous Europeans in far-off places: for example, by Clunies-Ross in the Cocos Island chain, by the real Lingard in Borneo, and by James (later Sir James) Brooke on Sarawak. Almost single-handedly, Brooke established himself as revered ruler of the indigenous people of Sarawak: he became 'the first White Rajah'; the land was declared his property, and on his retirement passed from one Brooke to another until eventually, in 1946, it was taken over by the British Government. Conrad wrote to the Lady Margaret Brooke, Dowager Ranee of Sarawak, in 1920: 'The first Rajah Brooke has been one of my boyish admirations, a feeling I have kept to this day strengthened by the better understanding of the greatness of his character and the unstained rectitude of his purpose' (*LCG*, p. 210). He drew heavily on the life of James Brooke (particularly as recorded in Rodney Mundy's *Narrative of Events in Borneo and Celebes*, 1848) when writing *Lord Jim* and *The Rescue*; and there is no doubt that Conrad could feel the romantic appeal of such daring, personal achievements. Yet he still, in the novels, consistently makes the point that 'fools rush in where angels fear to tread': in the long run, even the benevolent paternalist does more harm than good. In *Lord Jim*, although Jim helps his adopted tribe to conquer and prosper for a while, his presence provokes the massacre in which the old chief's son is slain; and, in *The Rescue*, though Lingard initially safeguards and supports his Malay friends Hassim and Immada, his infatuation with a white woman leads him to ignore their plight, and they, betrayed, perish. Even Kurtz in 'Heart of Darkness' leaves his tribal followers mourning and distraught by his decision to return with the Europeans.

The philosophical Stein of *Lord Jim* (p. 213) muses regretfully: 'This magnificent butterfly finds a little heap of dirt and sits still on it; but man he will never on his heap of mud keep still. He want to be so, and again he want to be so . . . .' His words, a comment on Jim and human nature, may serve also as a wry comment on imperialism.

Finally, we should notice the relationship between Conrad's attitudes to imperialism and his attitudes to racial and sexual prejudice – for these are interlinked matters. It could be argued that with the surface of his imagination he reflects and in some measure endorses imperialistic enthusiasms, but the depths of his imagination question and largely subvert them. Similarly, it often seems that at a superficial level his works reflect and in some measure endorse the prejudices (of white against black, of gentile against Jew, of male against female) which were taken for granted by most people of all classes in the Europe of his day; but it can be claimed that the more fully his imagination is engaged, the more those prejudices are challenged. Such defences have much validity, though they encounter textual resistance at certain points: notably, the depiction of Wait in *The Nigger of the 'Narcissus'*, the 'demonisation' of the jungle in 'Heart of Darkness', and the treatment of Hirsch in *Nostromo*.

Science and determinism

In the nineteenth century, science enjoyed greater prestige than ever before, and possibly more than it has enjoyed since. In the twentieth century, two world wars, in which scientific knowledge was so ingeniously employed to multiply slaughter and destruction, have shown that advances in science are far from synonymous with advances in civilisation, and that a decent quality of life is far more dependent on human kindness than on scientific qualifications. Nevertheless, in the nineteenth century the prestige of science was so great that even areas of thought which were little constrained by empirical experimentation (for example, the psychological speculations of Freud, or the political rhetoric of Marx and Engels) claimed to be 'scientific' and therefore 'objective'.

Today, we are much more aware that scientific laws change from age to age, and that scientific fact in one period may be fantasy in another. In the Middle Ages, it was 'scientific fact' that the sun went round the earth; but the cosmology of Ptolemy has been superseded by that of Copernicus, and Newton has been superseded by Einstein. Although there has been a gradual accumulation of new knowledge about the universe, it is also the case that we are far more aware that a scientist's conclusions are implicit in his or her premises, that scientific developments may help to support oppressive political systems, and that (as a distinguished nuclear physicist, Sir Denys Wilkinson, has declared) 'The world is real all right and it is not in the mind; on the other hand, it is, or is going to be, what the mind makes it.'

When Conrad was a young man, science seemed to be making vast progress in many areas: astronomy, biology, chemistry, physics, engineering; the burgeoning of European industrial technology was transforming Europe and changing the world. New weapons, new machines, new means of transport; and, dominating a receptive globe, a thriving and expanding 'workshop of the world'. Here, in the spectacular advances of the capitalist economies, lay some of the reasons for science's prestige and the sense that it was unfailingly objective. ('There are times when the tyranny of science and the cant of science are alarming', remarked Conrad.)

Some scientific laws are analytic propositions or deductions; they may resemble tautologies or the rules of a game. Other scientific laws are synthetic propositions, or inductions: they are often generalisations inferred from a number of experimental observations. These results are seldom rigid, binding and perennial: they are potentially refutable and may be revised, corrected or scrapped in the light of further observations. Again, though event is linked to event by a sequence of cause and effect, that sequence is not a binding, compelling sequence. In the nineteenth century, however, causality was sometimes confused with determinism, and this confusion had extensive consequences in the thought and the literature of the period. An intermittent but powerful sense of the universe as a soulless mechanism determining human lives was one of the obvious sources of Conrad's pessimism, as the following words to Cunninghame Graham indicate:

> There is a – let us say – a machine. It evolved itself (I am severely scientific) out of a chaos of scraps of iron and behold! – it knits. I am horrified at the horrible work and stand appalled. I feel it ought to embroider – but it goes on knitting . . . . . And the most withering thought is that the infamous thing has made itself; made itself without thought, without conscience, without fore-sight, without eyes, without heart. It is a tragic accident – and it has happened. You can't interfere with it. The last drop of bitterness is in the suspicion that you can't even smash it . . . . .
>
> It knits us in and it knits us out. It has knitted time space, pain, death, corruption, despair and all the illusions – and nothing matters. I'll admit however that to look at the remorseless process is sometimes amusing.
>
> (LCG, pp. 56–7)

If 'nothing matters', then man, as a moral being, is superfluous. And, as we shall now see, 'Superfluous Men' soon manifest themselves.

The Superfluous Man

The Superfluous Man is a distinctive type of man who is commonly found in Russian literature of the nineteenth century. He is the offspring of certain rather lonely, self-pitying and unlucky heroes of the Romantic period: notably Goethe's sorrowful young Werther and Byron's moody Childe Harold. In turn, he is the progenitor of certain neurotically self-conscious and rather impotent figures of twentieth-century literature: Rilke's Malte Laurids Brigge, Eliot's Prufrock, Sartre's Roquentin (for yesterday's Existentialist is last week's Superfluous Man), Camus's Clamence, Nabokov's Humbert Humbert, and numerous futile protagonists in Samuel Beckett's works.

The name of the type, established by Lermontov, was used by Conrad's favourite Russian novelist, Turgenev, in his tale 'The Diary of a Superfluous Man' (1850). Tchulkaturin, the central figure of that tale, is the son of fairly well-to-do landowners in Russia. The estate has been sold; he has enough money to live in idleness, but not enough to have power. He lives in the countryside, which is relatively inexpensive compared with Moscow, but excruciatingly boring. He is extremely egoistic: his 'sensibility' makes him self-conscious to the point of paralysis or derangement. A romantic without a cause, he is socially superfluous. His style combines sentimental self-absorption, emotional exhibitionism, and ironic, even comic, self-deflation:

> Farewell, life! . . . . . Farewell, Liza! I wrote those two words, and almost laughed aloud. This exclamation strikes me as taken out of a book. It's as though I were writing a sentimental novel and ending up a despairing letter . . .
>
> To-morrow is the first of April. Can I be going to die to-morrow? That would be really too unseemly. It's just right for me, though . . .
>
> How the doctor did chatter to-day!

Even Tchulkaturin's last words combine pathos with irony: 'Sinking into nothing, I cease to be superfluous.'

Characteristics of this type, then, are an egoistic (albeit intelligent) sensibility, rather decadent or neurotic in its oscillations of mood; a cynical or ironic quality; and, above all, that sense of being superfluous, without role or function; isolated from society. Other examples of the type are: Pechorin, central figure of Lermontov's *A Hero of Our Time* (1840), the eponymous protagonist of Turgenev's *Rudin*, the protagonist of Chekhov's 'A Moscow Hamlet', and a variety of prominent figures in Chekhov's plays – the hero of *Ivanov*, Vanya in *Uncle Vanya*, Cherbutykin in *Three Sisters*. Others can be found in the pages of Goncharov, Dostoyevsky and Tolstoy; and the Superfluous Man may also exist as a state of being through which pass various characters who may not eventually belong to this type.

If we ask why Superfluous Men are so numerous in *Russian* literature of the nineteenth century, they themselves provide numerous answers. One is that for various reasons (price inflation, the increase of labour costs after the emancipation of the serfs, the high cost of living in the fashionable cities of St Petersburg and Moscow) there then existed a large class of educated, idle, discontented, bored gentlemen. Sufficiently well-to-do not to be obliged to work, yet too poor to enjoy the pleasures of power; often forced to live in the countryside, which was inexpensive but, to their civilised natures, oppressively boring. Another reason is that the Russian state, autocratically ruled and with a rigid hierarchy, already virtually a police state with ruthless powers of censorship, offered few outlets for romantic idealism and radicalism. In the chilly vastness of Tsarist

Russia, it was easier for a man to feel 'superfluous' than in other parts of Europe. And the sense of fatalism that this engendered could make him particularly receptive to deterministic arguments.

In his powers of philosophical self-vindication, the narrator of Dostoyevsky's *Notes from Underground* seems by far the most fully developed of the Superfluous Men. However he looks at his situation, this morbid Hamlet feels himself threatened by 'the stone wall' of laws, whether they be those of the utilitarian economists or of evolutionary scientists; men can appear to him merely 'the keys of a piano, which the laws of nature threaten to control so completely'. He considers various responses to this sense of determinism. One is to be Hamlet-like: to shrug one's shoulders and do nothing, submitting to inertia. (If action is compelled, perhaps inaction manifests, perversely, a sense of independence.) The second way is to assert one's independence by acting in apparent defiance of rational laws: to be quixotic, using one's will wilfully; acting capriciously, even anarchically. If 'the direct, legitimate fruit of consciousness is inertia', nevertheless 'reason is nothing but reason . . . . . while will is a manifestation of the whole life'; 'caprice . . . . . preserves for us what is most precious and most important – that is, our personality, our individuality'; 'it is just his fantastic dreams, his vulgar folly, that he will desire to retain, simply in order to prove to himself . . . . . that men still are men and not the keys of a piano'; 'he will contrive destruction and chaos . . . . . only to gain his point'. The narrator actually adds, as though prophesying the coming of Conrad's Mr Kurtz, 'It may be at the cost of his skin, it may be by cannibalism!'

In his neurotic self-consciousness, his impotence and his habitation of a waste-land of boredom, the Superfluous Man anticipates many twentieth-century figures, from Eliot's Prufrock to the static Jeremiahs of Samuel Beckett. On the other hand, in his sense of absurdity and alienation, and in his idea that one could prove one's selfhood by some defiant, anarchic, seemingly irrational action, he anticipates Existentialist or Absurdist heroes: Sartre's Roquentin or Camus's Meursault and Clamence. We could perhaps say that the Existentialist is a Hamlet who chooses to become a Don Quixote.

To this tradition we can relate not only some of Conrad's characters but also Conrad himself in certain moods so eloquently registered in his more pessimistic letters.

The Hamlet/Don Quixote dichotomy

From the mid-nineteenth century onwards, the gradual erosion of religious belief reduced confidence that moral standards had absolute, objective warrant. One of the numerous cultural consequences was that Cervantes' Don Quixote came to be regarded not just as a lovable literary eccentric but increasingly as a symbol of modern idealism, for his idealism had patently lacked objective sanction. So in the latter half of the nineteenth century, a 'Cult of Don Quixote' developed in Europe. The number of translations of Cervantes' classic multiplied rapidly; and characters in literature or in life who manifested questing idealism were likely to be compared to Quixote. The cult's extreme was probably reached in 1906, when Miguel de Unamuno published *Our Lord Don Quixote*, a philosophical and religious commentary which proposed that we adopt Cervantes' deluded knight as the Christ for our times. 'I believe,' said Unamuno, 'we might undertake a holy crusade to redeem the Sepulchre of the Knight of Madness from the power of the champions of Reason.' In *Meditaciones del Quijote* (1914), by José Ortega y Gasset, the Don was termed 'a Gothic Christ, torn by modern anguish'.

This cult was anticipated by some of the Russian authors. We have noted that Dostoyevsky's Superfluous Man considered two contrasting responses to his plight: one that of passivity, a Hamlet-like response; the other that of irrational, rather Quixotic action. In another Russian writer of the time, this Hamlet/Don Quixote dichotomy became fully explicit as a means of analysis of contemporary states of mind. The writer was, again, Conrad's favourite Russian author, Turgenev; and the specific item is his influential lecture, 'Hamlet and Don Quixote' (1860), which in England was first published in 1894.

In the lecture, Turgenev claims that Hamlet and Don Quixote represent 'the twin antitypes of human nature, the two poles of the axle-tree on which that nature turns'. Shakespeare's Hamlet was a sceptical procrastinator: in him 'the native hue of resolution/Is sicklied o'er with the pale cast of thought'; and the Hamlet type is similarly a sceptical egoist, his will paralysed by reflection. Don Quixote, conversely, is an active campaigner, a credulous idealist: he can act, although (alas) he is often misguided or deluded: his giants are only windmills.

> So on the one side we see the Hamlets of this world – that is to say, types that are thoughtful and discriminating, persons of wide and profound understanding, but persons who are useless in the practical sense, inasmuch as their very gifts immobilize them – and, on the other, crack-brained Don Quixotes, who are only useful to humanity and can set its feet marching because they see but one sole point on the horizon, a point the nature of which is often not at all what it seems to their eyes.

A pessimistic disjunction, then: rationality that leads to inaction, versus activity that is deluded. (It recalls Schopenhauer's distinc-

The Second Sally *by William Strang.*
  Conrad's friend, Cunninghame Graham (see illustration on page 34), was the model for the Don in this picture from Strang's Series of Thirty Etchings . . . . . illustrating . . . . . 'Don Quixote' (1902).

tion, in *Die Welt als Wille und Vorstellung*, 1818, between reflection and will.)

Chekhov read and admired Turgenev's lecture, and it influenced the characterisation of his plays, most explicitly in *Ivanov*. Conrad, who warmly admired Turgenev's 'unerring instinct for the significant, for the essential in human life and in the visible world' (EG, p. 269), would have known the dichotomy through its use in Turgenev's novels and tales even if he had not known the lecture itself. What is certain is that the Hamlet/Don Quixote dichotomy has obvious application both to Conrad's janiform personality and to the loom of characterisation in his works.

We have seen that Conrad's tutor called him 'an incorrigible, hopeless Don Quixote' for his determination to go to sea, and that the Don figures almost as a patron saint in the autobiographical *Personal Record*; we have also seen that Conrad was reproached for being a brooding Hamlet by his 'aunt', Marguerite Poradowska, and that jeremiads about the native hue of resolution's being 'sicklied o'er with the pale cast of thought' are a recurrent feature of his letters. Again, we have seen that Conrad's closest literary friendship was with Cunninghame Graham, a man who was celebrated in his lifetime as 'a modern Don Quixote' (and who was called 'the Don Quixote' by Conrad); who often paid tribute to both Cervantes and Shakespeare, and who even posed as the Don for a series of etchings by Strang to illustrate Cervantes' masterpiece; and yet whose tales and letters (like this one to Edward Garnett in 1899) reveal a profound and often Hamlet-like scepticism about the value of action:

> Significance in things, Ha, Ha, why even atoms themselves are all in a jumble.
>
> Fornication, my masters, murder, adultery, cheating, lies, & the offertory, those are the leading motives of life, & ever will be . . . . . A dingy farce played by fools & harlots, on a poor stage, with an incompetent stage manager, & the only laugh in it, being at one's own antics & folly for continuing to act.
>
> (*LCG*, p. 27)

If we turn to Conrad's works, we find that the Hamlet/Don Quixote dichotomy is almost alarmingly applicable to a wide range of characters. I say 'almost alarmingly', since this fact implies a certain schematic ruthlessness in Conrad's approach to characterisation, and since we are thus reminded of Conrad's pessimistic emphasis on impotence and futility. Many of his patently honourable characters can be seen as quixotic either because their values are anachronistic or incongruous, given the nature of the environment in which those values operate, or because their idealism has the quality of a delusion or monomania. Both factors operate in the case of Tom Lingard, the brave adventurer with a fatal capacity for wishing to foster protégés. In *Almayer's Folly, An Outcast* and *The Rescue*, his well-intentioned schemes bring not only disappointment to himself but also bitterness, suffering and death to others. (And he is explicitly likened to Don Quixote, of course: D'Alcacer in *The Rescue* calls him 'a descendant of the immortal hidalgo errant upon the sea'.) More subtly, several of the major works, and *Nostromo* in particular, suggest that all conduct governed by pursuit of some ideal is quixotic both in the sense that it will be betrayed by the facts of harsh actuality – 'There was something inherent in the necessities of successful action which carried with it the moral degradation of the idea' (*N*, p. 521) – and in the sense that the quester will appear deranged in proportion to his devotion to that ideal – 'Every conviction, as soon as it became effective, turned into that form of dementia the gods send upon those they wish to destroy' (*N*, p. 200). When trying to sum up the political confusions of South America, Decoud in that novel says: 'There is a curse of futility upon our character: Don Quixote and Sancho Panza, chivalry and materialism, high-sounding sentiments and a supine morality . . . . .' (p. 171). A central thematic statement of *Under Western Eyes* is: 'Hopes grotesquely betrayed, ideals caricatured – that is the definition of revolutionary success' (p. 135).

Conrad has ambivalent feelings, of course, about quixotic individuals. The Romantic tradition, which confers high value on lonely, intense idealism, encourages Conrad to look with some sympathy on such characters; but various Augustan and Enlightenment traditions (commending balance, restraint and sociability) encourage him to look sceptically on conduct tending to the fanatical and extreme. An excellent resolution of this ambivalence is found in the characterisation of Charles Gould in *Nostromo*, whose courage, rectitude and sense of honour win measured respect, even though his progress towards what is virtually a cold monomania is systematically delineated. As the narrator remarks of Gould: 'A man haunted by a fixed idea is insane. He is dangerous even if that idea is an idea of justice; for may he not bring the heaven down pitilessly upon a loved head?' (p. 379).

Looking beyond particular characters, we can see that in his more sceptical moods Conrad could regard any and every apparently purposeful action as quixotic. If humans were predetermined beings, the puppets of causality, in a universe devoid of God, of responsiveness, of ultimate purpose, they were all, in a sense, quixotic: futile and deranged, the sense of effective action being only an illusion. The point is uncompromisingly made in the most famous epigram of *Nostromo*, an epigram which deploys dauntingly the words 'illusion' and 'helpless': 'In our activity alone do we find the sustaining illusion of an independent existence as against the whole scheme of things of which we form a helpless part' (p. 497). The idea is repeated with variations in *Nostromo* and in other writings of Conrad:

> Action is consolatory. It is the enemy of thought and the friend of flattering illusions.
>
> (*N*, p. 66)

> He [Anatole France] wishes us to believe and to hope, preserving in our activity the consoling illusion of power and intelligent purpose.
>
> (*NLL*, p. 34)

> Action, in which is to be found the illusion of a mastered destiny, can alone satisfy our uneasy vanity and lay to rest the haunting fear of the future . . . . .
>
> (*NLL*, p. 109)

One implication of these words was to be developed extensively later by Absurdist and Existentialist authors: the implication that man, as a moral and meaning-seeking creature, is an absurdity in the creation. And Conrad fully recognised this implication, as the following passages show:

> Humanity presses from all sides upon the narrow waters desecrating with the whisper of its hopes and fears, with the cry of its strife, with the sigh of its longings, the august unconcern of a limitless space.
>
> (MS of *The Rescue*)

> Man on this earth is an unforeseen accident which does not stand close investigation.
>
> (*V*, p. 196)

If we now consider the other half of the Hamlet/Don Quixote dichotomy, we see that Turgenev's Hamlet has sired many offspring in Conrad's pages. The most familiar example is probably *Nostromo*'s Decoud, the sophisticated sceptic who sees the follies of activities which others take seriously (though it must be said that his scepticism is frequently surpassed by the narrator's), and who, when isolated on an island, experiences 'the crushing, paralysing sense of human littleness', comes to doubt even his own individuality, and eventually shoots himself. A more extreme example is Axel Heyst, the hero of *Victory*. Heyst has been indoctrinated by his father, a cynical philosopher (probably based by Conrad on Schopenhauer) who with 'strange serenity, mingled with terrors', had contemplated 'the universal nothingness' and had taught his son that life was a cruel joke, a snare and a cheat. Consequently:

> The young man learned to reflect, which is a destructive process, a reckoning of the cost. It is not the clear-sighted who lead the world. Great achievements are accomplished in a blessed, warm mental fog, which the pitiless cold blasts of the father's analysis had blown away from the son.
> 'I'll drift,' Heyst had said to himself deliberately.
>
> (V, pp. 91–2)

Nevertheless, though he strives to be detached and uncommitted, he is twice drawn into involvement with his fellow humans, once through pity and once through a mixture of pity and sexual desire; and both acts conspire to bring about the disastrous dénouement in which the young woman who loves him, Lena, is killed. Heyst appears to disavow his father's sceptical philosophy with the words, 'Woe to the man whose heart has not learned while young to hope, to love – and to put its trust in life!'; but, having said this, he commits suicide. If the elder Heyst could be invited to comment on this novel, he would doubtless observe that the plot vindicates his cynicism, since his son's altruistic acts have actually provoked the final disasters; and, as if echoing his pronouncements on nothingness, the novel's last word is 'Nothing!'

Just as the more quixotic characters are only the extreme examples in an extensive discussion, within Conrad's fiction, of an essential quixotry in all human action, so the more Hamlet-like characters (intelligent, sceptical, distrustful of action) are only the extreme instances of an extensive preoccupation with the idea that reflection may paralyse will. In *The Shadow-Line*, when the narrator is afflicted with acedia (a sense of the pointlessness of action), his phrasing echoes the play *Hamlet* as he speaks of 'this stale, unprofitable world of my discontent', 'an undiscovered country', 'that force somewhere within our lives which shapes them this way or that' and 'the mortal coil'; and his imagination proves to be a subversive power which leads him almost to the point of mental breakdown on his ship.

Generally in Conrad's fiction, it seems to be the rule that the more reflective the man, the more likely he is to prove unreliable in action, and the more stolidly imperceptive the man, the more likely he is to prove resiliently dependable in action. If you wish to ally yourself to one who is consistent and seems designed for survival, you should ally yourself with Sancho Panza or Horatio rather than with their masters. In Conrad's pages, such dependables are represented by – among others – Singleton (*Nigger of the 'Narcissus'*),

MacWhirr ('Typhoon'), the boiler-maker ('Heart of Darkness'), Don Pepe (*Nostromo*), Wang (*Victory*) and Jörgenson (*The Rescue*). The tradition that they represent is explained in the following section.

Anti-rational primitivism

Writers are primitivists insofaras they say or imply that a relatively primitive state of being (in individuals or societies) is better than a relatively sophisticated state of being. Writers are anti-rational primitivists in so far as they say or imply that a relatively primitive state of consciousness is better than a relatively sophisticated one. Such a writer may, for example, commend instinctive awareness or 'blood consciousness' and condemn rational calculation or 'mental consciousness'. These writings often reveal a nostalgic chronological primitivism, too: nostalgia for some kind of golden age in the past, before the fall into our present unhappy state. The story of Adam and Eve in the Garden of Eden is, among other things, a myth of chronological anti-rational primitivism. (I phrase matters so as to evoke a wince at the jargon, which is adapted from the definitive studies by Arthur O. Lovejoy and George Boas; but even jargon may have its uses, as here.)

Consciousness imposes its gifts and its burdens on all of us; civilisation bestows on us amenities and problems. In every era, it seems, people have intermittently yearned for a release from the burdens of consciousness; in all civilisations, there has been some degree of nostalgia for the bygone simplicity of the imagined Golden Age. However, a remarkably strong burgeoning of anti-rational primitivism took place among numerous writers in the mid to late nineteenth century. The reasons are clear: this was a time when the vistas of thought were particularly depressing, since so many of the advances of science and technology seemed to blight faith in God and in a benevolent universe. Of the philosophers, Schopenhauer, Nietzsche, Kierkegaard, Sorel and later Bergson were among those who, in various ways, sought to disparage conventional rational awareness and to emphasise the potency of instinctual or anti-rational being. We have seen that in 1888 the young Bertrand Russell, who was later to enter a warm friendship with Conrad, could think of man as just 'a kind of machine endowed, unhappily for himself, with consciousness'; and seventy-three years later the same Bertrand Russell, reflecting on a long lifetime dedicated to rational enquiry, told me:

> I think I have always felt that there were two levels, one that of science and common sense, and another, terrifying, subterranean

and chaotic, which in some sense held more truth than the everyday view. You might describe this as a Satanic mysticism.

For Russell, this subterranean level appeared to hold not only 'more truth' but also more potency.

Amongst literary figures of the mid to late nineteenth century, anti-rational primitivism took a diversity of forms. Walter Pater, for example, looked back nostalgically to the instinctive awareness of the child and of the 'childhood of man' in Homeric Greece:

> A world . . . . . under Homeric conditions, such as we picture to ourselves with regret, for which experience was intuition, and life a continuous surprise, and every object unique, where all knowledge was still of the concrete and the particular, face to face delightfully.
>
> *(Plato and Platonism*, 1893)

Thomas Hardy knew Pater personally, and studied his works; and the narrator of *The Return of the Native* laments that 'thought is a disease of flesh': 'When standing before certain men the philosopher regrets that thinkers are but perishable tissue, the artist that perishable tissue has to think.' Samuel Butler, throughout his literary career, championed instinct and intuition as against conscious reflection and calculation. The following wry remarks, in *Life and Habit* (1877), are characteristic:

> Dog-fanciers tell us that performing dogs never carry their tails; such dogs have eaten of the tree of knowledge, and are convinced of sin accordingly – they know that they know things, in respect of which, therefore, they are no longer under grace, but under the law, and they have yet so much grace left as to be ashamed. So with the human clever dog; he may speak with the tongues of men and angels, but so long as he knows that he knows, his tail will droop . . . . . In that I write at all I am among the damned.

Anti-rational primitivism gained its fullest, richest and most complex expression in the novels, tales and essays of D.H. Lawrence, above all in *The Rainbow* and *Women in Love*. In his letters, particularly in those of 1915–16 to Bertrand Russell, Lawrence could reduce it to crude, stark terms:

> There is a blood-consciousness, with the sexual connection, holding the same relation as the eye, in seeing, holds to the mental consciousness. One lives, knows, and has one's being in the blood, without any reference to nerves and brain. This is one half of life, belonging to the darkness. And the tragedy of this our life, and of your life, is that the mental and nerve consciousness exerts a tyranny over the blood-consciousness . . . . .

> Do for your very pride's sake become a mere nothing, a mole,
> a creature that feels its way and doesn't think . . . . .
> When you make your will, do leave me enough to live on.

Russell, who was to outlive Lawrence by forty years, tartly observed: 'The only difficulty with this programme was that if I adopted it I should have nothing to leave.' He also claimed that Lawrence's doctrine of blood-consciousness 'led straight to Auschwitz'. This, however, does Lawrence some injustice. Anti-rational primitivism has contributed to every part of the spectrum of political beliefs, though it has been far more conspicuous as a contributor to politics of the extreme Left (libertarian anarchism) and extreme Right (fascism) than as a contributor to democratic liberalism. This diversity is not surprising when we recall that anti-rational primitivism is an important element in both the Augustan and the Romantic movements. The Augustan writer (for example, Swift in *Gulliver's Travels*, a work well known to Conrad) condemns abstruse, fanatical and seemingly impractical reasoning; in fact the so-called 'Age of Reason' was one which distrusted intense reasoning and commended instead common sense, a reasoning strictly controlled by criteria of practicality and social utility. The Romantic, on the other hand, condemns 'the mind-forg'd manacles', the meddling intellect which murders to dissect, and strives to defend the life of the emotions or instincts.

Primitivism offers both 'soft' and 'hard' ideals. 'Soft primitivism' occurs when the postulated Golden Age is a location of idleness and ease, like the legendary Land of Cockayne or the Isle of the Lotos Eaters. 'Hard primitivism' occurs when the postulated Golden Age is the location of toil and austerity. Insofar as he is an anti-rational primitivist, Conrad upholds the hard version. His simple, dependable, constructive types are workers: Singleton, the patriarchal helmsman of the *The Nigger of the 'Narcissus'*, the boiler-maker of 'Heart of Darkness', or Jörgenson in *The Rescue*. Once Cunninghame Graham sent Conrad a letter which evidently complained that Singleton was too much the ignorant Uncle Tom, the inarticulate loyal workman, and should have been granted an education. Conrad's response has become one of the most famous anti-rationalist statements in the history of modern literature:

> You say: 'Singleton with an education' . . . . . But first of all –
> what education? If it is the knowledge how to live my man
> essentially possessed it. He was in perfect accord with his life. If
> by education you mean scientific knowledge then the question
> arises – what knowledge, how much of it – in what direction? Is
> it to stop at plane trigonometry or at conic sections? Or is he to
> study Platonism or Pyrrhonism or the philosophy of the gentle

Emerson? Or do you mean the kind of knowledge which would enable him to scheme, and lie, and intrigue his way to the forefront of a crowd no better than himself? Would you seriously, of malice prepense cultivate in that unconscious man the power to think. Then he would become conscious – and much smaller – and very unhappy. Now he is simple and great like an elemental force. Nothing can touch him but the curse of decay – the eternal decree that will extinguish the sun, the stars one by one, and in another instant shall spread a frozen darkness over the whole universe. Nothing else can touch him – he does not think.

Would you seriously wish to tell such a man: 'Know thyself'. Understand that thou art nothing, less than a shadow, more insignificant than a drop of water in the ocean, more fleeting than the illusion of a dream. Would you?

(LCG, pp. 53–4)

It is a letter of characteristic rhetorical eloquence – characteristic in the way the argument gathers a rhythmic roll and surge of momentum. It demonstrates that Conrad's primitivism is strongly defensive and pessimistic, and therefore closer in spirit to the Augustan modes than to the Romantic. His reference to the 'frozen darkness' is further evidence that, in the late nineteenth century, anti-rationalism was in large measure an imaginative refuge from the bleak vistas offered by science.

In *The Nigger of the 'Narcissus'*, there is a claim that the Golden Age of simplicity was the age of the uneducated seaman, a breed of whom Singleton is the last representative:

Yet he was only a child of time, a lonely relic of a devoured and forgotten generation. He stood, still strong, as ever unthinking . . . . . The men who could understand his silence were gone . . . . . They were the everlasting children of the mysterious sea. Their successors are the grown-up children of a discontented earth. They are less naughty, but less innocent; less profane, but perhaps also less believing; and if they had learned how to speak they have also learned how to whine. But the others were strong and mute . . . . .

(NN, pp. 24–5)

In *Victory*, Heyst suggests that the Fall of Man occurred far earlier – and not when Eve ate the forbidden fruit but rather at the very moment when Adam gained conscious awareness of his surroundings:

That first ancestor . . . . ., as soon as he could uplift his muddy frame from the celestial mould, started inspecting and naming the animals of that paradise which he was so soon to lose.

77

Action – the first thought, or perhaps the first impulse, on earth! The barbed hook, baited with the illusion of progress, to bring out of the lightless void the shoals of unnumbered generations!

(*V*, pp. 173–4)

Conrad is not being wholly ironic when, in the 'Author's Note' to that novel, he remarks: 'The habit of profound reflection . . . . . is the most pernicious of the habits formed by the civilized man.' In another of the letters to Cunninghame Graham, he again shows how anti-rational primitivism is largely a defensive reaction against the bleak findings of nineteenth-century science – though this time it is Darwinian evolutionism rather than Kelvinian thermodynamics which is cited:

Systems could be built, and rules could be made – if we could only get rid of consciousness. What makes mankind tragic is not that they are the victims of nature, it is that they are conscious of it. To be part of the animal kingdom under the conditions of this earth is very well – but as soon as you know of your slavery the pain, the anger, the strife – the tragedy begins.

(*LCG*, p. 70)

Such preoccupations help to give the rich charge and swelling glow of symbolic suggestion to memorable Conradian passages like this one in *Nostromo*:

Nostromo woke up from a fourteen hours' sleep, and arose full length from his lair in the long grass. He stood knee deep amongst the whispering undulations of the green blades with the lost air of a man just born into the world. [But quickly the look of recognition came into his eyes.] Handsome, robust, and supple, he threw back his head, flung his arms open, and stretched himself with a slow twist of the waist and a leisurely growling yawn of white teeth, as natural and free from evil in the moment of waking as a magnificent and unconscious wild beast. Then, in the suddenly steadied glance fixed upon nothing from under a thoughtful frown, appeared the man.

(*N*, pp. 411–12)

This is, of course, an admirably written passage. (I include in square brackets a necessary sentence which appeared in the serial text but is regrettably absent from the book version.) It tells us much about the character of Nostromo and his fictional environment, but at the same time it reminds us of our own lives and tells us things about ourselves which we have often sensed but never quite been able to put into apt words. Shimmering within this vision of Nostromo awakening is another vision, of a savage tigerish Adam stirring ('with a leisurely growling yawn of white teeth'). It reminds us that humans are perennially divided creatures: part of the animal kingdom, yet alienated from it by the burden of consciousness. And the passage also tells us about our everyday transition from the pleasure of awakening, fully rested, to the pain of realisation of the day's tasks and problems. As in all great writing, we are at the intersection of the particular and the general, of the familiar and the strange.

Determinism and solipsism

Determinism is the belief that all events are determined, so that free will is an illusion. Solipsism is the belief that the individual self constitutes the sole reality. On the one hand, each person is the puppet of the universe and its causal laws; on the other, each person is a flame of awareness glowing in the midst of a dark flux of the unknown. These are contrasting, mutually contradictory notions; yet both flourished in the late nineteenth century; and both derive from the prestige of empiricism.

As we have seen previously, scientific empiricism, by postulating and verifying numerous causal laws, could instil in people who failed to distinguish between causality and compulsion the sense that each human is the passive subject of those laws. But solipsism, too, develops with the prestige of empiricism. Since the empirical outlook of science has the basic assumption that the foundation of all worthwhile knowledge is the evidence of the senses, recognition that the senses can deceive us appears to reveal a threat to the basis of all certainty. We are all familiar with optical illusions – with the apparent bending of a straight stick lowered into water, for example; and we all confuse illusion with reality when we dream. Because our senses deceive us some of the time, it is theoretically possible that they may deceive us all the time; in which case we can be certain only of our own existence, it seems, and of nothing beyond.

Common sense revolts against such a notion (and Dr Johnson expressed his revolt by kicking a stone), but philosophers have encountered remarkable difficulty when they have attempted to vindicate common sense. We could argue, perhaps, that our faith that the world is substantially as common sense assumes it to be rests not on any naïve belief in the infallibility of the senses but rather on the value-judgement that it is good for our assumptions about the status of the world to be fulfilled. We know that predictions based on the assumption that the world is as stable as common sense assumes it to be are, on the whole, sufficiently fulfilled; while predictions based on the assumption that the world is essentially 'private' or phantasmagoric tend not to be fulfilled. Such arguments are still open to challenge, though it is notable that the solipsist's case often seems to depend on a confusion of terminology: particularly a confusion of the 'self and world' convention with the 'sense-data' convention, as A.J. Ayer showed in *The Foundations of Empirical Knowledge*. Significantly, the most brilliant early expounder of the solipsist case, David Hume, recorded in his *Treatise of Human Nature* (1739–40) that when logic would not rescue him from solipsism,

> I dine, I play a game of backgammon, I converse, and am merry with my friends; and when after three or four hours' amusement, I wou'd return to these speculations, they appear so cold, and strain'd, and ridiculous, that I cannot find it in my heart to enter into them any farther.

Nevertheless, as scientific empiricism gained prestige in the nineteenth century, so the undercurrent of solipsistic fear grew. A diversity of philosophers gave varied expression to the notion of the world's insubstantiality. Friedrich Nietzsche anticipated (and possibly influenced) Conrad's more sceptical epigrams when he wrote: 'Truths are illusions of which we have forgotten that they are illusions.' Arthur Schopenhauer, a philosopher studied closely by Conrad, modulated towards solipsism when he emphasised 'the frailty, vanity and dreamlike quality of all things'; and in Walter Pater's *Marius the Epicurean* (which Conrad read in 1897), Marius reflects 'that the ideas we are somehow impelled to form of an outer world, and of other minds akin to our own, are, it may be, but a day-dream, and the thought of any world beyond, a day-dream perhaps idler still . . . . . '

Conrad's letters frequently express the contradictory paradigms. Sometimes, as we have noted, he talks of the universe as a hard, remorseless machine – the deterministic paradigm. Yet he can also talk of the individual as a solitary consciousness amid a mirage-like flux – the solipsistic paradigm:

> The machine is thinner than air and as evanescent as a flash of lightning . . . . . The ardour for reform, improvement[,] for virtue, for knowledge, and even for beauty is only a vain sticking up for appearances as though one were anxious about the cut of one's clothes in a community of blind men. Life knows us not and we do not know life – we don't even know our own thoughts . . . . . Faith is a myth and beliefs shift like mists on the shore . . . . .
>
> (*LCG*, p. 65)

There is a quality of emotive rhetoric about this passage: it develops a certain lyrical-descriptive momentum, even approaching the tone

of an incantation; and, in the last sentence, alliteration and asso-
nance set the prose singing. This is writing to convey a mood as
much as to define an argument. The fears, however, were genuine.
When Conrad told Cunninghame Graham, 'Sometimes I lose all
sense of reality in a kind of nightmare effect produced by existence',
he was telling the cold truth. 'All is illusion', he wrote to Garnett.

This sense of extreme subjectivity has numerous consequences in
the works of Conrad. There are direct expressions: Marlow in
'Heart of Darkness' says 'We live, as we dream – alone'; and one of
the phrases that Conrad liked to quote was Calderón's 'La vida es
sueño' ('Life is a dream'), which is recalled by Decoud's thought:
'All this is life, must be life, since it is so much like a dream' (*N*, p.
249.) Conradian narrators (particularly those of *Nostromo* and *Lord
Jim*) have the cynical habit of applying the term 'illusions' to ideals,
thoughts, observations and feelings – even love is termed merely
'the strongest of illusions' in *Nostromo*. Max Beerbohm acutely
parodied this tendency in his tale 'The Feast', with the splendidly
mock-Conradian lines:

> In his upturned eyes . . . . . the stars were reflected, creating an
> illusion of themselves who are illusions . . . . .
> Within the hut the form of the white man, corpulent and pale,
> was covered with a mosquito-net that was itself illusory like
> everything else, only more so.
>
> (*A Christmas Garland*, 1912, pp. 125, 126)

(Beerbohm thus solicits the paradox that if all is illusory, so is the
belief that all is illusory.) Conrad's solipsistic intuitions magnify his
awareness of the gulfs in comprehension between people who
ostensibly are in accord; and this awareness generates many Conradian ironies. In *The Secret Agent*, for instance, the recumbent
Verloc summons, in tones of sexual desire, the wife who is about to
stab him in the heart. Their different worlds, instead of coinciding,
collide lethally.

There is another, related, consequence. In the works of Walter
Pater, whom Conrad admired, we find both an eloquent presentation of the solipsist case and a nostalgia for a time when all
knowledge was 'of the concrete and the particular'. Pater's phrase,
and the criteria it commends, subsequently became clichés of
literary criticism in the period 1920–60; F.R. Leavis, for example,
frequently praised authors who provide 'the vivid evocation of the
concrete'. In *A Common Sky* (1974), A.D. Nuttall argued that the
modern taste for vivid concreteness in literature may have been
compensatory: it may have been caused by a widespread (and not
always fully recognised) fear that the solipsist case might be valid,
generating a demand for reassurance that the world retained

tangibly solid reality: 'If a man feels the real world slipping from him, he tightens his grip upon it.' Although Nuttall did not discuss Conrad, Conrad's work appears to provide an excellent illustration of his thesis. On the one hand, the explicit solipsistic comments are supported by descriptive passages which strongly emphasise a dreamlike, phantasmagoric quality of experience; yet, on the other hand, there are innumerable passages which emphasise the tangible solidity of our environment. Thus, the remarkably varied textural richnesses of Conrad's writing stem in part from his paradoxical imaginative sympathy with both determinism and solipsism.

I conclude this section, and anticipate the next, by quoting from *The Shadow-Line* two passages which respectively illustrate what Nuttall would term 'ontological security and insecurity'. In the first, the narrator seems to have a confident grasp of the world; in the second, the world seems treacherously to be vanishing from him.

> I went aft, ascended the poop, where, under the awning, gleamed the brasses of the yacht-like fittings, the polished surfaces of the rails, the glass of the skylights. Right aft two seamen, busy cleaning the steering gear, with the reflected ripples of light running playfully up their bent backs, went on with their work, unaware of me and of the almost affectionate glance I threw at them in passing towards the companion-way of the cabin.
>
> (*SL*, pp. 50–1)

> Ransome stepped back two paces and vanished from my sight.
> At once an uneasiness possessed me, as if some support had been withdrawn. I moved forward too, outside the circle of light, into the darkness that stood in front of me like a wall. In one stride I penetrated it. Such must have been the darkness before creation. It had closed behind me. I knew I was invisible to the man at the helm. Neither could I see anything. He was alone, I was alone, every man was alone where he stood. And every form was gone too, spar, sail, fittings, rails; everything was blotted out in the dreadful smoothness of that absolute night.
>
> (*SL*, pp. 112–13)

That the latter passage implies a grimly ironic commentary on the former is characteristic of the art of Conrad.

Darkness and the dying sun

In the 1850s William Thomson (later to be Lord Kelvin) had defined the Second Law of Thermodynamics: the law of entropy, which says that the amount of 'available' energy in the universe must gradually dwindle to nothing as heat flows from warmer into cooler masses until equalisation of temperatures prevails. The aspect of this law which most captured the popular imagination was the notion that the sun, instead of burning inexhaustibly, must inevitably burn itself out, like a great Victorian coal-fire in the sky, and that as it does so, the human race must perish as icy darkness palls the earth. (Later, scientists developed alternative notions: one being that the sun, like a perfect atomic reactor, might be able perpetually to replenish its energies, and another being that it might grow vaster, consuming the earth before collapsing.) Some writers in the twentieth century envisaged the ultimate doomsday as the blazing inferno of a nuclear holocaust; but for writers in the late nineteenth century (and particularly in the 1890s, when thoughts of *le fin de siècle* led to thoughts of *le fin du globe*) the foreseen doomsday was utterly dark and cold.

It stirred the imagination. Even a scientist, Professor Alexander Winchell, was moved to sombrely eloquent use of the pathetic fallacy in his article, 'The Sun Cooling Off', published in *Scientific American* in 1891:

> The treasury of life and motion from age to age is running lower and lower. The great sun which, stricken with the pangs of dissolution, has bravely looked down with steady and undimmed eye upon our earth ever since organization first bloomed upon it, is nevertheless a dying existence.

In *The Golden Bough* (1890 onwards), a massive study of myth, ritual, legend and intellectual evolution, Sir James Frazer wrote:

> In the ages to come man may be able to predict, perhaps even to control, the wayward courses of the winds and clouds, but hardly will his puny hands have strength to speed afresh our slackening planet in its orbit or rekindle the dying fire of the sun.

One of the most memorable descriptions of the dark doomsday comes in H.G. Wells's *The Time Machine* (1895; a tale which Conrad read, admired and remembered), when the Time Traveller voyages almost to the end of time:

> So I travelled, stopping ever and again, in great strides of a thousand years or more, drawn on by the mystery of the earth's fate, watching with a strange fascination the sun grow larger and duller in the westward sky, and the life of the old earth ebb away.
> . . . . . In another moment the pale stars alone were visible. All else was rayless obscurity. The sky was absolutely black.
> A horror of this great darkness came on me.

The idea of the dying sun obviously augmented Conrad's pessimism by suggesting the ultimate futility of all action in this alien universe; and it added importantly to the symbolic vistas of his imagination. In 1898 he told Cunninghame Graham:

> The mysteries of a universe made of drops of fire and clods of mud do not concern us in the least. The fate of a humanity condemned ultimately to perish from cold is not worth troubling about. If you take it to heart it becomes an unendurable tragedy. If you believe in improvement you must weep, for the attained perfection must end in cold, darkness and silence.
>
> (*LCG*, p. 65)

Yet when, seven years later, Conrad wrote his essay 'Henry James', the tone had modulated from the sardonically pessimistic to the stoically affirmative:

> When the last aqueduct shall have crumbled in pieces, the last airship fallen to the ground, the last blades of grass have died upon a dying earth, man, indomitable by his training in resistance to misery and pain, shall set this undiminished light of his eyes against the feeble glow of the sun. The artistic faculty, of which each of us has a minute grain, may find its voice in some individual of that last group . . . . . The artist in his calling of interpreter creates (the clearest form of demonstration) because he must. He is so much of a voice that, for him, silence is like death; and the postulate was, that there is a group alive, clustered on his threshold to watch the last flicker of light on a black sky, to hear the last word uttered in the stilled workshop of the earth.
>
> (*NLL*, pp. 13–14)

This passage from the essay has obvious affinities with Marlow's tale in 'Heart of Darkness', which also has the theme that in course of time all man's technology may be annulled by the non-human environment; and in both cases we have an artist-narrator speaking to a small group which is beset by an apparently all-encompassing darkness. Conrad is celebrated for his 'nightscapes': for descriptions like that of the black night in the Placid Gulf through which Decoud sails in *Nostromo*, the perilous approach to the looming obscurity of Koh-ring in 'The Secret Sharer', or the oppressive blackness of the night which palls the becalmed ship in *The Shadow-Line*. And such descriptions, which attribute an annihilating dynamism to the darkness, have a peculiarly haunting power. By these scenes Conrad conveys to us, directly or subliminally, a wide array of his fears: the fear that decency may be fighting a doomed rearguard action against barbarism, the fear that human rationality is opposed by a cruel irrationality in the universe, and the fear that an infinity of blank extinction awaits humanity as a race, just as surely as it awaits each person as a mortal individual. Nevertheless, as Conrad remarked in 'Henry James': 'The creative art of a writer of fiction may be compared to rescue work carried out in darkness . . . . . '

Darwinism

We have previously noted that evolutionary ideas were already current before Charles Darwin's *The Origin of Species* appeared in 1859; but this book, and its successor, *The Descent of Man* (1871), formed a culmination of Victorian evolutionary thought. Darwin held that humans had not been specially created (as the Bible said) but had gradually, over millions of years, evolved into their present form in accordance with natural laws. These laws he listed as follows: growth with reproduction; inheritance; variability; 'a Ratio of Increase so high as to lead to a Struggle for Life, and as a consequence to Natural Selection' – whereby those who are fittest for survival in the given environment prevail while the others perish. Herbert Spencer summed it up in the phrase, 'survival of the fittest'.

In its stress on ruthless competition, this theory of evolution is largely a product of its economic times. It appeared in the heyday of Victorian *laissez-faire* capitalism; and Darwin mentioned that he had been strongly influenced by the economic theories of the Reverend Thomas Malthus. Sternly utilitarian in outlook, Malthus believed that the rate of increase of population tends to outstrip increases in the food supply, so that mass starvation is a recurrent phenomenon; charity, therefore, should reward the poor who had few children and be withheld from those who had many. Darwin's theory appears to reflect the ethos of its day by over-emphasising competition and underestimating co-operation. Partly because of this reflection, *The Origin of Species* became rapidly and bleakly influential as a work of scientific fact. There is no doubt that its influence was, on the whole, a bleak one. George Bernard Shaw wrote: 'When its whole significance dawns on you, your heart sinks into a heap of sand within you. There is a hideous fatalism about it.' This was in spite of Darwin's endeavour, in the concluding pages of *The Origin of Species*, to give his theory a consolatory form by postulating a Creator who works (albeit deviously and somewhat wastefully) to raise ever higher forms of life:

> And as natural selection works solely by and for the good of each being, all corporeal and mental endowments will tend to progress towards perfection . . . . . Thus, from the war of nature, from famine and death, the most exalted object which we are capable of conceiving, namely, the production of the higher animals, directly follows. There is grandeur in this view of life, with its several powers, having been originally breathed into a few forms

or into one; and that, whilst this planet has been cycling on according to the fixed law of gravity, from so simple a beginning endless forms most beautiful and most wonderful have been, and are being, evolved.

During this deliberately consolatory peroration, Darwin had urged the reader to take heart from the contemplation of 'an entangled bank':

It is interesting to contemplate an entangled bank, clothed with many plants of many kinds, with birds singing on the bushes, with various insects flitting about . . . . . and to reflect that these elaborately constructed forms, so different from each other, ... have all been produced by laws acting around us.

Conrad responded deeply to Darwinism. His stories contain numerous 'entangled banks'. In his early novels and tales, in *Almayer's Folly, An Outcast*, 'An Outpost of Progress', 'Heart of Darkness' and *Lord Jim*, he is very fond – some critics have said too fond – of describing fecund jungly settings. Conrad is both Darwinian and anti-Darwinian. He emphasises the struggle for survival which is constantly taking place in these jungles; and, on the whole, though he sees the exotic beauty, he emphasises the savage violence and wastefulness of the struggle, rather than the achievement of 'forms most beautiful and most wonderful'. Thus in *Almayer's Folly*:

The intense work of tropical nature went on: plants shooting upward, entwined, interlaced in inextricable confusion, climbing madly and brutally over each other in the terrible silence of a desperate struggle towards the life-giving sunshine above – as if struck with sudden horror at the seething mass of corruption below, at the death and decay from which they sprang.

(*AF*, p. 71)

Such descriptions can soon become tedious and skippable; they have too much melodrama, too predictably emotive and insistent an application of adjectives and amplifications; yet they are characteristic of Conrad's early work in their depiction of an evolutionary struggle so ruthless as to appal, seemingly, even the plants that are involved in it.

In the late nineteenth century, many apologists for aggressive imperialism propped their arguments with illicit inferences from Darwinian principles – illicit, because Darwin was dealing with competition between species and species, or between species and environment, but not between nations or races. The illicit argument went like this: It is a law of nature that creatures should compete, and that the 'fittest' should survive and prevail over the 'unfit'.

Therefore, if Europeans seize Africa and subjugate the Africans, they are simply doing what they are naturally obliged to do: the fit cannot avoid proving their fitness. This argument was implicit in, for example, Lord Salisbury's distinction (which Conrad noted and derided) between 'living' and 'dying' nations:

> From the necessities of politics or under the pretence of phil-anthropy – the living nations will gradually encroach on the territory of the dying . . . . . It is not to be supposed that any one nation of the living nations will be allowed to have the profitable monopoly of curing or cutting up these unfortunate patients . . . . . We shall not allow Britain to be at a disadvantage in any re-arrangement.

$$(LCG, \text{p. } 129)$$

In 'Heart of Darkness', Conrad retorts by turning Darwinism against the political Darwinians. If a goal of the evolutionary process is an equilibrium between the creature and its environment (as *The Origin of Species* had suggested), that goal has been reached in Africa by the natives whom Marlow observes on the coast, who 'wanted no excuse for being there' and who blend with their setting, rather than by the Europeans, who appear absurdly anomalous and who perish rapidly there or survive as grotesques or brutal automata. Conrad is particularly good at showing that in a struggle for survival, the victors may simply be the more ruthless or cunning (or physically tough), like the manager in 'Heart of Darkness', rather than those who in any moral sense are 'fittest' or 'higher'. Similarly, Conrad is skilled at deflating the pride of those who think that civilised Europeans offer a complete contrast to indigenous Africans. From time to time (as here in 'An Outpost') he asserts that 'civilised' values are matters of social convention, without real roots:

> The courage, the composure, the confidence; the emotions and principles; every great and every insignificant thought belongs not to the individual but to the crowd: to the crowd that believes blindly in the irresistible force of its institutions and its morals . . . . .

$$(TU, \text{p. } 89)$$

More paradoxically, he can undercut Darwinian teleology by suggesting that the rifle is merely a more powerful version of the bow, fashionable dress an elaborated loin-cloth, romantic love a sophistication of carnal lust, and the appetite for roast meat a modern vestige of cannibalism. *Nostromo*'s Decoud reflects that whereas in the past, 'barbarism . . . . . went about yelling, half-naked, with bows and arrows', today it wears 'the black coats of politicians' (*N*, p. 231). In 'Heart of Darkness', *Lord Jim* and the tale 'Falk', Conrad describes civilised men who have probably or certainly become cannibals: in the first example, with Kurtz, the attitude taken by the narrator is largely one of dismay; in the second, Captain Robinson is depicted as a tottering grotesque; in the third, the narrator's attitude to Falk is one of cool acceptance – 'Don't be shocked', he says. Conrad even likes to hint that Christianity may differ little from the rites of tribespeople: Marlow describes the sound of distant drums as 'weird, appealing, suggestive, and wild – and perhaps with as profound a meaning as the sound of bells in a Christian country' (*Y*, p. 71). In some respects, indeed, the primitive may be morally preferable to the civilised: 'Not perhaps that primitive men were more faithless than their descendants of to-day, but that they went straighter to their aim, and were more artless in the recognition of success as the only standard of morality' (*N*, p. 386).

We have stressed that Conrad relishes paradox, and though at times he suggests that civilisation is just a hypocritical sophistication of savagery, at other times he will suggest that it is a precious achievement to be guarded. Such paradoxes often hinge on ambiguous key terms; and, as we elucidate the meanings of the ambiguous term (like those of 'civilisation' here), the apparent self-contradiction dwindles into sound sense. If civilisation is represented by a humane fellow like Marlow, then Conrad can see it as indeed a valuable achievement. If it is represented by jingoistic statesmen and the commercial exploitation of Africa, Conrad can see it as a hypocritical fraud.

Darwinism and psychology

In the final chapter of *The Origin of Species*, Darwin claimed that with the arrival of his theory of evolution, 'Psychology will be based on a new foundation'; and he was quite right. An eager devotee of Darwinian evolutionism was Sigmund Freud, who, as a young medical student, conducted zoological research which supported Darwinism by demonstrating continuity between the cell-structures of lower and higher animals. In later years, when he became the great pioneer of psychoanalysis, Freud was fond of equating himself with Darwin, claiming that just as Darwin had inflicted one great blow on man's pride by having 'robbed man of his peculiar privilege of having been specially created, and relegated him to a descent from the animal world, implying an ineradicable animal nature in him', so Freud had inflicted a further great blow by proving that every person's 'ego' is 'not even master in his own house', but must constantly battle with unruly sexual drives. Obviously, Freudian theory was, in its origins, largely an inference from Darwin's: for if

Darwin suggests that each of us has 'an ineradicable animal nature', it is plausible that beneath the conscious surface of our minds there may be numerous primitive urges and impulses linking us with more barbaric or bestial forebears. Hence Freud's bold 'conflict-model' of the human mind, with its constant tussle between the anarchic drives from the id and the controlling endeavours of the more prudent and civilised ego; or, in his later and quite inconsistent scheme, the tussle between life-affirming libido and life-denying death-wish. Hence, too, Freud's sceptical readiness to see ostensibly civilised phenomena as mere 'sublimations' – i.e., as respectable transformations of relatively base source-material.

It will already be clear that there are some interesting similarities between Conrad's notions and Freud's. The presentation of Mr Kurtz in 'Heart of Darkness' may suggest the Freudian conflict-model of the self by indicating that his civilised qualities were 'sublimated' versions of repressed barbaric powers which, in the wilderness, can display their original lustful and murderous nature. Again, Marlow indicates that a conflict-model is appropriate to his own character: for, in spite of his civilised outlook, something within him responds sympathetically both to the charisma of the fallen Kurtz and to the throbbing of drums on the bank. (One commentator, Albert Guerard, carried this idea to implausible extremes by suggesting that Kurtz is really meant to be the 'id' of Marlow.) On the other hand, there are ways in which the dramatisation of human psychology in 'Heart of Darkness' differs from the Freudian scheme, and here Conrad may be wiser than Freud. Many of the Europeans are depicted as conscienceless automata who carry death and exploitation abroad almost as a matter of mechanical habit; indeed, the tale emphasises that such men as the accountant at the central station, the manager and the brickmaker are 'hollow men', not men impelled by a striving id. This is a debatable matter, but arguably the psychology here is both un-Freudian and sound. The Nazi extermination camps of the 1940s (in which so many millions of Jews and Poles died) were, in many cases, run by individuals who, like Conrad's accountant, were prepared to do their duty without qualms, as a matter of routine, even when such duty entailed the administration of mass murder. Adolf Eichmann, for example, when captured by the Israelis after the war, betrayed no remorse at his trial and was inclined to shrug off the indictments. Incidentally, it is worth noting that one of Freud's precursors, William James (in his *Principles of Psychology*, 1890), commended the value of habit as a force which maintains social harmony. Conrad looks now with sympathy and now with deep suspicion on predictably habitual activity.

Even where there are similarities between Conrad's ideas and

Freud's, these are not the result of any direct indebtedness of Conrad to the elder man. When 'Heart of Darkness' was first published, Freud was virtually unknown in England, and by the time that Freud had established an international reputation (1909–10) most of Conrad's best work had been completed. Quite likely Conrad's first direct encounter with Freud's writings was the very late one, during a holiday on Corsica in 1921. There he met a French disciple of Freud, H.-R. Lenormand, who persistently (and irritatingly) urged him to psychoanalyse such characters as Lord Jim and Almayer. Conrad was predictably resistant: 'I'm nothing but a story-teller', he would say; 'I don't want to get to the bottom . . . . . I want to look on reality as something rough and coarse over which I pass my fingers. Nothing more.' Lenormand lent Conrad two of Freud's books, but Conrad, 'who spoke of Freud with scornful irony', returned them apparently unread, and urged the Frenchman to write a novel on 'the decline of men who had arrived at certainty'.

Conrad might have found Jung more congenial. Albert Guerard has suggested various ways in which Conrad's 'night journeys', linkages between 'doubles', and perilous voyages of discovery, all anticipate Jung's theories about the value of a compensatory descent into 'the night-side of life'. Certainly, Conrad's library contained Jung's *Psychology of the Unconscious* (1916). Again, however, the anticipation is complex and critical. 'Heart of Darkness' and even 'The Secret Sharer' have important political aspects which a Jungian reading tends to neglect.

Atavism and doubles

The Freudian conflict-model of the human psyche emerged from that great mass of writing which explored with varying degrees of plausibility the possible implications of evolutionary theory. Atavism (the reversion to an ancestral or primitive type) and the fear of atavism became important subjects for fiction-writers, who seized rapidly on the dramatic notion that in individuals civilisation and even humanity might be only skin-deep.

A richly symbolic (and revealingly racist) forerunner of the later fictional treatments is Herman Melville's *Benito Cereno* (1855), in which a crew of supposedly docile and deferential blacks prove to be cunning, vengeful killers who, rising from slavery, have murdered the white crewmen and taken the Spanish captain hostage. In England, H.G. Wells, in *The Island of Doctor Moreau* (1896), offered one of the most subversive and starkly antitheistic discussions of the atavistic theme. Moreau acts on the assumption that since humans have evolved from beasts, he should be able, by means of skilled vivisection, to convert various animals – pumas, apes, etc. – into the likeness of humans. He has some success: victims of his experiments can pass for people at a distance and shamble around docilely enough, Moreau having indoctrinated them with the notion that he is their God and can punish disobedience with inflictions of pain like those the creatures have already suffered beneath his scalpel. But, of course, these humanoids gradually regress; every experiment seems doomed; and eventually Moreau himself is killed in a rebellion by the very creatures he had thought to dominate as God. It is in the epilogue that the narrative modulates most steeply into the subversive. The narrator, a traveller who by chance had witnessed the crisis on the island, returns to Europe – and finds that ordinary people have frightening resemblances to the humanoids of Dr Moreau:

> I could not persuade myself that the men and women I met were not also another, passably human, Beast People, animals half-wrought into the outward image of human souls, and that they would presently begin to revert, to show first this bestial mark and then that . . . . .
>
> I would go out into the streets to fight with my delusion, and prowling women would mew after me, furtive craving men glance jealously at me, weary pale workers go coughing by me, with tired eyes and eager paces like wounded deer dripping blood . . . . . Then I would turn aside into some chapel, and even there, such was my disturbance, it seemed that the preacher gibbered Big Thinks even as the Ape Man had done; or into some library, and there the intent faces over the books seemed but patient creatures waiting for prey. Particularly nauseous were the blank expressionless faces of people in trains and omnibuses; they seemed no more my fellow-creatures than dead bodies would be, so that I did not dare to travel unless I was assured of being alone. And even it seemed that I, too, was not a reasonable creature, but only an animal tormented with some strange disorder in its brain, that sent it to wander alone, like a sheep stricken with the gid.

This ending has some affinities with the conclusion not only of Swift's *Gulliver's Travels* but also of Conrad's 'Heart of Darkness': particularly with the passage in which Marlow, on his return to Europe, experiences a partly deranged hostility to the masses of people in the streets, who seem ludicrous, arrogant and stupid in their failure to comprehend the abyss which is so near, the abyss of corruption or atavism into which Kurtz has fallen. Again, Moreau's humanoid animals may remind us that in Conrad's *Victory* the hero's island sanctuary is invaded by three beings who seem to represent three stages of evolution: Gentleman Jones is an intelligent but decadent, enfeebled and sterile villain; his henchman Ricardo seems more tiger (or wildcat) than man in movements, outlook and mannerisms; and their servant Pedro is so ape-like that his knuckles almost brush the ground. 'Here they are before you', says Heyst; 'Evil intelligence, instinctive savagery, arm in arm. The brute force is at the back.' Atavism of a kind – some reversion of 'civilised' men to the savage or bestial when they are taken from the familiar supports offered by urban Europe – is a theme in *Almayer's Folly*, when the isolated Almayer descends to the stupor of opium addiction; in 'An Outpost of Progress', as Kayerts and Carlier cast aside tolerance and restraint, becoming slave-traders and finally fighting each other to the death; and in 'Falk', in which two seamen battle so that the victor may eat the flesh of the vanquished.

Atavism permeated the pseudo-science of Conrad's day. In Italy, Cesare Lombroso claimed that criminals and madmen were actually instances of atavism, throwbacks in the evolutionary sequence. These various types of degeneration, he alleged in *L'uomo delinquente* (1876), were physically identifiable: for example, they often had crinkly hair, thick lips and a Mongoloid slant to the eyes. Conrad knew Lombroso's theories, and in *The Secret Agent* he plays an elaborate game of ironic endorsement and mocking reversal of them. Ossipon, the parasitic anarchist, is a disciple of Lombroso, and accordingly detects in the young Stevie all the physiological characteristics of the 'mongoloid degenerate' defined by the Italian. The first irony is that Stevie, in his innocent benevolence, is a living contradiction of the doctrine; the second is that Ossipon totally fails to see that he himself, with his crinkly hair, flattened nose, and mouth 'of the Negroid type', is a perfect example of the 'negroid degenerate' described by his racially-prejudiced master. And the third is that though Mr Vladimir had justified the attack on Greenwich Observatory by claiming that science was the 'sacrosanct fetish' of the respectable middle classes, the blindest worshipper of 'science' is in fact Ossipon himself in his devotion to Lombroso.

In England, the chief disciple of Lombroso was Max Nordau, who corresponded with Conrad in 1898. (He wrote to praise *The Nigger of the 'Narcissus'*; Conrad, a little embarrassed, remarked 'Praise is sweet, no matter whence it comes.') Nordau was author of *Degeneration*, a best-selling pseudo-scientific work of 1895. In this, there is a type-description of the 'ego-maniac', which appears to have influenced Conrad's depiction of the Professor in *The Secret Agent*; and Nordau also discusses the 'highly-gifted degenerate', a type in whom some mental gift is exceptionally developed at the expense of the remaining faculties, and who may be exceptionally tall. Nordau says: 'Highly-gifted degenerates . . . . . corrupt and delude; they do, alas! frequently exercise a deep influence, but this is always a baneful one . . . . . They are guides to swamps like will-o'-the-wisps, or to ruin like the ratcatcher of Hammelin.' This account probably provided elements of the character of Kurtz in 'Heart of Darkness'. Kurtz has the gift of exceptional eloquence; he signally possesses the magnetism of the Pied Piper; he is the guide to a swamp of corruption; and he even has the characteristic of exceptional height, for to Marlow 'he looked at least seven feet long'.

Evolution, Aestheticism and sex

Aestheticism was a movement amongst English and French writers and artists which flourished (if that is not too robust a term) in the period 1850–1905 and particularly in the 1890s. It can be traced back to the Romantic Movement's emphasis on the importance of private, intense experience and on the role of the artist as a seer who is not to be judged by mundane laws. Of the English Romantics, the chief forerunner of Aestheticism is John Keats, whose work is quiveringly self-conscious (often depicting the vocation of the poet as a high mystery to be entered only by the Elect), exalts the quest for beauty, and is rich in sensuous description yet poor in social, political and moral debate. (Indeed, this isolation of the sensuous makes Keats seem more sensuous than he really is: Ben Jonson, in various plays, is equally sensuous in descriptions but is doing many other things at the same time.) One of the most famous slogans of the Aesthetes, 'Art for Art's sake', derives from Théophile Gautier's 'l'Art pour l'Art', which in turn derives from Victor Cousin's 'Il faut de la religion pour la religion, de la morale pour la morale, de l'art pour l'art' ('We need religion for religion's sake, morality for morality's sake and art for art's sake'). It seems to have been coined originally by Henry Crabb Robinson, who knew Keats personally.

If an Aesthete is one who believes that the artist should be devoted to the creation of beautiful works of art, it would at first appear that there is nothing at all objectionable in this belief, since artists down the ages have striven to create objects of beauty. What matters, though, is what the Aesthete thinks should be sacrificed, ignored or rejected in that pursuit of the beautiful. An art which achieves its identity largely by means of massive exclusions can become a very trivial art. Perhaps the most revealing 'Aesthete's Creed' is that offered by Oscar Wilde in the Preface to *The Picture of Dorian Gray* (1890–91):

> The artist is the creator of beautiful things.
> To reveal art and conceal the artist is art's aim . . . . .

> There is no such thing as a moral or an immoral book. Books are
> well written, or badly written. That is all . . . . .
> The moral life of man forms part of the subject-matter of the
> artist, but the morality of art consists in the perfect use of an
> imperfect medium. No artist desires to prove anything. Even
> things that are true can be proved.
> No artist has ethical sympathies. An ethical sympathy in an artist
> is an unpardonable mannerism of style . . . . .
> All art is quite useless.

It's a splendidly insolent, provocative preface, and it makes very
good sense when we consider which enemies Wilde had in mind.
He is opposing not only the censoriously moralistic critics of his
day, but also critics of a utilitarian disposition, who would value art
only in proportion to its evident social utility; he sets his face against
Victorian propriety and practicality. In its opposition to censorship
and social control, Wilde's epigrammatic preface is shrewdly polemical. Yet such a creed can encourage a trivial, narcissistic art which
turns its back on much of life and thus debases itself. The most
characteristic works of the Aesthetic Movement are usually slight
and ephemeral: poetry variously languorous or precious, hinting at
decadent vice or murmuring of lethargic raptures amid veiled
somnolent vistas of melancholy twilight. In the largely forgotten
poems of Lionel Johnson, Ernest Dowson, Arthur Symons or
Theodore Wratislaw, for example, as in the essays of Richard le
Gallienne or Hubert Crackanthorpe, the predictably narcissistic
connoisseurship of a limited range of experience continues. However, though most of the work of the Aesthetes was ephemeral, the
movement helped to generate a number of 'Preter-Aesthetes': artists
who in various ways grew through and beyond Aestheticism, having
some sympathies with it yet also an increasing sense of its
limitations.

The great Preter-Aesthetes include W.B. Yeats, whose early
poetry so often sounded the melancholy, languorous and lethargic
tones of Aestheticism, yet who came to quarrel with the movement
and to exploit the tension between Aesthetic egotism and public
political awareness. Another Preter-Aesthete was James Joyce,
whose *Portrait of the Artist as a Young Man* is very much a portrait of
the student as a would-be Aesthete, but whose *Ulysses* looks in
criticism as well as sympathy on Stephen Dedalus, who after all has
produced no significant work of art and who could not conceivably
produce a work with the vitality of *Ulysses* itself. A third was Ezra
Pound, whose 'Hugh Selwyn Mauberley' sequence regards with
pity and scorn the narcissistic poet: significantly, commentators
have experienced great difficulty in distinguishing between parts of

the poem which represent Mauberley's work and parts which represent Pound's comments on Mauberley. And Conrad, too, can be related to this august company.

In his famous Preface to *The Nigger of the 'Narcissus'*, Conrad says of the true artist:

> He . . . . . cannot be faithful to any one of the temporary formulas of his craft. The enduring part of them – the truth which each only imperfectly veils – should abide with him as the most precious of his possessions, but they all: Realism, Romanticism, Naturalism, even the unofficial sentimentalism (which, like the poor, is exceedingly difficult to get rid of), all these gods must, after a short period of fellowship, abandon him – even on the very threshold of the temple – to the stammerings of his conscience and to the outspoken consciousness of the difficulties of his work. In that uneasy solitude the supreme cry of Art for Art, itself, loses the exciting ring of its apparent immorality. It sounds far off. It has ceased to be a cry, and is heard only as a whisper, often incomprehensible, but at times and faintly encouraging.

So even 'the supreme cry of Art for Art, itself,' eventually sounds merely as a 'faintly encouraging' whisper behind the dedicated artist as he proceeds on his lonely and agonisingly difficult quest – seeking 'by the power of the written word to make you hear, to make you feel . . . . ., to make you *see*', and to 'awaken in the hearts of the beholders that feeling of unavoidable solidarity . . . . . which binds men to each other and all mankind to the visible world'. Thus, although Conrad shows respect for the spirit of priestly dedication to one's art which Aestheticism may conjure, his emphasis on social solidarity indicates clearly enough his Preter-Aestheticism. And it is quite typical of Conrad's janiformity that the very preface which upholds the duty of establishing solidarity between humans should also make the plight of the creative artist seem an arduously solitary one. 'Art is long and life is short, and success is very far off.'

The extent to which Aestheticism was a defensive reaction against evolutionary ideas has been underestimated. Yet the connection seems quite clear. In the writings of Baudelaire and Huysmans, of Pater and Wilde, there is heavy emphasis on the value not only of art but also of the artificial and the sterile; and one reason for this initially novel and puzzling emphasis is that Darwin and the evolutionists had made the natural and the fecund seem, to some sensitive observers in some moods, a bloody battleground – 'Nature, red in tooth and claw'. Such observers might reflect that if nature is a battleground, man proves his superiority by detaching himself from it as far as possible. This partly explains the decadents' connoisseurship of the artificial in literature and in life-style, and even their preoccupation (in literature and in life) with sterile forms of sexuality: for example, heterosexuality whose object is a courtesan, or homosexuality. ('Woman is natural – which means abominable', claimed Baudelaire.)

This post-Darwinian imaginative recoil from the implications of fecund procreative sexuality is strongly evident in Conrad's work: sometimes he even seems to anticipate Jean-Paul Sartre's bizarre assertion that 'the sexual act is the castration of the man'. Again and again in Conrad's pages, a passionate sexual encounter seems, paradoxically, to emasculate the man, to be subversive, making him bewildered and self-doubting, and it sometimes results in his destruction. This pessimistic pattern extends from the earliest novel, *Almayer's Folly*, to much later ones like *Victory* and *The Rescue*. In *Almayer's Folly*, the young warrior, Dain, feels that because of his passion for Nina, 'he had lost faith in himself, and there was nothing else in him of what makes a man'; and, when he copulates with her, 'the heavens were suddenly hushed up in the mournful contemplation of human love and human blindness'. In *Victory*, we are told that Heyst 'used to come out of her [Lena's] very arms with the feeling of a baffled man', and he too finds that attachment to Lena has sapped his power to defy the invaders of his island.

In this preoccupation of Conrad's there is some common sense: a man with marital responsibilities is less likely to rush into a duel than is an unattached bachelor. There is also the ex-seaman's notion that if a man brings his wife aboard, he cannot be giving undivided loyalty and energy to his work. ('I was never married myself. A sailor should exercise self-denial', says Captain Mitchell in *Nostromo*.) A more sophisticated influence is Schopenhauer's *The World as Will and Idea*, which argued that the woman, whose prime loyalty is to the life-force and its procreative drive, is basically in opposition to the man, who at his highest should be a stoical spectator of nature's battles. And the influence of the post-Darwinian recoil from fecund nature is made clear when Conrad describes passionate native consorts as though they were emanations from the torrid jungle, as in this passage of second-rate Conradese in 'Heart of Darkness': 'The immense wilderness, the colossal body of the

Right: *Drawing by Conrad:* Woman with Serpent.
'Both his writings and his drawings are liberally sprinkled with references to birds and snakes . . . . . When Lena [in Victory*] finally succeeds in inducing [Ricardo] to surrender his knife, the writer observes: "The very sting of death was in her hands; the venom of the viper in her paradise, extracted, safe in her possession".' (Bernard C. Meyer,* Joseph Conrad: A Psychoanalytic Biography, *1967, p. 331.)*

This sketch must have been done
between the years of 1892 - 1894
They came into my possession
at my marriage in 1896.
                    Jessie Conrad

Drawing by Conrad: The Diffident Suitor. ;
'*A remarkable pictorial re-affirmation of the bizarre and distorted relationships encountered in his love stories . . . . . As if retreating from both beast and lady, the man sits retracting his pigeon-toed feet, his knees pressed firmly together like a well-behaved girl, with his left forearm guarding the vicinity of his genitals.*' (*Meyer,* Joseph Conrad: A Psychoanalytic Biography, *1967, p. 329.*)

fecund and mysterious life seemed to look at her, pensive, as though it had been looking at the image of its own tenebrous and passionate soul' (*Y*, p. 136). (As has been noted, Conrad's inhibitions in dealing with the sexual sometimes result in second-rate writing like this.)

If the passionate mistresses resemble emanations from the jungle, the idealised heroines resemble·emanations from the world of art. In Shakespeare's *The Winter's Tale*, the statue of Hermione comes, apparently miraculously, to life; but we soon realise that Hermione has been flesh and blood all the time and has only been *imitating* a statue. In Conrad's fiction, it is tempting to say, the reverse is apparent: several of his beautiful heroines purport to be flesh and blood but evidently belong to the condition of statuary. They linger in the imagination as a series of statuesque poses and gestures, soliciting classical or allegorical titles. Examples include the Intended in 'Heart of Darkness', light shining on her white brow; Antonia, 'lovely like an allegorical statue', in *Nostromo*; Felicia Moorsom in 'The Planter of Malata', who resembles 'a being made of ivory and precious metal'; Alice Jacobus, 'a seated statue' in 'A Smile of Fortune'; and Hermann's niece in 'Falk', who 'appeared to look at the world with the empty white candour of a statue' and who 'could have stood for an allegoric statue of the Earth'.

Feminists may rightly see misogynistic implications in this dichotomy, in which idealised beauty is made statuesque while passionate sexuality is associated with dangerously fecund nature. A crucially problematic detail occurs in 'Heart of Darkness', when the Intended stretches out her arms towards the Kurtz of memory, in a gesture which exactly duplicates that of Kurtz's tribal consort. Does the duplication of gesture indicate a 'common humanity', or does it accentuate the remaining differences? Does it subvert the dichotomy or symmetrically reinforce it?

Literary influences

We have noted that Conrad's father was a poet and an accomplished linguist: a translator into Polish of works by Shakespeare, Victor Hugo and others. Thus Conrad, from his early years, became familiar with a wide range of French and English literary texts as well as with Polish works, and in later years he retained a habit of wide (indeed voracious) reading, studying material ancient and modern, popular and specialised. Whether among poetry or prose, drama or essays, his range was impressive. He recalled being 'fed on French and English literature', and claimed to have bought, with his first earnings in England, a thick, green-covered volume of Shakespeare. The epigraphs to his works give some idea of the diversity of his interests as a reader: they are taken from Amiel, Shakespeare, Spenser, Boethius, a nursery rhyme, Chaucer, Milton, Sir Thomas Browne, Novalis, Samuel Pepys, Baudelaire . . . . . So a full discussion of possible literary influences would be a book in itself; and that book would probably not have room for all the memoirs, biographies, autobiographies, travel accounts and ephemera consulted by Joseph Conrad during the writing of his own works. Here, however, we may note selectively some aspects of Conrad's literary heritage.

Polish writing

We have seen that Conrad's very name – Konrad, anglicised as Conrad – is a mnemonic of the long tradition of Polish patriotic writing, often romantically lyrical or religiose, which has its culmination in Mickiewicz's *Konrad Wallenrod* and *Dziady*. In Conrad's 'Prince Roman', 'The Crime of Partition' and 'Poland Revisited' there can be found a note of intense patriotism which might have gladdened Mickiewicz. As previously noted, the eponymous hero of *Konrad Wallenrod* lures his German followers into a disastrous campaign against Lithuania: loyalty to his homeland entails betrayal of his troops. Wallenrod is depicted as a brooding, bitter figure, rendered harsh and saturnine by his duplicitous ambition: eventually he commits suicide. In this concern with the psychological burden of patriotic treachery, *Konrad Wallenrod* foreshadows *Under Western Eyes*; and it brings to mind the maxim of *Nostromo* – 'There was something inherent in the necessities of successful action which carried with it the moral degradation of the idea.' Furthermore, its use of various 'tales within the tale' may be one source of Conrad's preoccupation with this narrative technique.

In Mickiewicz's epic poem, *Pan Tadeusz*, the protagonist (Jacek Soplica) is a man who once had helped the Russian foe by killing a loyal Polish magnate; subsequently he was tortured by his own conscience and by the general suspicion that he was a traitor; but, to atone for his crime, he then works as a secret agent, helping the French and Polish forces in their campaign against the Russians. The theme of heroic atonement for past disgrace anticipates Conrad's *Lord Jim* and has connections with the depiction of Monygham in *Nostromo* and Razumov in *Under Western Eyes*. A small but significant link between the two authors is that Yankel, the patriotic Polish–Jewish innkeeper of 'Prince Roman', is clearly a literary reincarnation of Yankiel, the patriotic Polish–Jewish innkeeper of *Pan Tadeusz*.

Various further debts have been cited by scholars. The plot of Conrad's 'Karain' is partly based on Mickiewicz's ballad, 'Czaty'; and verbal echoes of *Konrad Wallenrod* have been detected in *Almayer's Folly* and *An Outcast*. Other Polish authors have left their marks, too. Bobrowski's *Memoirs* were used in *A Personal Record*; and Conrad's *Victory* derives some of its melodramatic features (a seemingly homosexual villain, a feline henchman and a self-sacrificing 'fallen woman') from Stefan Żeromski's novel, *Dzieje grzechu* (*The Story of a Sin*). Conrad's literary ambitions were undoubtedly strengthened by the international acclaim accorded in the 1890s to Henryk Sienkiewicz, the Polish novelist who, in 1905, was to win the Nobel Prize for Literature.

French influences

Polish commentators have remarked that Conrad's syntax often seems reminiscent of Polish usages, as when he employs asyndeton (the omission of conjunctions) or anaphoric parallelism (repetition of the same word at the beginning of two or more parallel phrases). Examples of the former could be: 'An empty stream, a great silence, an impenetrable forest. The air was thick, warm, heavy, sluggish' (HD). An example of the latter could be: 'the sea, blue and profound, remained still, without a stir, without a ripple, without a wrinkle – viscous, stagnant, dead' (*Lord Jim*). That second quotation could equally well, in fact, be cited as an instance of Gallic influence, for, as was common in French writing, its adjectives are arranged in pairs and triplets after the noun: one of the parody-inviting signs of 'Conradese'. Jocelyn Baines has suggested that Conrad's over-fondness for polysyllabic privative adjectives ('inconceivable', 'inscrutable', 'impenetrable') may have been encouraged by the inflated phraseology of Pierre Loti.

Though not accurate in French, Conrad was so fluent in that language that he sometimes unthinkingly used Gallic words or idioms as if they were English. In *The Nigger*, for example, a heap of nails is 'more inabordable than a hedgehog' ('inabordable' is French for 'unapproachable'); and, in *Lord Jim*, a patient 'held the doctor for an ass'. In correspondence with British acquaintances, Conrad readily turned to French (a) when offering courteous gallantries, (b) when expressing highly sceptical or cynical ideas ('la société est essentielment [*sic*] criminelle' – society is essentially criminal), or (c) when expressing some of his own positive moral convictions – as in a letter to Sir Sidney Colvin in 1917:

> The humorous, the pathetic, the passionate, the sentimental *aspects* come in of themselves – mais en vérité c'est les valeurs idéales des faits et gestes humains qui se sont imposés à mon activité artistique. [But truly my artistic activity has been governed by the ideal values of human facts and deeds.]
>
> (*LL*, II, p. 185)

Conrad's shifts to French indicate sometimes a desire for a more confidential, intimate mode, and sometimes a need for the language which lends courtliness to politeness and which invests abstract terms with greater sonority than English can.

Of the French authors, it was probably Gustave Flaubert (1821–80) who had the greatest influence on Conrad. Flaubert set the standard of extreme literary dedication: for him, literature was the central responsibility of life, and the great writer was the one who was prepared to sacrifice all other concerns in order to build the fictional world laboriously, phrase by phrase, with intense concentration and zeal for *le mot juste*. Conrad's attitudes to his art form a protean cluster, but part of that cluster is certainly a note of Flaubertian dedication, an obsession with literary truth and beauty, and a related contempt for those who would prostitute literature on the altars of commerce. (Inevitably, he compromised.) Flaubert's strengths as a writer were much in his mind at the very beginning of his literary career, for, in a letter of 1892, while he was slowly building *Almayer's Folly*, he wrote in French to Marguerite Poradowska:

> I have just re-read *Madame Bovary* with respectful admiration.
> Now here is a man who had enough imagination for two realists. There are few authors who are as creative as he. One never for a moment questions the characters or the events in his pages; one would rather doubt one's own existence.
>
> (*CL*, I, p. 109. My translation.)

Flaubert had striven for cool lucidity in seeing life as it is, warts and all; he brought a new scrupulous diligence of attention to ostensibly mediocre lives in mediocre settings. Though he scandalised some early readers – he was prosecuted for offending public morals – and seemed to some subsequent readers a life-denying Aesthete, a new honesty and human poignancy emerge from his apparently ruthless texts. Certainly, Flaubert strengthened Conrad's preoccupation, so evident in *Almayer's Folly*, with blighted communication, egoistic delusion and frustrated ambition. As Ian Watt has remarked, 'Almayer is a Borneo Bovary.' The range can be extended: Almayer, Willems, Lingard, Jim, Kurtz, Gould: all of them, in various ways, are impelled by dreams, and all are ambushed by recalcitrant circumstances. The naïvely incompetent endeavours of the heroes of Flaubert's *Bouvard et Pécuchet* constituted one of the sources of Conrad's mordant tale, 'An Outpost of Progress'.

Another feature in which Flaubert was of the literary vanguard was the use of starkly ironic counterpoint or juxtaposition. For example, when Rodolphe deploys his eloquence to seduce Emma Bovary, his words are juxtaposed with cries from the Agricultural Show beyond the window:

> 'A hundred times I've wanted to abandon you, and yet I've always followed and stayed by you!'
> 'Manure!'

At the book's climax, Emma has poisoned herself and is lying in her death-pangs:

As the death-rattle grew louder, the priest hurried his prayers;
they blended with Charles Bovary's stifled sobs . . .

Suddenly, on the pavement outside, there was a clacking of big
clogs and the scraping of a stick, and a harsh voice rose, singing:
'When the hot sun shines above,
A young girl often dreams of love . . . . .
The wind blew very hard that day –
Her petticoat flew far away!'

Against the pious words of the priest, a bawdy song from a beggar.
This technique of discordant juxtaposition is incisively ironic, often
jarring and cruelly aggressive in effect, like a callous practical joke.
Among English writers, it is Conrad's contemporary, Thomas
Hardy, who, particularly in *Jude the Obscure* (notably in the sequence
depicting Jude's death), comes closest to this Flaubertian example;
but in Conrad's work there are many kindred effects. In *Almayer's
Folly*, Lakamba's decision to have Almayer poisoned is counter-
pointed by Verdi's *Il Trovatore* played on a barrel-organ amid the
jungles of Sambir: 'The Trovatore fitfully wept, wailed, and bade
good-bye to his Leonor[a] again and again in a mournful round of
tearful and endless iteration.' In *Nostromo*, the temporising rhetoric
of the politicians is interrupted by the squawk of 'Viva Costaguana!'
from a parrot. In *The Secret Agent*, the Professor's sinister discussion
with Ossipon is concluded by a selection of 'national airs' (including
'The Blue Bells of Scotland') on the automatic pianola.

Another French writer admired by Conrad was Guy de Maupassant (1850–93), the prolific author of drily ironic tales. Conrad
claimed to be 'saturé de Maupassant' – saturated by him; when
established in his literary career, Conrad provided a genial introduction to a selection of Maupassant's tales; and various debts have
been noted by scholars. The Heyst–Lena relationship in *Victory* is
partly foreshadowed in Maupassant's *Fort comme la mort*; the Preface
to *The Nigger of the 'Narcissus'* owes some debts of phrasing to
Maupassant's Preface to *Pierre et Jean*; and *The Nigger* itself derives
occasional descriptive touches from the novel *Bel-Ami* – particularly
at the death of James Wait, which has similarities to that of
Forestier. Conrad's 'A Smile of Fortune' repeatedly echoes Maupassant's 'Les Sœurs Rondoli': the nonchalant, slatternly yet seductive
Alice seems a reincarnation of Francesca. Curiously, the tale by
Conrad which, in subject and treatment, most resembles one of
Maupassant's is not particularly successful. This tale is 'The Idiots'
(*TU*), a drably pessimistic account of a blighted marriage amid the
harsh environment of the Breton coast. (Conrad wrote it during his
honeymoon . . . . .)

In two book-reviews (in *The Speaker* for 16 July 1904 and in *The*

English Review for December 1908), Conrad paid tribute to the 'princely' genius, the sceptical humanity, of Anatole France (1844–1924). From the pages of France, Conrad derived not only reinforcement of his own bleak view of history and human nature but also instances of lucidly epigrammatic phrasing. In the essay 'Mérimée', for example, France sums up as follows the character of the novelist Prosper Mérimée:

> What should he regret? He had never recognised anything but energy as virtue or anything but passions as duties. Was not his sadness rather that of the sceptic for whom the universe is only a succession of incomprehensible images . . . . . ?

Years later, in *Nostromo*, the narrator sums up as follows the character of Decoud:

> What should he regret? He had recognised no other virtue than intelligence, and had erected passions into duties . . . . . His sadness was the sadness of a sceptical mind. He beheld the universe as a succession of incomprehensible images.

This may look like plagiarism, but the shift of mode (non-fiction into fiction) and of context largely vindicates Conrad. As Shakespeare took ideas and phrases from Plutarch and Holinshed, seizing and reanimating, so Conrad used his French mentors.

American influences

Conrad maintained considerable affection for the works of James Fenimore Cooper (1789–1851), declaring that from his boyhood he had regarded Cooper as one of his masters. In particular, Cooper showed how 'the sea inter-penetrates with life'; and his descriptions have 'the magistral ampleness of a gesture indicating the sweep of a vast horizon'. Another American writer of the sea, Herman Melville (1819–91), incurred his hostility, however. *Moby Dick* he deemed 'a rather strained rhapsody': 'He knows nothing of the sea'; 'It's fantastic, ridiculous.' Perhaps, like his antipathy to Dostoyevsky, this vehement response indicates some repressed affinities; certainly, critics have repeatedly seen anticipations in Melville of Conrad's highly symbolic treatment of voyages and certain voyagers. Conrad was happier to acknowledge Mark Twain's *Life on the Mississippi*, which he had recalled when voyaging up the Congo; and he praised the 'authentic' detail of Edgar Allan Poe's tale, 'MS. Found in a Bottle'.

If we seek specific debts, it is significant that *The Nigger of the 'Narcissus'* several times recalls R.H. Dana's *Two Years before the Mast* (1840). Both works note: the popularity of Bulwer-Lytton's novels among seafarers; the harsh régime on American vessels; the benefits of seeking the cook's friendship; the likelihood that faithful seamen will be corrupted by education and political information; the superstition that Finns have supernatural powers; and the superstition that a foreign seaman may be able to avert favourable winds. Both texts feature a cook who, being excessively devout, upbraids the crew for their ungodly ways and warns them of being unprepared for sudden death.

English influences

One of the many possible English examples is Coleridge's visionary, nightmarish poem of the sea, 'The Rime of the Ancyent Marinere' (1798), which influenced *The Shadow-Line*. In both, an accursed ship is a place of torment for the central figure. In the poem, the mariner bears a burden of guilt and feels that he is subject to reproachful gazes from the crew; so does the young captain in the novel. Above all, Conrad's work rivals Coleridge's in its attempt to render the horror of a becalmed ship. The captain reflects:

> No confessed criminal had ever been so oppressed by his sense of guilt . . . . . The sun climbs and descends, the night swings over our heads as if somebody below the horizon were turning a crank . . . . . This death-haunted command . . . . . I had had visions of a ship drifting in calms and swinging in light airs, with all her crew dying slowly about her decks.

At the climax of the poem, there comes a sudden rain and wind, and the dead crewmen begin to haul on the ropes. At the climax of the novel, there comes a sudden rain and wind, and the crew – virtually all of whom have been very ill – man the ropes like ghosts: 'Those men were the ghosts of themselves, and their weight on a rope could be no more than the weight of a bunch of ghosts.'

In the 'Author's Note' to *The Shadow-Line*, Conrad repudiated the supernatural in fiction: 'This story . . . . . was not intended to touch on the supernatural . . . . . which (take it any way you like) is but a manufactured article, the fabrication of minds insensitive to the intimate delicacies of our relation to the dead and to the living . . . . . ' Yet it is typical of Conrad's janiformity that in spite of this repudiation, just as supernatural motifs are strongly evident in *The Nigger*, 'Heart of Darkness' and 'The Secret Sharer', so in *The Shadow-Line* there are counterparts to the supernatural elements of Coleridge's poem. Though Conrad may not consciously have intended this to happen, his novel can in part be read, like the poem, as a religious allegory of guilt and redemption through suffering and divine grace. In both cases the descriptive strength lies mainly in the vivid evocation of the nightmarish journey of an apparently accursed ship. In *The Shadow-Line* the captain's most loyal helper is a fellow who is mysteriously immune to fever, who is uncannily attentive and calm, and whose 'grace' (a term connoting both physical and metaphysical beauty, both ease of movement and spiritual virtue) is repeatedly and explicitly emphasised; and this fellow is called Ransome. In the particular context that Conrad provides, the name Ransome evokes memories of the Christ who suffered to redeem man from sin, the Christ whom the Bible describes as man's ransom: in Matthew 20: 28 and Mark 10: 45 ('the Son of man came . . . . . to give his life a ransom for many'), and in 1 Timothy 2: 5–6 ('Christ Jesus . . . . . gave himself a ransom for all'). Of course, at the end of the novel, the supernatural suggestions fade like ghosts at cock-crow, and we recall that Ransome's grace of movement is largely a consequence of his weak heart, which makes him move cautiously; but those ghosts were deliberately conjured up, to enrich the texture and meaning of the story, by Conrad's creative imagination.

There is no doubt that Conrad was familiar with 'The Rime of the Ancyent Marinere': one of his letters, to John Livingstone Lowes, the Coleridge scholar, complains that an albatross in a seaman's yarn by P.J. Pigors had been borrowed from the poem. Nevertheless, both Conrad and Coleridge could draw on a traditional fund of legends of the sea, legends about becalmed, haunted or crewless ships (like the *Marie Céleste*) or of protracted purgatorial voyages inflicted on a sinful mariner: a tradition as old as Jonah, and which culminates in the legend of the Flying Dutchman. Conrad, who admired Wagner's music, must have known his opera, *Der fliegende Holländer*, and there are explicit references to the Flying Dutchman both in *The Shadow-Line* and in 'Falk'.

Among novelists, it is probable that the Englishman whose work Conrad most enjoyed was Charles Dickens. As a boy, he had read Dickens in Polish: 'My first introduction to English imaginative literature was *Nicholas Nickleby*. It is extraordinary how well Mrs Nickleby could chatter disconnectedly in Polish' (*PR*, p. 71); and Conrad's letters and literary works are sprinkled with Dickensian references. Thus in *Chance* (p. 162), the narrator notes that once de Barral had clung to his child beside his wife's grave and later walked hand in hand with his daughter at the seaside, and comments: 'Figures from Dickens – pregnant with pathos.' In *A Personal Record* (p. 124), Conrad remarks that a forbidding acquaintance of his Marseille days, Madame Delestang, reminded him of Lady Dedlock in *Bleak House*. And in 'Poland Revisited' (*NLL*, p. 152) he says that his first visit to London was in order to call at a shipping office:

A Dickensian nook of London, that wonder city, the growth of which bears no sign of intelligent design, but many traces of freakishly sombre phantasy the Great Master knew so well how to bring out by the magic of his understanding love. And the office I entered was Dickensian too. The dust of the Waterloo year lay on the panes and frames of its windows . . . . .

'Freakishly sombre phantasy': the similarity between the two writers lies mainly in their powers of creation of grotesquerie. In *The Secret Agent* particularly, Conrad makes London a place of savage farce by using the Dickensian technique of investing the inanimate with an unexpected degree of life (a pianola plays spontaneously, houses have apparently strayed from their correct locations), while investing the animate – the men and women – with an alarming degree of automatism. (Henri Bergson's theory of comedy thus gains evidence.) Again, there is a rather Dickensian quality to Conrad's atmospheric rendering of London in that novel: to live there is like living at the bottom of a filthy, muddy and stagnant aquarium (the slimy London of *Bleak House* comes to mind); and the scene in which Winne Verloc's bewigged mother crosses the city in a rattling cab drawn by an emaciated horse approaches a Dickensian vividness.

It is still not a *very* close approach: there are important differences between the two men. Dickens has a rich creative exuberance, an eruptive fecundity of comic and absurd invention, which the more austere and laborious Conrad lacks; and Conrad has a more mature control of the elements of his works than the relatively manic and erratic Dickens possesses. One un-Dickensian subtlety of *The Secret Agent* is that the virtue which prevails is distinctly sullied: the right thing is done, but for wrong reasons: the Assistant Commissioner expels Mr Vladimir, but he does so partly in order to protect Michaelis, because Michaelis is the protégé of a wealthy and influential hostess who, in turn, is a friend of the Assistant Commissioner's wife.

Both Charles Dickens and Dickens' admirer, Thomas Carlyle (whose *Sartor Resartus* Conrad knew), provided British precedents for some aspects of Conrad's political radicalism. Dickens and Carlyle were passionately eloquent when exposing and denouncing the injustice and brutality of industrialism in the nineteenth century, yet their attack proceeded not from socialist premises but from 'organicist conservative' premises: they sought a hierarchic society in which the concept of *noblesse oblige* guides the high, while grateful deference guides the low – an attempt to convert industrial society into an idealised harmonious feudal state. And certainly, in *The Nigger of the 'Narcissus'* Conrad came close to recommending that

Part Two
The Art of Conrad

3   Conrad on his art

From the Preface to *The Nigger of the 'Narcissus'*, 1897:

> A work that aspires, however humbly, to the condition of art
> should carry its justification in every line. And art itself may be
> defined as a single-minded attempt to render the highest kind of
> justice to the visible universe . . . . . My task which I am trying to
> achieve is, by the power of the written word to make you hear, to
> make you feel – it is, before all, to make you *see*.

From a letter to William Blackwood, proprietor of *Blackwood's
Magazine*, 12 February 1899 (*CL*, II, p. 164):

> The cheque for *£60* now received and the previous one of *£40* on
> account of the same tale ['Heart of Darkness'] will probably
> overpay it as I do not think it will run to 40000 words. I did write
> that number or even more but I've been revising and compressing
> the end not a little.

From a letter to Edward Sanderson, 12 October 1899 (*CL*, II, pp.
204–5):

> I am at it day after day and I want all day, every minute of a day
> to produce a beggarly tale [i.e. tally] of words or perhaps to
> produce nothing at all . . . . .
>
> And oh! dear Ted, it *is* a fool's business to write fiction for a
> living. It is indeed.
>
> It is strange. The unreality of it seems to enter one's real life,
> penetrate into the bones, make the very heart beats pulsate
> illusions through the arteries. One's will becomes the slave of
> hallucinations . . . . .

From a letter to John Galsworthy, 20 July 1900 (*CL*, II, p. 284):

> The end of *L.J.* [*Lord Jim*] has been pulled off with a steady drag
> of 21 hours . . . . . A great hush. Cigarette ends growing into a
> mound similar to a cairn over a dead hero. Moon rose over the
> barn[,] looked in at the window and climbed out of sight. Dawn
> broke, brightened. I put the lamp out and went on, with the
> morning breeze blowing the sheets of MS all over the room. Sun
> rose. I wrote the last word and went into the dining room. Six

o'clock. I shared a piece of cold chicken with Escamillo [the dog]
. . . . .

From a letter to the *New York Times*, 2 August 1901 (*CL*, II, pp. 348–9):

Fiction, at the point of development at which it has arrived, demands from the writer a spirit of scrupulous abnegation. The only legitimate basis of creative work lies in the courageous recognition of all the irreconcilable antagonisms that make our life so enigmatic, so burdensome, so fascinating, so dangerous – so full of hope. They exist! And this is the only fundamental truth of fiction.

From a letter to William Blackwood, 31 May 1902 (*CL*, II, p. 418):

I am *modern*, and I would rather recall Wagner the musician and Rodin the Sculptor who both had to starve a little in their day – and Whistler the painter who made Ruskin the critic foam at the mouth with scorn and indignation. They too have arrived. They had to suffer for being 'new'. And I too hope to find a place in the rear of my betters. But still – my place.

From a letter to H.G Wells, 7 February 1904 (*CL*, III, p. 112):

I've started a series of sea sketches [*The Mirror of the Sea*] and have sent out P [Pinker, the agent] on the hunt to place them. This must *save* me. I've discovered that I can dictate that sort of bosh without effort at the rate of 3000 words in four hours. Fact! The only thing now is to sell it to a paper and then make a book of the rubbish. Hang!

From 'Henry James', January 1905 (*NLL*, p. 13):

Action in its essence, the creative art of a writer of fiction may be compared to rescue work carried out in darkness against cross gusts of wind swaying the action of a great multitude.

From 'Books', July 1905 (*NLL*, pp. 7–8, 9):

Liberty of imagination should be the most precious possession of a novelist. To try voluntarily to discover the fettering dogmas of some romantic, realistic, or naturalistic creed in the free work of its own inspiration, is a trick worthy of human perverseness which, after inventing an absurdity, endeavours to find for it a pedigree of distinguished ancestors . . . . .
To be hopeful in an artistic sense it is not necessary to think that the world is good. It is enough to believe that there is no impossibility of its being made so . . . . . I would wish him [the

artist] to look with a large forgiveness at men's ideas and prejudices . . . . .

From 'A Familiar Preface', 1912 (*PR*, pp. xix–xx):

At a time when nothing which is not revolutionary in some way or other can expect to attract much attention I have not been revolutionary in my writings. The revolutionary spirit is mighty convenient in this, that it frees one from all scruples as regards ideas. Its hard, absolute optimism is repulsive to my mind by the menace of fanaticism and intolerance it contains. No doubt one should smile at these things; but, imperfect Esthete, I am no better Philosopher.

From a letter to Sir Sidney Colvin, 18 March 1917 (*LL*, II, p. 185):

I have been called a writer of the sea, of the tropics, a descriptive writer, a romantic writer – and also a realist. But as a matter of fact all my concern has been with the 'ideal' value of things, events and people. That and nothing else.

From a letter to Barrett H. Clark, 4 May 1918 (*LL*, II, pp. 204–5):

My attitude to subjects and expressions, the angles of vision, my methods of composition will, within limits, be always changing – not because I am unstable or unprincipled but because I am free. Or perhaps it may be more exact to say, because I am always trying for freedom – within my limits . . . . . A work of art is seldom limited to one exclusive meaning and not necessarily tending to a definite conclusion. And this for the reason that the nearer it approaches art, the more it acquires a symbolic character.

4 The pressure towards paradox

Conrad's most distinctive works display a tendency towards paradox in matters large, small and intermediate; sometimes this becomes an impulsion which results in self-contradiction. These are aspects of what we have termed his 'janiformity'.

To begin with small matters: even in his habits of phrasing, that predilection for the paradoxical can be discerned. Conrad likes an oxymoronic construction which can be rendered by the formula: $A = B + (-B)$. Examples in 'Heart of Darkness': the cry of the Intended is 'an exulting and terrible cry . . . . . the cry of inconceivable triumph and of unspeakable pain'; and the words of Kurtz are 'the bewildering, the illuminating, the most exalted and the most contemptible, the pulsating stream of light, or the deceitful flow from the heart of an impenetrable darkness'. (As these examples suggest, the device can become facile and automatic.)

In larger matters, the sense of paradox underlies Conrad's interest in the oblique narrative technique which offers 'a tale within a tale', a second narrator being introduced by the first narrator. 'Youth', 'Heart of Darkness', *Lord Jim*, 'Falk', *Under Western Eyes* and *Chance* provide examples. At its most extreme, as in 'Heart of Darkness' and *Lord Jim*, this procedure enables one narrator's viewpoint to be undercut or questioned by another's; it emphasises relativism of perception; and it makes problematic the process of transmission and comprehension of experience. Though oblique narration was a common device in fiction of the late nineteenth century, Conrad exploited its potentialities more fully than did his contemporaries.

If we turn to his descriptive methods, we see that Conrad has a predilection for a variety of techniques which lend an air of absurdity, futility or nightmare to what, presented by more orthodox means, would appear quite rational and natural. Such techniques are sometimes called 'impressionistic', but 'absurdist' is more appropriate, particularly when we recall that Conrad usually regarded literary impressionism as vivid but shallow – he said that Stephen Crane was *'the only* impressionist and *only* an impressionist'. One of these absurdist techniques is the use of the *reductive perspective*: a viewpoint that offers a reductive view of human activities. It may be a bird's-eye view or, so to speak, a star's, jungle's or mountain's view of humans. Here is an example from *Nostromo*, describing a battle:

Horsemen galloped towards each other, wheeled round together, separated at speed . . . . . The movements of the animated scene were like the passages of a violent game played upon the plain by dwarfs mounted and on foot, yelling with tiny throats, under the mountain that seemed a colossal embodiment of silence.

(*N*, pp. 26–7)

Another absurdist technique is the use of the *frustrating context*: the given context appears to render unattainable the goal of an activity: the actions appear blind or impotent. A good example is the account of the railway construction in 'Heart of Darkness': 'A heavy and dull detonation shook the ground, a puff of smoke came out of the cliff, and that was all. No change appeared on the face of the rock' (*Y*, p. 64). This and the previous technique combine when, in the same tale, Marlow describes a French warship shelling the African coast:

In the empty immensity of earth, sky, and water, there she was, incomprehensible, firing into a continent. Pop, would go one of the six-inch guns; a small flame would dart and vanish, a little white smoke would disappear, a tiny projectile would give a feeble screech – and nothing happened. Nothing could happen. There was a touch of insanity in the proceeding, a sense of lugubrious drollery in the sight . . . . .

(*Y*, pp. 61–2)

A third absurdist technique – and one which is of immense importance, as it applies to large-scale matters as well as to local descriptive passages – is that of *delayed decoding*. (The term is Ian Watt's, though I extend its application.) Here the writer confronts us with an *effect* while delaying or withholding knowledge of its *cause*; and the eventual explanation may not entirely erase the strong initial impression of the event's strangeness. In 'Heart of Darkness' (which contains a remarkably large number of such examples):

Something big appeared in the air before the shutter, the rifle went overboard, and the man stepped back swiftly, looked at me over his shoulder in an extraordinary, profound, familiar manner, and fell upon my feet. The side of his head hit the wheel twice, and the end of what appeared a long cane clattered round and knocked over a little camp-stool. It looked as though after wrenching that thing from somebody ashore he had lost his balance in the effort.

(*Y*, p. 111)

Not until several lines later is the decoding supplied: the man has been slain by a spear hurled by a tribesman on the riverbank. To be aware of the technique of delayed decoding is to discover the secret of much vivid, immediate writing by Conrad and by others. The impressions are often appropriate to those of a mind under stress or illness, when the awareness of events outstrips the ability to understand or interpret those events. Works of fiction which frequently use this device are likely to raise one of the defining questions of Modernism: Is it the case that all life, truly perceived, is absurd and senseless? (Later novels, by Jean-Paul Sartre and Albert Camus, carried to extremes this 'defamiliarisation device'.)

Where characterisation is concerned, the impulsion to paradox has various consequences. One is the presence of characters who themselves are walking paradoxes. There is Mr X, for example, the aristocratic revolutionary, the elegant firebrand, of the tale 'The Informer'. (Evidently he was prompted by Cunninghame Graham, an aristocratic revolutionary in real life.) Then there is Mr Kurtz, the crusading idealist who becomes a savage god. In *The Nigger of the 'Narcissus'*, James Wait is a black seaman from St Kitts who yet speaks with the accents of an English gentleman ('Won't some of you chaps lend a hand with my dunnage?'), and who claims to be ill when he is relatively well, but well when he is mortally ill. As we have noted earlier, Conrad is fond of the *Doppelgänger* motif, in which complicity is established between apparently contrasting characters: for instance, between the apparently law-abiding captain and the murderous fugitive in 'The Secret Sharer', between Heyst and Jones in *Victory*, and even between Gould and the bandit Hernández in *Nostromo*; indeed, *Nostromo* is bound by a network of such connections. It should be noted, though, that Conrad's conventions of characterisation may vary from work to work as the imaginative environment of the characters changes. Thus, in *Nostromo* the narrator is able to epitomise the characters with laconic aphorisms, whereas in the earlier 'Heart of Darkness' the emphases fell rather on the mysteriousness of personality: there we encountered numerous characters who had a vivid question-raising exterior and an answer-frustrating inner opacity. Conrad's interest in this *opacity factor* is another of his anticipations of Modernism.

A further anticipation is provided by his interest in the *covert or elided plot-sequence*. Conrad likes to conceal or withhold narrative elements that a more orthodox novelist would have made evident and prominent. Two or more readings may be needed before the full sequence is perceived. Examples include the covert murder plot of 'Heart of Darkness', the wiles of Alfred Jacobus in 'A Smile of Fortune', and the attempt to defraud the hero of his first command in *The Shadow-Line*. A particularly cunning example is provided by

Almayer's Folly, in which Abdulla successfully intrigues to destroy Almayer, his trade rival. On other occasions, as in *Nostromo* and *The Secret Agent*, the anonymous narrator, by juggling with the sequence of events or leaving large elisions in his representation of them, obliges us to do a great deal of reconstitution; delayed decoding then takes place on a large scale. This contrasts markedly with what happens in detective fiction. In a typical detective novel, we soon know what the crime is, and our interest lies in fitting together the clues to identify the criminal. In Conrad's work, we may be unaware of any 'crime' and we may not be consciously engaged in any 'detection'. Sometimes we share the experiences of a protagonist who is at first unaware that he is the object of machinations or manipulations by others; events strike him as odd rather than as sinister; and only tardily may realisation come to him and to us of the scheme being woven about him. The narrative both illustrates and generates deceived comprehension. So this method of the 'covert plot' may initially give a strong sense of absurdity and later a strong sense that the world is a place of ambushes in which virtue needs to be vigilant.

Some Conradian narrative sequences are covert in the sense that they span two or more texts, so that a reader who is familiar with only one of the texts will lack valuable information. These sequences, which are usually centred on a recurrent character, I term *transtextual narratives*. For example, the story of Tom Lingard unfolds (in reversed order) in *Almayer's Folly*, *An Outcast* and *The Rescue*, and we see the repeated frustration of his paternalistic schemes, which always seem to result in misfortune rather than happiness. The story of Charles Marlow, as told in 'Youth', 'Heart of Darkness', *Lord Jim* and *Chance*, proved poignant, for he who had felt love for Kurtz's fiancée never marries but settles into a long lonely bachelorhood. At the end of *Chance* we find the ageing Marlow begging Mrs Anthony not to remain trapped in her love for a man who is now dead, but to live for the present by marrying Powell, her young admirer. Marlow is saying, on behalf of Powell, what he perhaps should have said long ago on behalf of himself. To perceive a transtextual narrative is to register extended irony.

Numerous other characters appear in two or more texts, among them Abdulla, Almayer, Babalatchi, Lakamba, Blunt, Burns, Dominic Cervoni, Daman, Ellis, Ford, Gambril, Hamilton, Hollis, Hudig, Jim-Eng, MacWhirr, Ortega, Rita, Schomberg, Thérèse and Vinck; and sometimes they appear in Conrad's autobiographical writings as well as in the works of fiction. A large-scale moral paradox thus emerges. Conrad's literary output, which so strongly emphasises human isolation, alienation and separation, is also characterised by an exceptional endeavour to interconnect texts,

5 The covert plot: three examples

1. Abdulla's defeat of Almayer in Almayer's Folly

Almayer's collaborator, Dain, is betrayed to the Dutch authorities while smuggling gunpowder. He escapes from the ambush but is pursued; and this precipitates his hasty elopement with Nina Almayer. The *overt* plot concentrates on Almayer's response to these events, and particularly his increasing disillusionment and demoralisation on realising not only that, without Dain's help, his hopes of finding gold in the jungle are dashed, but also that his beloved daughter prefers Dain to himself and will depart for ever. He becomes an opium addict and dies. The *covert* plot is the story of Abdulla's complicated scheme to eliminate his trading rival, Almayer; and this provides the dynamism of the novel's story, but is so reticently presented that only a close reading of details reveals it. For example, in Chapter 8, two lines of dialogue reveal that the ambush of Dain resulted from a warning sent to the authorities by 'an Arab trader of this place' – who can only be Abdulla. All the subsequent main events stem from this warning. At the end of the novel, when Abdulla looks on the corpse of Almayer, victor confronts victim, and the covert plot confronts the overt plot which it has stealthily shaped.

2. The conspiracy against Kurtz in 'Heart of Darkness'

When Marlow approaches the Central Station, he expects to take command of a paddle-steamer which will voyage upstream to aid Kurtz. But, on arrival, he finds that the steamer has been wrecked. Looking back on that time, he reflects: 'I did not see the real significance of that wreck at once. I fancy I see it now, but I am not sure – not at all. Certainly the affair was too stupid – when I think of it – to be altogether natural.' The circumstances of the wrecking are peculiar: two days before Marlow's arrival, 'They had started . . . . . in a sudden hurry up the river with the manager on board, in charge of some volunteer skipper, and before they had been out three hours they tore the bottom out of her on stones.' At Marlow's first interview with him, the manager suggests that the repair will take three months. 'Afterwards . . . . . it was borne in upon me startlingly with what extreme nicety he had estimated the time requisite . . . . .'

The repair is delayed because there are no rivets at the Central Station. There are many rivets at the Outer Station, but though Marlow requests them they are not delivered. Later we learn that the manager has been in a position to censor the requests.

We gradually infer what Marlow has come to suspect. Before Marlow had arrived at the Central Station, the manager had persuaded 'some volunteer skipper' to steer the vessel on to rocks, and had then impeded the repairs for three months by withholding materials. A further two months are taken by the steamer's eventual journey. By the time relief arrives, the ailing Kurtz, who has thus been isolated for well over a year, is dying.

Conrad succeeds in eating his cake and saving it. The reticently elliptical presentation of this plot enables him to maintain the general atmosphere of futile, pointless activity; while the plot, when we eventually perceive it, makes a bitter comment on the evolutionary doctrine of the 'survival of the fittest' and on the political doctrine that the white man has a moral right to rule in Africa.

3. *The attempt to defraud the hero in* The Shadow-Line

> He couldn't see me anywhere this morning. He couldn't be expected to run all over the town after me.
>
> 'Who wants you to?' I cried. And then my eyes became opened to the inwardness of things and speeches the triviality of which had been so baffling and tiresome.
>
> (*SL*, p. 26)

At this point the hero at last begins to realise that the 'inwardness' of things at the Officers' Sailors' Home at Singapore has included a trick to defraud him of his first command. The master of a British ship has died at Bangkok, and the Consul has cabled to the Harbour-Master at Singapore for a new captain. The Harbour-Master, knowing that the hero, a first mate with excellent references, has no ship at present, sends word to the Sailors' Home that the job is available. The shifty steward at the Home decides to pass the message not to our hero but to Hamilton, his motive being a desire to get rid of Hamilton, who has not been paying his bills. Luckily, the observant Captain Giles perceives the trick and warns the hero, who eventually secures the command of the beautiful sailing-ship at Bangkok. Heavy irony stems from the fact that our man initially fails to see the point of Giles' hints and is slow to realise that Giles, far from being irritatingly inane, is in fact astutely safeguarding his interests. There is also a subtle suggestion that Giles, by securing the command for the young man, saves him from degenerating into the states of surly dishonesty, torpor or dissipation manifested by other people at the Home.

One of Conrad's strengths as a narrator lies in engaging our interest in a protagonist who has much to learn and who is aware of facts which he is only tardily learning to comprehend. The elliptical mode of narration obliges the reader to share that process of tardy comprehension. Conrad thus emphasises the contrast between meaning which is correctly *construed* and meaning which is erroneously *constructed*.

6 Textual commentaries

The opening of Almayer's Folly *(1895)*

'Kaspar! Makan!'

The well-known shrill voice started Almayer from his dream of splendid future into the unpleasant realities of the present hour. An unpleasant voice too. He had heard it for many years, and with every year he liked it less. No matter; there would be an end to all this soon.

He shuffled uneasily, but took no further notice of the call. Leaning with both his elbows on the balustrade of the verandah, he went on looking fixedly at the great river that flowed – indifferent and hurried – before his eyes. He liked to look at it about the time of sunset; perhaps because at that time the sinking sun would spread a glowing gold tinge on the waters of the Pantai, and Almayer's thoughts were often busy with gold; gold he had failed to secure; gold the others had secured – dishonestly, of course – or gold he meant to secure yet, through his own honest exertions, for himself and Nina. He absorbed himself in his dream of wealth and power away from this coast where he had dwelt for so many years, forgetting the bitterness of toil and strife in the vision of a great and splendid reward. They would live in Europe, he and his daughter. They would be rich and respected. Nobody would think of her mixed blood in the presence of her great beauty and of his immense wealth . . . . .

Such were Almayer's thoughts as, standing on the verandah of his new but already decaying house – that last failure of his life – he looked on the broad river. There was no tinge of gold on it this evening, for it had been swollen by the rains, and rolled an angry and muddy flood under his inattentive eyes, carrying small driftwood and big dead logs, and whole uprooted trees with branches and foliage, amongst which the water swirled and roared angrily.

The novel's title will prove to be characteristically ambiguous. 'Almayer's Folly' is both name and fact. It is the name jocularly given to the shell of a large building erected to accommodate the traders and workmen of the British Borneo Company; but the company had to leave to the Dutch this area of Borneo, so the building (like most architectural follies) remains empty. And

'Almayer's Folly' also refers to Almayer's habit, throughout his life, of making foolish misjudgements: his loveless marriage for gain, his belief that his Eurasian daughter should be bred to European ways, his faith in the trading-station and the coming of the British; and now, as the tale opens, his faith that with the help of Dain Maroola, a trader and prince from Bali, he can equip an expedition to find gold in the interior of Borneo and thus return proudly to Europe with his daughter.

The quoted passage bears one sign of Conrad's uncertainty with English idioms ('dream of splendid future') and several signs of being the opening of a 'first novel': the author is cramming in rather too much expository information. Nevertheless, the scene is well set: we see the European against an oppressive exotic background which is ominously turbulent, and that driftwood in the river will later figure significantly in the plot. The passage is rich in latent ironies. 'Kaspar! Makan!' means 'Kaspar Almayer! Come to dinner!', and the shrill tones are those of Almayer's wife, whom he now despises. She had been a Malay girl, an orphan benevolently adopted by the adventurous trader, Tom Lingard; and Almayer had agreed to marry her at Lingard's suggestion. He had calculated that though it was demeaning (in his view) to marry a dark-skinned woman, the marriage would win him Lingard's favour and a share in Lingard's fortune – 'And then she may mercifully die', he had reflected. But the fortune has not yet materialised, and the wife has lived on to be a cunning schemer who opposes him secretly, arranging for his beloved daughter to elope with Dain.

The trading-post which at first seemed to promise such wealth to Almayer has become a trap, an ambush to his ambitions. The British never arrive, but leave control of the region to the less enterprising Dutch, and what trade there is in the locality goes to his rivals, the shrewd Arabs; and Lingard, who has travelled to Europe to raise money for his schemes, seems lost without trace. Therefore Almayer dreams of an expedition with Dain to find gold – and with gold, freedom. What happens, of course, is a multiple disillusionment for Almayer. The expedition never takes place, because Dain, after a fight with the Dutch authorities, escapes to Bali; and Nina, who has gained bitter experience of white people's hypocrisies, elopes with him. Almayer actually helps them to flee, claiming that it would be a disgrace for white men to find his daughter with a Balinese. Having lost his daughter and his supposed ally, Almayer burns down his house and lives in the Folly. An opium-smoking Chinaman joins him, and Almayer too becomes addicted to opium; the Folly is renamed 'The House of Heavenly Delight', and Almayer sinks into a drug-addict's death. The covert plotter, Abdulla, has won.

Thus, in the opening pages of his first novel, Conrad has introduced the themes which he will develop in so many later works: (1) The theme of human isolation, physical and psychological, in an exotic setting. (2) The theme that men seek opiates for existence, having a capacity for romantic dreams that may tantalise them or lure them on to disaster or defeat. (3) The theme that even where humans appear to be close and interdependent, they may be scheming against each other. (4) The theme that no one of the competing nations or races may be essentially worthier than another.

Those readers who attribute racial prejudice to Conrad should notice that the crux of *Almayer's Folly* – the moment when a 'happy ending' seems a real possibility – comes when Almayer is tempted to abandon both his jealousy and his racial prejudice so as to join Nina in her flight with Dain: 'What if he should suddenly take her to his heart, forget his shame, and pain, and anger, and – follow her! What if he changed his heart if not his skin and made her life easier between the two loves . . . . .' As much as anything, therefore, it is racial pride that destroys Almayer. And connoisseurs of leitmotifs will notice that the river which carries Dain and Nina to a new life across the sea is the very river on which Almayer used to stare, dreaming of the gold that lay upstream and which one day might bear him and Nina to a new life across the sea.

The ending of 'An Outpost of Progress' (1897)

The Managing Director of the Great Civilizing Company (since we know that civilization follows trade) landed first . . . . . The captain and the engine-driver of the boat followed behind. As they scrambled up the fog thinned, and they could see their Director a good way ahead. Suddenly they saw him start forward, calling to them over his shoulder: – 'Run! Run to the house! I've found one of them. Run, look for the other!'

He had found one of them! And even he, the man of varied and startling experience, was somewhat discomposed by the manner of this finding. He stood and fumbled in his pockets (for a knife) while he faced Kayerts, who was hanging by a leather strap from the cross. He had evidently climbed the grave, which was high and narrow, and after tying the end of the strap to the arm, had swung himself off. His toes were only a couple of inches above the ground; his arms hung stiffly down; he seemed to be standing rigidly at attention, but with one purple cheek playfully posed on the shoulder. And, irreverently, he was putting out a swollen tongue at his Managing Director.

(*TU*, pp. 116–17)

There are obvious connections with *Almayer's Folly*. This time there are two men, not one, in the jungle outpost; the jungle is African and not Bornean; but, again, fond hopes and dreams give way to disillusionment and death.

In the tale, Kayerts and Carlier come to their African trading-station, complacently deeming themselves the vanguard of civilisa-tion, bringing 'Quays, and warehouses, and barracks, and – and – billiard rooms. Civilization, my boy, and virtue – and all'; and naturally they hope to make a lot of money from trade as well. But although they begin affably enough, the isolation and their incom-petence tell on their nerves; they connive in slavery and killing in the region (the station being managed in practice by a black, Makola); and eventually the two whites quarrel bitterly over a spoonful of sugar. One chases the other round the hut; a shot is fired; and Kayerts, horrified to discover he has killed Carlier, finally hangs himself from a cross. Thus an emissary of Christian civilisa-tion has killed his partner and died by means of the symbol of Christianity; by a further irony, it is the cross that marks the grave of his white predecessor at the station; and, moreover, that cross had been erected by the Managing Director and made straight and firm by Carlier, the victim of the man who now dangles from it. A distinctive atmosphere of mordantly harsh comedy is created by Conrad's sardonic vividness of phrasing: 'one *purple* cheek *playfully posed*'; 'irreverently, he was putting out a *swollen* tongue'. In such phrases, Conrad proves himself to be a major intermediary between the Flaubertian realism of the nineteenth century and the shock tactics of Modernism in the twentieth.

The narrator of 'An Outpost of Progress' has earlier pronounced the contemptuous epitaph of Kayerts and Carlier in words which offer an indictment of urban civilisation as a whole:

> They were two perfectly insignificant and incapable individuals, whose existence is only rendered possible through the high organization of civilized crowds. Few men realize that their life, the very essence of their character, their capabilities and their audacities, are only the expression of their belief in the safety of their surroundings. The courage, the composure, the confidence; the emotions and principles; every great and every insignificant thought belongs not to the individual but to the crowd: to the crowd that believes blindly in the irresistible force of its insti-tutions and of its morals, in the power of its police and of its opinion. But the contact with pure unmitigated savagery, with primitive nature and primitive man, brings sudden and profound trouble into the heart.

(*TU*, p. 89)

The ideas here may derive partly from Thomas Carlyle, whose 'Signs of the Times' declared:

> For the 'superior morality', of which we have heard so much, we too would desire to be thankful; at the same time, it were but blindness to deny that this 'superior morality' is properly rather an 'inferior criminality', produced not by greater love of Virtue, but by greater perfection of Police; and of that far subtler and stronger Police, called Public Opinion.

Though it is possibly indebted to Carlyle and certainly indebted to Flaubert's *Bouvard et Pécuchet*, 'An Outpost of Progress' remains a distinctive study in mordant Conradian irony and an evident precursor of the subversive masterpiece, 'Heart of Darkness'. In its references to the corruptive power of the 'pure unmitigated savagery' of Africa, the tale belongs to its Victorian times; but in its indictment of the arrogance and naïvety of colonialism, it heralds the future.

A passage from 'Heart of Darkness' (1899)

'I came upon a boiler wallowing in the grass, then found a path leading up the hill. It turned aside for the boulders, and also for an undersized railway-truck lying there on its back with its wheels in the air. One was off. The thing looked as dead as the carcass of some animal. I came upon more pieces of decaying machinery, a stack of rusty rails. To the left a clump of trees made a shady spot, where dark things seemed to stir feebly. I blinked, the path was steep. A horn tooted to the right, and I saw the black people run. A heavy and dull detonation shook the ground, a puff of smoke came out of the cliff, and that was all. No change appeared on the face of the rock. They were building a railway. The cliff was not in the way of anything; but this objectless blasting was all the work going on.

'A slight clinking behind me made me turn my head. Six black men advanced in single file, toiling up the path. They walked erect and slow, balancing small baskets full of earth on their heads, and the clink kept time with their footsteps. Black rags were wound round their loins, and the short ends behind waggled to and fro like tails. I could see every rib, the joints of their limbs were like knots in a rope; each had an iron collar on his neck, and all were connected together with a chain whose bights swung between them, rhythmically clinking. Another report from the cliff made me think suddenly of that ship of war I had seen firing into a continent. It was the same kind of ominous voice; but these men could by no stretch of imagination be called enemies. They were called criminals, and the outraged law, like the bursting shells, had come to them, an insoluble mystery from the sea. All their meagre breasts panted together, the violently dilated nostrils quivered, the eyes stared stonily up-hill. They passed me within six inches, without a glance, with that complete, deathlike indifference of unhappy savages. Behind this raw matter one of the reclaimed, the product of the new forces at work, strolled despondently, carrying a rifle by its middle. He had a uniform jacket with one button off, and seeing a white man on the path, hoisted his weapon to his shoulder with alacrity. This was simple prudence, white men being so much alike at a distance that he could not tell who I might be. He was speedily reassured, and with a large, white, rascally grin, and a glance at his charge, seemed to take me into partnership in his exalted trust. After all, I also was a part of the great cause of these high and just proceedings.'

(*Y*, pp. 63–5)

Marlow has been telling his hearers on the yawl *Nellie* about his journey through the Congo some years previously; here he recalls his arrival at the Company's Outer Station. The most obvious and important point to be made about this passage is that it conveys a controlled but intense indignation against racial exploitation and the hypocrisy of the imperialists: there is no doubt of Marlow's sympathy for the exhausted and emaciated blacks of the chain-gang. Conrad had seen actual instances of such ill-treatment during his Congo journey in 1890; and we should not forget that this tale appeared in the year when the Boer War recommenced, with the British and the Afrikaners competing violently for the spoils of Africa. At this time in Britain, the vast majority of Tories, the majority of Liberals, and at least a minority of those who deemed themselves Socialists, were pro-imperialist: the Fabians were, and of course Marx and Engels had seen imperialism as a progressive (though predatory) phase of history. Such bravely humane writings as Conrad's 'Heart of Darkness' and Cunninghame Graham's '"Bloody Niggers"' were pioneering works in their forthright condemnations of racial exploitation.

In a lecture of 1975, the Nigerian novelist, Chinua Achebe, alleged that 'Heart of Darkness' revealed Conrad to be 'a bloody racist'. Achebe said that the tale depicts Africans as dehumanised, denied speech, and associated with evil. Africa is seen as 'a foil to Europe . . . . ., a place of negation . . . . . in comparison with which Europe's own state of spiritual grace will be manifest'. Other 'Third World' writers, including Wilson Harris (from Guyana), C.P. Sarvan, Ngugi wa Thiong'o, Lewis Nkosi and Mathew Buyu, subsequently defended the tale, arguing that on the whole its tendency was progressive. Frances B. Singh shrewdly postulated a conflict between the 'historical' and the 'metaphysical' dimensions of the text: 'Historically Marlow would have us feel that the Africans are the innocent victims of the white man's heart of darkness; psychologically and metaphysically he would have us believe that they have the power to turn the white man's heart black.'

Certainly, some of Marlow's attitudes could, more than seventy years after the tale's publication, seem patronising or misguided. Nevertheless, judged historically in the appropriate context of its times, 'Heart of Darkness' can be seen predominantly as a powerfully anti-imperialist text. There is evidence that it contributed to the international protest-campaign which eventually resulted in the curbing of Belgian excesses in King Leopold's Congo. E.D. Morel, leader of the Congo Reform Association, stated that 'Heart of Darkness' was 'the most powerful thing ever written on the subject'; and Conrad sent encouraging letters to his acquaintance (and Morel's collaborator in the campaign), Roger Casement, who in 1904 published a parliamentary report documenting the atrocities committed by the Belgian administrators. On 21 December 1903, for instance, Conrad wrote to Casement:

> You cannot doubt that I form the warmest wishes for your success. A King, wealthy and unscrupulous, is certainly no mean adversary . . . . .
>
> It is an extraordinary thing that the conscience of Europe which seventy years ago has put down the slave trade on humanitarian grounds tolerates the Congo State to day. It is as if the moral clock has been put back many hours . . . . .
>
> And the fact remains that . . . . . there exists in Africa a Congo State, created by the act of European Powers[,] where ruthless, systematic cruelty towards the blacks is the basis of administration . . . . .
>
> I do hope we shall meet before you leave. Once more my best wishes go with you on your crusade. Of course You may make any use you like of what I write to you.
>
> (*CL*, III, pp. 95–7)

The passage from 'Heart of Darkness' quoted at the beginning of this section holds a characteristic ironic contrast. On one side we see instances of the inefficiency, wastefulness and futility of the imperialists' endeavours – objectless blasting, upturned trucks; and on the other side we see the price in human terms of these activities: the emaciated blacks of the chain-gang, starved slave-labourers. The juxtaposition makes a telling indictment of the folly, hypocrisy and callousness of the so-called emissaries of progress, the 'pilgrims' who, nominally Christians, are idolators before ivory.

However, the passage has greater resonance than this. The rather surrealistic landscape, in which the boiler is wallowing in the grass like a metal animal from another planet, seems to hint of a future time when all man's technology will be annulled by the non-human environment. Similarly, the depiction of the treatment of the Africans implies searching questions: we are led to ask, 'Who are the real "savages" here, the blacks or the Europeans?' This encounter with the chain-gang is just one of the many shocks that Marlow is to experience as he travels deeper into Africa, further towards the Inner Station, deeper into a continent – and into human nature. These shocks oblige him, and the reader, to ask repeatedly, 'What, if anything, justifies imperialism? On what does civilisation rest? And what are the foundations of moral conduct?'

Another important feature of this passage is its development of the tale's linguistic theme. Clichés are invoked and ironically undercut. After an account of a futile and ugly muddle of machinery, after a pointless explosion, comes the explanation: 'They were building a railway.' We are shown black slaves; and then comes the official jargon: Marlow reports that 'They were called criminals'. In his attention to the uses and abuses, the seductions, ambiguities and limitations of language, Conrad anticipates a major preoccupation of Modernist literature and of twentieth-century philosophy; indeed, the reader of 'Heart of Darkness' will be well prepared for Ludwig Wittgenstein's demonstrations that 'our language determines our view of reality, because we see things through it'.

Marlow had observed a French ship conducting 'one of their wars' by shelling 'enemies' (i.e. firing shells at the people of Africa); an African degraded by the Europeans is 'one of the reclaimed'; the European 'Workers' (ironically dignified by the capital W) are generally destructive and often slothful; Kurtz's slain victims are 'rebels'; Kurtz's megalomanic depravity is, according to the manager, the 'vigorous action' for which 'the time was not ripe': 'unsound method'. If the Europeans were presented as *consciously* hypocritical, the tale would be less incisive, for conscious hypocrisy entails recognition of the truth. But what Marlow notes around him amongst the Europeans is the credited lie, a sincerity in the use of euphemistic jargon – jargon that sanctions destruction and callousness. Conrad seems prophetic when we consider the proliferation of such political euphemisms in the twentieth century, whether by the Nazis with their 'final solution of the Jewish problem' (i.e. mass murder) or by those tyrannies which conferred on themselves such hypocritical titles as 'People's Republic' or 'Democratic Republic'.

Conrad's attitude to language is janiform: he can see it as truth-revealing or truth-concealing. Marlow strives to convey the truth, though he frequently suggests the inability of language to convey the essential: 'Do you see anything? It seems to me I am trying to tell you a dream – making a vain attempt, because no relation of a dream can convey the dream-sensation . . . . .' Kurtz, on the other hand, wields a charismatic eloquence: a power to corrupt others, and himself, through words. Another seemingly prophetic aspect of 'Heart of Darkness' is that through the emphasis on the seductive eloquence of Kurtz, who might have made a successful political leader 'on the popular side', the tale offers a warning against the kind of demagogy that would eventually bring Hitler to power.

The art of Conrad is an art of ambush. In his works we see protagonists variously ambushed by circumstances; and his techniques may lead the reader to be ambushed by the text. In the passage cited, we see how Marlow is treated as an accomplice of the exploiters by that African who guards the slaves and who 'with a large, white, rascally grin, and a glance at his charge, seemed to take [Marlow] into partnership in his exalted trust'. After all, Marlow reflects sardonically, 'I also was a part of the great cause of these high and just proceedings.' The tale concerns complicity. Marlow, as an employee of the company and even by simply being a European with a European's acceptance of ivory commodities, is involved in the exploitation he detests. The tale's structure may ambush the reader in modes of imaginative complicity. The narrative has not one narrator but two. At first, we may think that the patriotic anonymous narrator speaks with Conradian authority; but his words are undercut by the entry of Marlow, with his 'And this also . . . . . has been one of the dark places of the earth', and for a while we may be uncertain of our bearings. Then, as Marlow's narration predominates, and as we come to terms with his personality, we tend to accept his authority; so that when he records his fascination by Kurtz we are drawn into a complicated moral entanglement. Again, Marlow may initially flatter the British reader by talking of the British empire as an area where you know that some 'real work' is being done; but Marlow's ensuing narrative, by never explicitly calling the company Belgian or the region the Congo, and by stressing that 'all Europe' – including England – 'contributed to the making of Kurtz', soon dispels the flattery and associates Britain with exploitation. 'Kurtz had been educated partly in England . . . . . His mother was half-English, his father was half-French.' The tale portrays a choice of evils: between the thoughtless corruption of the Europeans who exploit the Africans callously, and the intense corruption of Kurtz,

who becomes a savage god, adored by the Africans among whom
he lives.

Jim's jump: Lord Jim *(1900)*

'"With the first hiss of rain, and the first gust of wind, they
screamed, 'Jump, George! We'll catch you! Jump!' The ship
began a slow plunge; the rain swept over her like a broken sea;
my cap flew off my head; my breath was driven back into my
throat. I heard as if I had been on the top of a tower another wild
screech, 'Geo-o-o-orge! Oh, jump!' She was going down, down,
head first under me . . ."

'He raised his hand deliberately to his face, and made picking
motions with his fingers as though he had been bothered with
cobwebs, and afterwards he looked into the open palm for quite
half a second before he blurted out –

'"I had jumped . . ." He checked himself, averted his gaze . . .
"It seems," he added.

'His clear blue eyes turned to me with a piteous stare . . . . .'

(*LJ*, pp. 110–11)

The narrator is Marlow; the blue-eyed speaker is Jim. That jump is
the jump that has ruined Jim's reputation and brought public
scandal upon him. He had been chief mate in an over-crowded
pilgrim-ship; the ship had hit an obstacle and begun to sink; the
other European officers had lowered a boat alongside and urged a
friend, George, to jump in. Instead, Jim leaps; the boat reaches
shore; the pilgrim-ship is reported sunk by the captain; but the ship
has not sunk. With all its hundreds of Muslim passengers, it has
been safely towed to harbour, and now Jim has faced the public
disgrace of the inquiry. One great irony is that Jim is an egoistic
romantic who has long nursed dreams of glory for himself, and if he
had only stayed on that ship he would be the hero of the hour; but,
instead, he is branded a coward and a traitor to the seaman's ethic
of service. Later, in the jungles of Sumatra, he will appear to redeem
himself by being a paternalistic governor to the natives; eventually,
however, a white brigand, whose life Jim spares, will treacherously
kill some of those natives, including the chief's son, and Jim will
surrender his life in atonement to that chief.

The quoted passage is part of the novel's leitmotif (or recurrent
topic) of 'the jump'. As a cadet on a training-ship, Jim had missed
his chance of glory because he had failed to jump when other boys
leapt into a cutter to take part in a rescue-operation. In the pilgrim-
ship episode, in contrast, he *does* jump – and again deprives himself
of glory. The next leap is the one that frees him from captivity in a

stockade on his arrival in Patusan, the start of his apparently redemptive adventures there. Later, when Patusan is invaded by the brigand, Gentleman Brown, and Jim faces this murderous opponent, we are told:

> 'They met, I should think, not very far from the place, perhaps on the very spot, where Jim took the second desperate leap of his life – the leap that landed him into the life of Patusan, into the trust, the love, the confidence of the people.'

In a telling irony, when Brown is seeking to negotiate favourable terms, he uses metaphors which infallibly though unintentionally remind Jim of Jim's past disgrace:

> ' "This is as good a jumping-off place for me as another. I am sick of my infernal luck. But it would be too easy. There are my men in the same boat – and, by God, I am not the sort to jump out of trouble and leave them in a d—d lurch." '

By these accidental reminders of his guilty past, Jim's negotiating position is weakened, and his consequent lenience to Brown precipitates the deaths of local inhabitants; but it is also the case that by letting Brown go instead of killing him, Jim has acted with honour. Typically, the novel invites us to see the difficulty of choosing between an honourable course which may be risky and a practical course which may appear dishonourable.

The passage quoted at the head of this section, the 'I had jumped . . . . . it seems' passage, also focuses another subtlety of the text. The brave side of Jim is there in the frank admission of cowardice, 'I had jumped' – he faces the facts, as he faces the inquiry; and the egoistic, evasive side of Jim, the Jim who seeks an excuse and would blame circumstances for this bad luck, is there in the 'it seems'. That double perspective (was the jump voluntary or involuntary, a decision or a reflex?) characterises so much of the novel, in which Conrad has dramatised brilliantly the disparity between the external view of an action (for instance, the view that the Court of Inquiry takes of Jim's leap from the pilgrim-ship) and the internal view of it (the entirely different perspective of Jim, moment by moment during the time of crisis). What Conrad explores here was to form the basis of another fine novel by a later novelist (*L'Etranger* by Albert Camus): the sense that there is a radical disparity between crucial actions as conventionally, circumstantially and morally perceived, and the same actions as actually experienced by the agent. Conrad's recounting of the subjective experience of those fateful moments is so vivid that we may empathise with Jim's paralysis, uncertainty, bewilderment and impulsiveness; conventional moral judgements of cowardice or irresponsibility seem inappropriate; we may think: 'There, but for the grace of God, go I.' Yet when Jim says, 'There was not the thickness of a sheet of paper between the right and wrong of this affair', Marlow incisively remarks, 'How much more did you want?', and we are reminded of the force of authority and common sense that stands behind those traditional circumstantial moral judgements.

The novel both asserts that Jim was 'one of us' and asks whether he was 'one of us'. The phrase is a leitmotif with many meanings. It means variously: 'a fellow gentleman', 'a white gentleman', 'a white man', 'a good seaman', 'a seemingly-honest Englishman', 'an ordinary person' and 'a fellow human being'. The phrase echoes the words that God uttered to the angels when Adam ate the forbidden fruit: 'Behold, the man is become as one of us, to know good and evil.' The biblical text is a reminder that *Lord Jim* is a novel not merely about the moral situation of one particular individual but also about the situation of humans generally as moral beings, pulled this way by ideals that tantalise and that way by realities that demean. Which are truer: the confusing messages of immediate reality or the subsequent 'decodings' by moral rationality?

The ending of 'The Secret Sharer' (1910)

> Walking to the taffrail, I was in time to make out, on the very edge of a darkness thrown by a towering black mass like the very gateway of Erebus – yes, I was in time to catch an evanescent glimpse of my white hat left behind to mark the spot where the secret sharer of my cabin and my thoughts, as though he were my second self, had lowered himself into the water to take his punishment: a free man, a proud swimmer striking out for a new destiny.

This paragraph concludes 'The Secret Sharer' (*TLAS*), which is probably the most highly acclaimed of Conrad's shorter tales. The story is lucid, engrossing, entertaining and exciting; yet it is also enigmatic, and has provoked a great diversity of interpretations, Freudian and Jungian accounts being prominent among them. Its morality holds a grittily resistant feature which may cause critics to secrete around it the putative pearl of a smoothing exegesis.

'The Secret Sharer' succeeds in being at once satisfyingly straightforward and intriguingly mysterious. The story is told in the first person by a fictional narrator, a young captain on his maiden voyage as commander of a sailing-ship. A fugitive from justice (Leggatt), who has killed a seaman on his own ship, swims at night to the captain's vessel, and immediately the young man senses a bond of complicity and comradeship with the lawbreaker;

he conceals the fugitive, and takes the ship perilously close to a rocky shore so that Leggatt, under cover of darkness, can swim to freedom.

In the paragraph quoted, Leggatt is described as 'the secret sharer of my cabin and my thoughts, as though he were my second self'. This is a tale in the *Doppelgänger* tradition of Poe's 'William Wilson' or Dostoyevsky's 'The Double': uncanny complicity, a symbiotic relationship, is established between two ostensibly contrasting characters. The captain says that Leggatt 'was not a bit like me, really'; yet Leggatt also seems 'part of myself', 'my other self', 'my secret self' and 'my double'. Conrad's enduring interest in kinship between a protagonist and an outlaw gains here its most explicit presentation. Some of the reasons for the bond between the hero and Leggatt are obvious enough: both are young British 'gentlemen-officers' who have served on the training-ship *Conway*; they are bound by caste and class. The bond is also a matter of immediate, intuitive understanding. As is 'love at first sight' in the realm of emotions (instant, strong, irrational), so is their empathy in the realm of ethics. The stress on strange kinship has encouraged some critics to see Leggatt as some kind of Freudian 'id' or Jungian 'anima', as a repressed part of the hero's psyche, but this endeavour is resisted by the tale's predominant realism, which establishes fully the external existence of Leggatt. The tale does, however, adumbrate lightly (as a flickering glow of suggestion around the strongly realistic narrative) a supernatural covert plot, in which Leggatt seems a ghostly nocturnal visitant to be encountered and exorcised. The quoted passage, for instance, maintains the emphasis on Kohring (the island to which Leggatt swims) as an Erebus, Erebus being the gloomy cavern by which, according to classical mythology, the souls of the dead entered the underworld of Hades. 'It would never do for me to come to life again', Leggatt had remarked, provoking the comment: 'It was something that a ghost might have said.'

The narrator says that Leggatt swims away 'to take his punishment'. At the realistic level, this remark is true only in the sense that Leggatt has chosen to begin a self-imposed exile as a fugitive. In the most obvious sense, however, the remark is a lie, since Leggatt is fleeing the punishment that would assuredly await him if he were put on trial for killing a man. Indeed, one of the most enigmatic features of the tale is that the narrator never seems to appreciate the moral enormity of his own readiness to help a felon to elude justice. Leggatt killed a man who impeded his endeavour to set a sail during a storm. He believes himself to be entirely justified in his homicidal action, since the sail saved the imperilled ship. The hero unquestioningly accepts Leggatt's view. An unsavoury moral implication is clearly that some men constitute a bold élite with the right to override long-established moral and legal principles. One elegant structural and ethical irony of the tale is that whereas Leggatt had thought it right to kill a man in order to save a ship and her crew, the hero thinks it right to imperil a ship and her crew in order to save a man. As Leggatt resembles a complementary mirror-image of the hero, so the eventual crisis on the young captain's vessel resembles a complementary mirror-image of the crisis on Leggatt's vessel.

The structural elegance of the tale is also illustrated by that detail of the 'white hat' in the sea. When Leggatt was about to escape overboard, the captain had impulsively pushed his own floppy white hat on to the fugitive's head (so that it might later shield him from the tropical sun ashore); but the hat, falling off as Leggatt plunges into the waves, forms the salutary marker which, by showing that the ship is gathering sternway, helps the captain to avert shipwreck in the darkness. (*Conway* cadets were taught that a white straw hat could be used 'to mark the sea'.) The kindly gift has rewarded the giver, just as the captain's aid to Leggatt has resulted in a test of seamanship which enables the captain to gain confidence in his own authority over the ship. Like *The Shadow-Line*, this is a story of initiation by ordeal into maturity. Lucid, adroit, economical, elegant, 'The Secret Sharer' is both a vivid yarn and a tantalising rune. By depicting complicity with a violent outlaw as a near-mystical imperative with a valuably positive outcome, it displays in extreme form the defiantly Romantic and almost Nietzschian aspect of Conrad's paradoxical temperament. The tale complements *Under Western Eyes*, in which a fugitive is betrayed and the betrayer undergoes protracted anguish.

Conrad once remarked, 'Fraternity means nothing unless the Cain – Abel business'; in 'The Secret Sharer', the hero fraternally befriends a modern Cain. Perhaps E.M. Forster recalled the story when he declared: 'If I had to choose between betraying my country and betraying my friend, I hope I should have the guts to betray my country.'

Two Conradian cruces

A literary crux occurs when a word, phrase, passage or sequence offers extreme difficulty to commentators. Two notorious cruces in Conrad's fiction are Kurtz's words, 'The horror! The horror!', in 'Heart of Darkness', and Stein's 'Destructive Element' speech in *Lord Jim*. The concept of janiformity enables us to resolve both problems together.

Kurtz's words, 'The horror! The horror!'

These are Mr Kurtz's last words, and Marlow makes much of their significance. Some commentators find them affirmative, others find them nihilistic, others find them obscure. If we look closely at the text, we find that Marlow suggests the following meanings for 'The horror! The horror!': (1) Kurtz condemns as horrible his corrupt actions, and this 'judgment upon the adventures of his soul' is 'an affirmation, a moral victory'. (2) Kurtz deems hateful but also *desirable* the temptations to which he had succumbed: the whisper has 'the strange commingling of desire and hate', and therefore is not a moral victory after all, it seems. (3) Kurtz deems horrible the inner natures of all humans: 'no eloquence could have been so withering to one's belief in mankind as his final burst of sincerity', when his stare 'penetrate[d] all the hearts that beat in the darkness'. (4) Kurtz deems horrible the whole universe: 'that wide and immense stare embracing, condemning, loathing all the universe . . . . . "The horror!"'

Until this point in the tale, Kurtz has been a janiform character: to put it simply, he has been both a hollow man and a full man. Marlow has explicitly called him hollow: the whisper of the wilderness 'echoed loudly within him because he was hollow at the core'. This Kurtz seems to be the ultimate in a long line of hollow men who, though nominally civilised, lack moral backbone; and the emphasis on his apparent virtues, his idealism, his energy, his eloquence, serves to show that even a seeming exception only proves the rule about a vacuity at the heart of civilisation. (The emphasis on his eloquence should remind us of the Shakespearian maxim, 'The empty vessel makes the greatest sound'.) Yet, on the other hand, Marlow has also presented him as the replete *contrast* to the long line of hollow men: a being who, in contrast to the 'flabby devils', has at least, for all his corruption, lived vividly, violently, spectacularly; and, if he has sold his soul, he has at least had a soul to sell. As the end of 'Heart of Darkness' approaches, Conrad is under an obvious pressure of convention: the convention that a tale should offer final clarification, final resolution of its mysteries and paradoxes. At his best, Conrad is rather more proficient in generating and dramatising paradoxes than in resolving them: his imagination offers resistance to the idea of final simplification. So what he offers is a pseudo-resolution: a dramatic statement by Kurtz which seems to promise that grand *finale* of revelation but which, on closer examination, proves to be itself a compressed paradox, an oxymoron: a statement which mirrors, and does not reduce, the extreme ambiguity of the characterisation.

If we consider the texture of the prose at that climactic point in

'Heart of Darkness', we will find that it is not authoritative. Marlow seems over-insistent, and the elements of contradiction in his analyses of Kurtz's words make him seem rather glibly hyperbolic and emotively portentous. We may speculate whether Marlow is here the mouthpiece of a Conrad who is under strain, or whether, on the contrary, a coolly lucid Conrad is deploying an over-insistent and confused Marlow. Twice previously, Marlow's narrative had been interrupted by sceptical, disgruntled sounds from his audience on the yawl *Nellie*. If Conrad had wished to establish a critical distance between Marlow and himself at this point, he could have done so by means of a further sceptical interruption from Marlow's hearers. As there is none, it seems probable that Marlow's confusion is largely shared by Conrad, an author divided between sympathy for the charismatic rebel and allegiance to civilised decency.

Although crucial passages like these (which reveal ideological contradictions) naturally tend to engross much of the attention of commentators, the reader may reflect that passages in which the prose is rather insistent and hyperbolic (as when Marlow empha-sises the significance of Kurtz's phrase) usually convey less of the moral and imaginative force of a work than does a passage which is less problematic but more vivid – for example, the depiction of the chain-gang or the description of the voyage down the African coast.

Stein's 'destructive element' speech

In chapter 20 of *Lord Jim*, Marlow seeks advice about Jim from wise old Stein, a retired trader. Stein utters the oft-quoted words:

> 'A man that is born falls into a dream like a man who falls into the sea. If he tries to climb out into the air as inexperienced people endeavour to do, he drowns – *nicht wa[h]r?* . . . No! I tell you! The way is to the destructive element submit yourself, and with the exertions of your hands and feet in the water make the deep, deep sea keep you up. So if you ask me – how to be? . . . . .
>
> In the destructive element immerse . . . . . To follow the dream, and again to follow the dream – and so – *ewig – usque ad finem* . . .'

('*Nicht wahr?*' and '*ewig*' are German for 'Isn't that true?' and 'for ever', respectively; '*usque ad finem*' is Latin for 'to the very end'.)

Most commentators find this passage enigmatic, and some resolve the enigma by claiming that it means 'You should pursue at all costs the goal suggested by your idealism.' This interpretation (according to which, of course, Stein is looking sympathetically on Jim's romantic if egoistic ambitions) is sanctioned mainly by the fact that 'dream' can mean 'romantic goal or ideal'.

In function, the passage bears some resemblance to the crux of

'Heart of Darkness' that we have just considered. Jim, like Kurtz, has been presented in an extremely ambiguous light. He has been shown to be more sensitive, imaginative and idealistic than the average seaman, which seems to suggest that he is better than they; but his daydreams distract him from his immediate duty, his idealism is strongly egoistic, and he is capable of bringing disgrace upon himself and his profession. Stein's words, like Kurtz's 'The horror!', provide a memorable, climactic statement which, on close examination, proves to mirror and not to resolve the paradoxes of judgement with which we have been faced.

On the one hand, such words as 'In the destructive element immerse . . . . . To follow the dream . . . . . *ewig – usque ad finem*' sound like a rallying cry to all romantic crusaders. Be a Quixote; charge on; don't count the cost; risk your life. This interpretation is encouraged by our recollection that *usque ad finem* was the proud family motto that Bobrowski reiterated to his nephew, Konrad Korzeniowski. On the other hand, if we follow Stein's speech closely, this contrasting meaning also emerges: When we are born, we fall into the dream of life as if we were falling into a sea. So we should resemble good swimmers. An inexperienced person, immersed in the sea, tries to climb up out of it in panic – and, for snatching at the sky, pays the penalty of drowning in the depths. The sensible person co-operates with the water instead of fighting it: he exploits buoyancy, and lets the water carry him while he swims steadily. Thus he survives. In other words, we should be practical realists, ready to adapt to life and make the most of what it offers; we shouldn't be idealists who try to climb up out of ordinary life towards some transcendental goal.

Stein's speech accordingly resolves itself into the janiform recommendation: Be an idealist, and be a realist instead of an idealist. No wonder Marlow records some bewilderment. These self-contradictory features of the speech express the character of the speaker, Stein; for he is not only a practical man of action but also a brooding philosopher, connoisseur and idealist. A few minutes later, he will say of Jim: 'He is romantic – romantic . . . . . And that is very bad – very bad . . . Very good, too.' This is another instance of Conrad's 'A = B+(−B)' formulations.

To the reader who likes a narrative which proceeds by decisive steps, such sibylline paradoxes or oxymora will seem vapidly evasive; but other readers may feel that by such means Conrad usefully focuses in sharp definition the problems of human nature and cultural inscription that the work at large has been exploring.

The ending of *Lord Jim* preserves the enigma. Jim offers up his life as atonement to the natives who feel he betrayed them; yet, in doing so, he rejects the pleas of his devoted lover and his loyal bodyguard.

The narrator says that Jim may have regarded his self-sacrifice as 'an extraordinary success', but adds that he can see him as a man summoned by 'his exalted egoism':

> He goes away from a living woman to celebrate his pitiless wedding with a shadowy ideal of conduct . . . . .
>
> He is gone, inscrutable at heart, and the poor girl is leading a sort of soundless, inert life in Stein's house. Stein has aged greatly of late. He feels it himself, and says often that he is 'preparing to leave all this; preparing to leave . . .' while he waves his hand sadly at his butterflies.

In *Nostromo*, with the depiction of Charles Gould, Giorgio Viola and others, Conrad would explore more extensively the ways in which a man may turn from a living woman to 'a shadowy ideal of conduct'.

7 *Nostromo*

Genesis and production

In the 'Author's Note' to *Nostromo*, Conrad says that around 1902 he came upon the memoirs of an American seaman who had once served on a schooner owned by a thief: 'The fellow had actually managed to steal a lighter [a large open boat, laden] with silver, and this, it seems, only because he was implicitly trusted by his employers, who must have been singularly poor judges of character.' Conrad reflected on this account of the theft, and:

> It was only when it dawned upon me that the purloiner of the treasure need not necessarily be a confirmed rogue, that he could be even a man of character, an actor and possibly a victim in the changing scenes of a revolution, it was only then that I had the first vision of a twilight country which was to become the province of Sulaco, with its high shadowy Sierra and its misty Campo . . . . .

Conrad was at work on *Nostromo* by the beginning of 1903. Originally he envisaged it as a short piece: he referred to it as 'a tale in the "Karain" class'; and, in May, he told Cunninghame Graham that though set 'in Sth America in a Republic I call Costaguana', the work 'is however concerned mostly with Italians', which suggests that it dealt centrally with Nostromo's involvement with the Viola family. As had happened with *Lord Jim*, the tale burgeoned into a novel as Conrad proceeded. Eventually it appeared as a serial in the popular magazine, *T.P.'s Weekly*, between 29 January and 7 October 1904; and in the same October it was published as a book by Harper & Brothers (London and New York).

The early versions differed considerably. For the book, Part III was considerably expanded, but various earlier parts of the serial were cut; and, in some cases, the cuts are regrettable. Although, on the whole, the book is superior, occasionally the *T.P.'s Weekly* text is preferable. The book text was subsequently modified by Conrad and house editors, so that while various errors were corrected, some interesting material in the first edition did not appear in later editions.

Sources

> Didn't it ever occur to you, my dear Curle, that I knew what I was doing in leaving the facts of my life and even of my tales in

the background? Explicitness, my dear fellow, is fatal to the glamour of all artistic work, robbing it of all suggestiveness, destroying all illusion.

(Conrad to Richard Curle, 24 April 1922)

Richard Curle had written, for the *Times Literary Supplement,* an account of Conrad's works which emphasised their autobiographical qualities; and Conrad's testy rebuke is partly the response of a proud old man who seeks to guard his privacy, and partly the response of a dedicated artist who seeks to avert reductive simplification of the works. A list of the source materials of a literary masterpiece can sometimes appear to 'explain away' that masterpiece, but it may sometimes give the reader a keener eventual sense of the work's imaginative integrity. Any such list has to be ruthlessly selective. An exhaustive list would be interminable: it might include such matters as the author's preference for certain syntactical rhythms or for certain pictorial lighting effects in descriptions, and the causes of such preferences. The short lists that follow are conventional in range; I omit from them source materials in an unconventional sense (e.g. thematic preoccupations and dialectical impulses), which are discussed in a later section.

Personal encounters

The 'Author's Note' tells us that Antonia Avellanos is modelled on Conrad's 'first love', a proudly nationalistic young woman who was admired by Conrad and his schoolmates. This explanation may well be truthful, though Antonia is partly a familiar fictional type

Overleaf, pp. 142–3: *The beginning of the manuscript of* Nostromo.
Conrad made many revisions, small and large, to the whole text as it evolved via serialisation in T.P.'s Weekly *into the eventual book. In this opening paragraph, 'never been anything more' became 'never been commercially anything more'; 'salt fish and oxhides' became 'ox-hides and indigo'; 'on her three-knot way' was deleted; and 'sombre festoonings [of cloud]' became 'mourning draperies . . . . .' The change of 'Sulaco seemed to have found an inviolable sanctuary' to 'Sulaco had found an inviolable sanctuary' actually reduces the original ironic precision.*

The first paragraph introduces several important themes: economic evolution; the contrast between human acquisitiveness and nature's serene dignity; and the potential defilement of sanctuary. The emphasis on the calm of the Placid Gulf also prepares us for the episode when Decoud and Nostromo are becalmed in their vessel at night. Thus the opening paragraph of the novel is as deliberate as the concluding one, which so carefully incorporates the phrase 'a mass of solid silver' in the description of the nocturnal sky.

Fragments of Parts 1 & 2

NOSTROMO..

1.

Part First

The Silver of the Mine

~~The Isabels~~.

I

Through all the ages of Spanish rule and for many years afterwards the town of Sulaco (the luxuriant beauty of the orange gardens bears witness to its antiquity had never been anything important than a coasting port with a petty trade in salt fish and ox hides. The clumsy ~~get~~ deep sea galleon of the conquerors, that, needing a brisk gale to move at all would lie helplessly becalmed where your modern sailing

2

ship built on clipper lines
forges ahead on her three-
knot way by the mere flapping
of her sails, never had been
barred out of Sulaco by
the calms prevailing calms of
its gulf. Some harbours of
the earth are made difficult
of access by the treachery
of sunken rocks and the
tempestuous character of
their shores: Sulaco seemed
to have found an inviolable
sanctuary from the temptations
of the world in the solemn
hush of the deep Golfo Placi-
do as if within an enormous
semicircular and unroofed
temple open to the
the ocean, while its walls of
lofty mountains remain hidden
under the sombre festoonings of

(the noble, ardent and beautiful heroine who suffers stoically), and she owes her name and her emancipated spirit to a woman encountered by E. B. Eastwick and described in his book *Venezuela*.

Conrad's note about Antonia strengthens one's sense that Martin Decoud is based largely on the younger Conrad. We can readily imagine that Decoud's mixture of cynicism, romanticism and patriotism closely resembles Conrad's own, and that the 'idle boulevardier' of Paris has much in common with a former prodigal boulevardier of Marseille; and Decoud's suicidal pistol-shot re-echoes in the imagination when we recall that the young Conrad had once put a pistol to his own breast and pulled the trigger.

The 'Author's Note' also explains that Nostromo himself derives partly from the thief described in the source tale and partly from Dominic Cervoni, the Mediterranean sailor, tough and capable, who was the first mate of the *Saint-Antoine*, and with whom Conrad claimed to have attempted gun-running. The researches of Norman Sherry (*CWW*, pp. 163–5) confirm the historic existence of Dominic, who belonged to 'the Brotherhood of the Coast – a kind of Mafia'.

The fictional landscape of Costaguana is established with such a convincing richness and seeming knowledgeability of detail that the reader may be surprised to discover that the much-travelled Conrad actually saw very little of the South American continent. Conrad told Cunninghame Graham in 1903: 'I just had a glimpse 25 years ago – a short glance. That is not enough pour bâtir un roman dessus [to build a novel upon].' And to Richard Curle he remarked that he had gone ashore for about twelve hours at Puerto Cabello and about two-and-a-half to three days at La Guaira – 'and there were a few hours in a few other places on that dreary coast of Ven[ezue]la'. This was during the period of the *Saint-Antoine* voyage (1876–7), when, according to Jerry Allen (in *The Sea Years of Joseph Conrad*) the vessel carried arms for the Conservative rebels against the Liberal government in the Colombian Civil War, which was then raging. Allen's claim lacks verification; though, in the 'Author's Note' to *Victory*, Conrad hints that he was engaged in some lawless activity at that time.

The topography of Costaguana derives from Conrad's recollection of the Venezuelan coast, perhaps his glimpses of the West Indies to some minor extent, and what he had heard or read of Colombia, Argentina, Chile and other places. He told Cunninghame Graham: 'Costaguana is meant for a S. Am^{can} state in general; thence the mixture of customs and expressions.' As it has both Pacific and Atlantic seaboards and a city called Santa Marta, geographically it resembles Colombia; though, the more we sense that Costaguana represents 'a S. Am^{can} state in general', the more we may recognise the novel's general implications concerning economic imperialism, history and human nature.

Conrad's friend Cunninghame Graham was an authority on South and Central America, having spent several years travelling and working there. He claimed to have seen action, in his youth, with a revolutionary army; certainly, he had journeyed through a devastated Paraguay in the aftermath of the war of 1865–70 conducted by the brutal dictator, Francisco Solano López. Graham provided Conrad with anecdotes and recollections (e.g., the 'dentist' anecdote of Part III, Chapter 9), with books by himself, his wife and others, which provided accounts of American life, and with an introduction to Pérez Triana, the Colombian Ambassador.

Norman Sherry (*CWW*, p. 149) has suggested that Charles Gould is based partly on Cunninghame Graham: 'Both are given Spanish names – Don Roberto, Don Carlos; both are remarkable for their flaming hair and moustaches; both have early family connections with the country in a political sense . . . . .' In addition, both men have wives who sketch and who accompany their husbands on exhausting journeys in America. We might add that Cunninghame Graham, like Gould, was a celebrated equestrian figure, was fluent in Spanish, and had prospected (for gold if not silver) in ancient mine-workings; and his marriage, too, proved childless. Some of Cunninghame Graham's political attitudes (his scepticism about economic imperialism and modern 'progress' in general) differ markedly from Gould's, but resemble those of the narrator of *Nostromo*.

During his exploration of the Paraguayan wilderness in 1873, Cunninghame Graham had been lent a gun by an Italian named Enrico Clerici, who kept a tavern at Itapua. Fierce and leonine, this former follower of Garibaldi appears in four of Graham's tales and is clearly a progenitor of Giorgio Viola in *Nostromo*. He refers to Garibaldi as 'my saint', and, like Viola, keeps a picture of this Italian leader on his wall.

From Conrad's letters (*LCG*, pp. 157–8) we know that Don Santiago Pérez Triana contributed to the book. He was the son of a Liberal President of Colombia who had been ousted during a revolution; and his numerous publications, including *Down the Orinoco in a Canoe* (1902) and his contribution to the *Cambridge Modern History*, Vol. XII (1910), show that he was a patriot who regarded with sadness the confusion and misrule of Colombia's past, and hoped that foreign investment (in particular, by Britain) might establish a future of peace and justice. His ideals doubtless contributed to those of Don José Avellanos in the novel. In appearance, however, Pérez Triana was short and stout, and much unlike the ageing, ailing, elder statesman of Costaguana; so it is possible that while he lent his ideas to Avellanos, he lent his body to Don Juste López, the eventual President of independent Sulaco.

Literary sources

1. 'F.B. Williams' (pseudonym of H.E. Hamblen): *On Many Seas: The Life and Exploits of a Yankee Sailor* (1897). This gave the story of Nicolo, the silver-thief: the basis for the narrative of Nostromo's theft of silver.

2. G.F. Masterman: *Seven Eventful Years in Paraguay* (1869). This provided many names of people and places: Don Carlos Decoud, Mitchell, Padre Corbelán, Gould, Barrios, Captain Fidanza, the Blancos, and 'the Cerro Santo Tomás, a bold square mountain' (equivalent to the square San Tomé mountain in *Nostromo*). Conrad's descriptions of Guzmán Bento and Pedrito Montero may derive partly from Masterman's description of the tyrant López. The torturing of Monygham and others by the sadistic priest, Father Berón, was probably suggested by Masterman's account of his own tortures at the hands of Padre Román. The parrot that cries 'Viva Costaguana' in the novel is the offspring of the parrot that cries 'Viva Pedro Segundo' in Masterman; and even Decoud's phrase 'Gran bestia!' can be found in *Seven Eventful Years*.

3. E.B. Eastwick: *Venezuela* (1868). This offered various names: Mount Higuerota, Sotillo, Guzmán, Ribera (adapted as Ribiera) and Amarilla; and its description of Puerto Cabello provided a basis for the description of Sulaco harbour and the Golfo Plácido beyond. More interestingly, Eastwick recalls the 'reigning beauty' of Valencia, Antonia Ribera, a Europeanised, well-educated, emancipated young woman with blue eyes and rich brown hair, who is said to wish to marry nobody but a foreigner: evidently a relative of Antonia Avellanos.

Eastwick also recalls an embarrassing moment at a banquet when the Venezuelan President toasted him with the vulgar words: 'I drink to the gentleman who has brought us thirty thousand pounds.' Conrad magnifies this incident in Part I, Chapter 8: 'I drink to the health of the man who brings us a million and a half of pounds', says Montero. In Eastwick, there is an account of the Venezuelan army: 'lean old scarecrows and starveling boys not five feet high, the greater number half naked, with huge strips of raw beef twisted round their hats or hanging from their belts.' Conrad, avid for unexpected and therefore vivid detail, pounced on the beef: his version is: 'Emaciated greybeards rode by the side of lean dark youths, marked by all the hardships of campaigning, with strips of raw beef twined round the crowns of their hats.'

4. Other books. Ramón Páez's *Wild Scenes in South America* (1863) provided descriptions of flora and fauna and anecdotes about

General Páez. (Conrad's selective use of this minor source will be discussed in a later section.) Garibaldi's memoirs provided the name Anzani, hints for the character Hernández, details of Garibaldi's career, and particularly the account of the torture by strappado which was the basis for Conrad's description of Hirsch's torture. Anatole France's essay 'Mérimée', as we have noted previously, contributed to the characterisation of Decoud. Cunninghame Graham's *A Vanished Arcadia* and *Hernando de Soto* repeatedly suggested that modern 'progress' might really entail the despoliation of South America. R.F. Burton's *Letters from the Battle-fields of Paraguay* (1870) describes the havoc wrought by the campaigns of the tyrant Francisco Solano López, and mentions a Don Juan Decoud, the promising son of a distinguished family, who edits a Liberal newspaper. Conrad's description of Linda Viola derives details from Flaubert's description of Mademoiselle Vatnaz in his *L'Education sentimentale*; when Nostromo calls Giselle 'his star and his little flower', he is cribbing King Balthasar's address to Balkis in Anatole France's *Balthasar*; and various philosophical generalisations in *Nostromo* have been borrowed from France's *Le Lys rouge*, *L'Anneau d'améthyste* and *Les Opinions de M. Jérôme Coignard*.

5. Newspapers and periodicals. In the decade before the publication of *Nostromo*, items by Conrad had appeared in the magazines *Cosmopolis*, *Blackwood's* and *The New Review*; he took *The Times* and was an avid reader of *The Saturday Review* (which published material by such acquaintances of his as Graham, Shaw and Wells). Anyone who devotes some time to browsing among those periodicals soon recognises that *Nostromo* emerges from the international news and political debates of the day with the inevitability of a battleship emerging from the clamour and bustle of a wartime shipyard.

Imperialism, both martial and economic, was the dominant topic, as Britain found that her power was being challenged by new rivals, particularly by the United States and Germany; and, around the turn of the century, Central and South American affairs figured prominently in the news. In 1895–96, the American President, Grover Cleveland, sided with Venezuela in the long-standing frontier dispute with Britain over the boundaries with British Guiana; and in 1898 the United States declared war on Spain, and eventually won control of the Philippines, Guam, Puerto Rico and (for a while) Cuba. Four years later, Venezuela was subject to naval blockades by Britain, Germany and Italy; and in 1903 the United States intervened to ensure the secession of Panama from Colombia. Of course, the turbulent unrest in the unstable South American republics (and the perils of investing in them) had often enough, during the mid to late nineteenth century, been a topic of regretful comment in the British papers; prominent coverage had been given to the war between Chile, Peru and Bolivia over the Atacama nitrate fields (1879–84), the war mentioned in Part I, Chapter 6, of *Nostromo* (p. 76). One of the keynotes of the novel is the recurrent phrase 'material interests', and this phrase was a cliché of political debates in the press. On 24 February 1900, for example, the Liberal magazine *The Speaker*, which subsequently published work by Conrad, contained an article by George Russell ('The Revival of Imperialism') which says: 'Today . . . . . We see lust of territory, lust of gold, lust of blood; the idolatry of material interests; the shameless repudiation of all moral appeals.'

The treatment of the source materials

> It dissolves, diffuses, dissipates, in order to re-create; or where this process is rendered impossible, yet still at all events it struggles to idealize and to unify. It is essentially *vital*, even as all objects (*as* objects) are essentially fixed and dead.
>
> > (Coleridge on the 'secondary imagination':
> > *Biographia Literaria*, Chapter 13)

From the heterogeneous source materials, Conrad derived names and phrases, bits of plot, palettes of 'local colour', historical references, political arguments and thematic motifs. Conrad's creative imagination strove to co-ordinate and unify this material, to heighten its vividness and to charge it with moral signficance. His aims were mimetic – to offer an evocation of the life that might be found in a South American state; they were cathartic, for his personal fears and tensions also sought expression; they were dialectical, for he was engaged in a complex debate with his cultural environment; and they were symbolic, for his urge to compress and relate significances generated symbols.

Here is just one instance of Conrad's ability to vivify his source material. Among his books was Ramón Páez's *Wild Scenes in South America*, a memoir of South American life with numerous descriptions of the flora and fauna. Páez writes:

> Less imposing than the preceding [the tiger owl] – although more terrifying in their way – are the *ya acabó* and the *pavita* – two other species of owl considered harbingers of calamity or death, when heard fluttering around a house. The first portends an approaching death among the inmates, and is therefore looked upon with dread even by men who would not flinch at the sight of the most formidable bull or jaguar. Yet that appalling cry, *ya acabó! ya acabó!* – it is finished! it is finished! – seems so fraught with evil mystery, that few hear it unmoved.

In Part III, Chapter 8, of Conrad's novel, Nostromo, having swum ashore from the gulf, wonders whether Teresa Viola may be still alive.

> As if in answer to this thought, half of remorse and half of hope, with a soft flutter and oblique flight, a big owl, whose appalling cry: 'Ya-acabó! Ya-acabó! – it is finished; it is finished' – announces calamity and death in the popular belief, drifted vaguely like a large dark ball across his path. In the downfall of all the realities that made his force, he was affected by the superstition, and shuddered slightly. Signora Teresa must have died, then. It could mean nothing else. The cry of the ill-omened bird, the first sound he was to hear on his return, was a fitting welcome for his betrayed individuality. The unseen powers which he had offended by refusing to bring a priest to a dying woman were lifting up their voice against him. She was dead . . . . . A man betrayed is a man destroyed. Signora Teresa (may God have her soul!) had been right. He had never been taken into account . . . . . The anger of her denunciations appeared to him now majestic with the awfulness of inspiration and of death. For it was not for nothing that the evil bird had uttered its lamentable shriek over his head. She was dead – may God have her soul!
>
> (pp. 418–19, 420)

The echoes of phrasing ('appalling cry', 'it is finished!', 'calamity and death') make quite clear that Conrad imported the owl from Páez's text. But whereas Páez was simply noting the bird-life of South America, Conrad incorporates this detail not merely to provide plausible local colour but also to make varied comment on its context, so that the owl gains symbolic force. The bird's cry suggests to Nostromo that Teresa must be dead; by reminding him of her, it recalls to him Teresa's repeated claims that he was betraying himself by serving Mitchell and Gould; and his increasing sense that she was right is reinforced by guilt, for instead of fetching the priest whom the dying woman had needed, he had served the company by sailing the silver-boat. The emergence of superstitious credulities from beneath his egoistic scepticism is part of that demoralising process which will cause him to abandon Decoud and steal the silver. The owl's ominous cry is one of many supernatural elements in the narrative: the first of them being introduced in the novel's opening pages, with their story of the haunted Punta Mala. Conrad's treatment of source material, then, tends not only to heighten significance but also to multiply ironies. The bird's 'It is finished' is taken by Nostromo to refer to Teresa's life; but it refers also, in a sense, to Nostromo's: for now his career, as an honest, untroubled overseer and factotum, is finished for ever.

Nostromo *and the meanings of its techniques*

In this discussion, I initially offer some reminders of *Nostromo*'s problematic techniques; next, I discuss the plot, or rather the view of history suggested by a plot summary; thirdly, by looking closely at two important passages, I bring together the previous findings; and finally, I deal with some recent criticisms. What emerges is a political reading of the novel's techniques which indicates a closer and more constructive relationship between technique and plot than some influential commentators have discerned.

Problematic mobility

When we first begin *Nostromo*, one of our strongest impressions is of a bewildering mobility – a kaleidoscopic quality accompanied by an extremity of irony and a conceptual jaggedness. There are repeated shifts in perspective: we're shifted from person to person, from area to area, from one time to another; there's a bright vividness and knobbly concreteness of description, yet also a commentary of aloofly sceptical generalisations. At one minute we're down in the thick of the crowd, being jostled against Nostromo's silver saddle-gear, and at the next we're taking a bird's-eye view of events and places, looking far along the coast and out across the Golfo Plácido. There's an epic scope and a solipsistic undertow. What is prominent and solid in one section dissolves and fades in the next. The wheels of the carts aren't simply wooden: they're discs of wood marked with 'the strokes of the axe' – they're *that* solid; yet during the night in the Placid Gulf, the world and the self seem about to dissolve into mere blackness.

Tolstoy's *War and Peace* has comparable scale and scope, a similar desire to relate great events to small, public to private, and general to particular; but its exposition is relatively smooth and steady, whereas *Nostromo* is jumpy, pouncy, twisting. One of the characteristics of *Nostromo* which clearly differentiates it from previous novels, British and continental, is an extreme *mobility of viewpoint and focus*. And under that general heading could be listed the following four subheadings:

1. TEMPORAL mobility. There are unexpected juxtapositions of events from different times; and Conrad is fond of delaying our decoding of large and small effects: experiences are thrust at us before we are in a position to comprehend their significance.

2. VISUAL mobility. As noted, there are both vertical and lateral shifts. Sometimes the viewpoint is low, looking up; sometimes high

and olympian, looking down. Now it is close to people on land; now it is miles away, at sea. It is one of the features which makes *Nostromo* remarkably cinematic, even though the cinema was then in its clumsy infancy.

3. NARRATORIAL mobility – mobility between informants. Towards the end of the book, much essential information is provided by Captain Mitchell's address to a visitor, and we have to allow for ways in which the information may be distorted by his personality or falsified by his ignorance. At another point, we are dependent on a letter being written by Decoud, and we have to make similar allowances. It is true that for much of the time we have the guidance of, ostensibly, an omniscient anonymous narrator whose outlook we may be tempted to identify as Conrad's; yet, at the opening of Chapter 8 in Part I, this narrator actually identifies himself as a mere character, a visitor to Costaguana: one of those 'whom business or curiosity took to Sulaco in these years before the first advent of the railway'. As the narrator soon resumes the customary spectral mobility of most impersonal fictional narrators (eavesdropping on solitaries, drifting through skulls), we may wonder why Conrad bothered briefly to give him a local habitation and identity. The reason is partly psychological: Conrad, like Eliot in *The Waste Land*, needs to don a mask, however transparent, in order to speak most eloquently. In 'Heart of Darkness', many subversive things are said in the course of Marlow's tale; and Conrad, if criticised for such observations, retained the right to say: 'Look again: the opinions are identified as Marlow's; they are not necessarily mine.'

Another aspect of narratorial mobility is Conrad's use of what in German is termed '*erlebte Rede*' and in French '*style indirect libre*': tacitly reported speech or thought. This occurs when, although the text does not there include quotation marks or the phrases 'he said that' or 'she thought that', we infer that the novel's ubiquitous narrator is not offering his own reflections but is reporting the speech or reflections of a character. Often the inference is easy and rapid; sometimes, however, tacit reportage is a possibility lacking confirmation, so that the degree of authority of a statement remains unresolved.

4. FOCAL or ANALOGICAL mobility: the postulation of analogies between different characters or entities. When we are observing one character, an unexpected analogy may oblige us to relate our observation to another character. We think we're looking at A, and suddenly find we're simultaneously looking at B. This is quite a common device (George Eliot was particularly skilled in its use), but *Nostromo* exploits it dextrously. The critic Cleanth Brooks once

said that in *The Waste Land* we are repeatedly shown apparent similarities which reveal underlying contrasts, and apparent contrasts which reveal underlying similarities. In *Nostromo* this technique interlinks numerous characters and historical phases. For example: Nostromo and Gould, though outwardly so different from each other, are both corrupted by their possession of silver (or in their possession by it); and Dr Monygham's love for Mrs Gould is compared with a secret store of unlawful treasure, so Monygham is thus linked to the Nostromo whom he distrusts. Decoud, shortly before his death by pistol-shot, repeatedly thinks of himself as a man suspended by both hands from a tense, thin cord; thus we are reminded of Hirsch, who, before his own death by pistol-shot, was suspended by both hands from the tense, thin rope of the strappado. Don Carlos Gould, the financial 'King of Sulaco' who is so frequently seen as a proudly equestrian figure, is juxtaposed with the equestrian statue of King Carlos IV of Spain, the last of the Spanish emperors of South America: which prompts the reflection that perhaps, for all the appearances of progress, the old story is being repeated: the story of exploiters and exploited, of overlords and the subjugated, of imperialism whether martial or economic. As Gould succeeds, he becomes more stonily statuesque himself; and, when he prevails, the old statue of King Carlos is removed as 'an anachronism'.

Marxism and the history of Costaguana

In their various ways, the novel's techniques throw us about, ambush and exercise us. When we have emerged from those ambushes and can look back on *Nostromo*, the main pattern of Costaguana's history emerges clearly enough; and the pattern has some distinctive similarities to that detected in (or imposed on) history by Marxists. We have noted that from 1897 onwards, Conrad's closest literary friendship was with R. B. Cunninghame Graham. This celebrated – indeed notorious – campaigner was he whom Friedrich Engels described as 'Communist, Marxian, advocating the nationalisation of all means of production'. In his books on South American history (which Conrad read with great pleasure) Cunninghame Graham had sardonically drawn parallels between the boldly predatory activities of the Spanish *conquistadores* long ago and the obliquely predatory activities of British, European and North American economic imperialists in modern times. Of course, even before he had met Cunninghame Graham, Conrad's writings had displayed some of those features which give a seemingly Marxist quality to *Nostromo*. We have seen that from the start, in *Almayer's Folly* and *An Outcast of the Islands*, he had taken a deeply sceptical view of various political and economic activities: he had distrusted idealistic and pious rhetoric and had been prompt to suggest the power of economic self-interest operating behind a smoke-screen of noble talk. However, it is not coincidental that with the arrival of Cunninghame Graham a new incisiveness enters Conrad's political thought.

In *Nostromo*, numerous aspects of the plot bring Marxism to mind. First, there is the recurrent emphasis on economics as a key to history, with the quest for material gain providing the main structure beneath the cultural superstructure. As Conrad remarked later: 'It may be that the noblest tradition is but the offspring of material conditions' (*NLL*, p. 183). Secondly, there is the related suggestion that even if men are not the puppets of a method of production ('Your very ideas', said Marx and Engels, 'are but the outgrowth of the conditions of your bourgeois production'), in the long run the success of men's schemes depends upon the compatibility of those schemes with international economic forces. Consider the following example. Decoud conceives the idea that Sulaco should secede from Costaguana, thus becoming an independent state, and his scheme comes to fulfilment: an individual's imagination seems to have changed history. But his scheme succeeds because, among other reasons, there is a show of force by the United States: we are told that the US warship *Powhattan* was the first to salute the flag of Sulaco; and the reason for this North American show of force is that a lot of North American capital is invested in the Sulaco silver-mine. The immediate historical precedent for this part of the novel was the secession of Panama from Colombia in 1903, a secession ensured by the arrival of US warships: thus the United States effectively seized control of Panama and its canal. 'What do you think of the Yankee Conquistadores in Panama? Pretty, isn't it?', wrote Conrad sarcastically to Cunninghame Graham.

A third feature of *Nostromo* which brings Marxism to mind is the book's emphasis on the ways in which a state's political apparatus can be manipulated in the interests of the wealthy. The best example is provided by Gould's increasing power. Initially, when he plans to redevelop the silver-mine, he says:

> 'What is wanted here is law, good faith, order, security. Any one can declaim about these things, but I pin my faith to material interests. Only let the material interests once get a firm footing, and they are bound to impose the conditions on which alone they can continue to exist. That's how your money-making is justified here in the face of lawlessness and disorder. It is justified because the security which it demands must be shared with an oppressed

people. A better justice will come afterwards. That's your ray of hope.'

(p. 84)

However, in order to get the mine established, Gould has to resort to bribery on such a large scale that it soon looks as though the cheaper option will be to finance a revolution which will bring to power a so-called dictator, Ribiera, who is pledged to serve the cause of the mine and of foreign investors generally. Yet this in turn engenders a further revolution: the Montero brothers, seeking wealth and power for themselves, are able to exploit nationalist feeling against the foreign investors, racial hostility against the whites, and class feeling against the aristocratic land-owning class. Ribiera is overthrown, and Pedro Montero invades the rich province of Sulaco. For a while the fate of the province hangs in the balance, but eventually the Monterist army is repulsed, the independence of Sulaco is assured, and the new state seems to prosper. Nevertheless, near the end of the novel, bitter reflections on Gould's initial hopes for a new era of justice are cast by two of the most reliable commentators on events. Dr Monygham says:

'There is no peace and no rest in the development of material interests. They have their law, and their justice. But it is founded on expediency, and is inhuman; it is without rectitude, without the continuity and the force that can be found only in a moral principle. Mrs. Gould, the time approaches when all that the Gould concession stands for shall weigh as heavily upon the people as the barbarism, cruelty, and misrule of a few years back.'

(p. 511)

And Mrs Gould accepts his wisdom:

She saw the San Tomé mountain hanging over the Campo, over the whole land, feared, hated, wealthy; more soulless than any tyrant, more pitiless and autocratic than the worst Government; ready to crush innumerable lives in the expansion of its greatness.

(p. 521)

Now it is certainly true that against these oft-quoted pessimistic pronouncements we have to set, among other things, the optimism of Captain Mitchell. He looks with complacent pride on new Sulaco, with its railways, department-stores and clubs; and, to him, an era of poverty and bloody civil wars seems finally to have been superseded by a tranquil era in which, under parliamentary government, property-owners like himself can look forward to a peaceful retirement enhanced by the income from their shares in the mine, while, in his view, the masses can enjoy peace, security and a steadily improving material standard of living. Still, we have been given many indications that the inner stability and composure of Mitchell depend on a certain thickness of skull: he is honest, generous and reliable, but fails to see the inner pattern of events. Near the end of the novel, the political situation in Sulaco is this: the mine-workers have reached the stage of critical class-consciousness; we are told that they are not likely ever again to take up arms to defend the owners. A Communist Party has developed, and the workers are being urged to rise against the capitalist exploiters. There are predictions of warfare on two fronts. Antonia Avellanos, Cardinal-Archbishop Corbelán and the political refugees from inland Costaguana are plotting a further revolution which would annex Costaguana to Sulaco; and meanwhile Hernández, the ex-bandit who had once supported Gould and is now Minister of War, has offered himself as military leader to the agitators who hope to 'raise the country with the new cry of the wealth for the people'.

So far, so Marxist: apparently an exemplary demonstration of the way in which capitalism, emerging from feudalism, reshapes in its own interests the political institutions of a country, thrives and prospers for a while, but eventually, through the tendency to monopoly and the creation of a vast and discontented work-force, reaches the phase of internal contradiction which (according to the old theory) ensures its own downfall. But, of course, this janiform novel offers shrewd complications.

The most obvious complication is provided by the very pejorative presentation of the revolutionary agitator, evidently a Marxist, who sits by the bedside of the dying Nostromo. (He's a later version of Donkin, who in *The Nigger of the 'Narcissus'* sits at the bedside of the dying negro, waiting to steal his money.) The agitator is 'pale . . . . ., small, frail, bloodthirsty'. He asks Nostromo to bequeath his wealth to the cause, saying: 'Do not forget that we want money for our work. The rich must be fought with their own weapons.' This may seem an eminently practical request: more practical than offering prayers for a change of hearts, for an increase in benevolence and brotherly feeling. Yet the silver had been regarded as a weapon by Gould, too; and he had discovered that it was a double-edged weapon, 'dangerous to the wielder'. Who guards the guardian? The novel has offered numerous examples of men's judgements being corrupted by the possession of the silver, or by the prospect of possessing it; and all too often the material means to some imagined good has perverted the end or become an end in itself: Gould had reached the point of preferring to be blown sky-high with his mine rather than let the wealth fall into anyone else's hands. One of the factors which makes the weapon of wealth two-edged and dangerous is the short-sightedness of the wielder. The Marxist looks like being even more short-sighted than Gould, for while sitting at Nostromo's bedside he says: 'You have refused all aid from that doctor. Is he really a dangerous enemy of the people?' The reason for Nostromo's refusal of aid from Dr Monygham is primarily guilt: the doctor rightly suspects that Nostromo has stolen the missing silver, and Nostromo senses the suspicions. An obvious irony implicit in the Marxist's question is the possibility that Dr Monygham, who in the past had suffered crippling torture on the orders of a dictator, may in the future suffer again – at the hands of one who proclaims the liberation of the oppressed. Conrad acutely anticipates the Marxist tyrannies to emerge long after *Nostromo* was written: for another and more general implication of these closing pages is that the old story of the manipulation and exploitation of the many by the few may extend a long time into the future: there may be changes of slogans and changes of masters, but the rapacity, the bloodshed and the parasitism will continue.

And this possibility brings us to the next complication, the matter of the time-shifts. One of the most influential commentators on this novel, Jocelyn Baines, offered this theory to account for the shifts: 'The elimination of progression from one event to another . . . . . has the effect of implying that nothing is ever achieved. By the end of the book we are virtually back where we started; it looks as if the future of Costaguana will be very similar to her past' (Baines, p. 301). 'Nothing is ever achieved.' A technical innovation is, according to this theory, translatable into a conservative political recommendation: people should resign themselves to the fact that they are incapable of making improvements in their condition. We can test this opinion by looking at two of the most striking instances of the time-shifts in *Nostromo*.

The time-shifts: two examples

The first selected example is the presentation of Dictator Ribiera's escape. We initially hear of this in Part I, Chapter 2. We have been introduced to Captain Mitchell, and we eavesdrop on some of his recollections (which the narrator reports with a fine relish of political and rhetorical absurdity):

> The political atmosphere of the Republic was generally stormy in these days. The fugitive patriots of the defeated party had the knack of turning up again on the coast with half a steamer's load of small arms and ammunition. Such resourcefulness Captain Mitchell considered as perfectly wonderful in view of their utter

destitution at the time of flight. He had observed that 'they never seemed to have enough change about them to pay for their passage ticket out of the country.' And he could speak with knowledge; for on a memorable occasion he had been called upon to save the life of a dictator, together with the lives of a few Sulaco officials . . . . . belonging to an overturned government. Poor Señor Ribiera (such was the dictator's name) had come pelting eighty miles over mountain tracks after the lost battle of Socorro, in the hope of out-distancing the fatal news – which, of course, he could not manage to do on a lame mule. The animal, moreover, expired under him at the end of the Alameda, where the military band plays sometimes in the evenings between the revolutions . . . . .

. . . . . As the Dictator was execrated by the populace on account of the severe recruitment law his necessities had compelled him to enforce during the struggle, he stood a good chance of being torn to pieces. Providentially, Nostromo – invaluable fellow – with some Italian workmen, imported to work upon the National Central Railway, was at hand, and managed to snatch him away – for the time at least. Ultimately, Captain Mitchell succeeded in taking everybody off in his own gig to one of the Company's steamers . . . . .

. . . . . To the very last he had been careful to address the ex-Dictator as 'Your Excellency.'

'Sir, I could do no other. The man was down – ghastly, livid, one mass of scratches.'

(pp. 11, 12, 14)

And the chapter concludes by telling us how the indispensable Nostromo and his men had dispersed the mob.

There the person reading the novel for the first time is likely to conclude that that little episode of history is closed. He or she will naturally think that the account of Ribiera's flight has just two simple functions: to set the scene generally by exemplifying the past political turmoil of the region, and to illustrate the characters of Mitchell and Nostromo, who may be important figures in the subsequent plot. Now certainly the information about Nostromo and Mitchell is very useful; but what is deceptive is the impression that the Ribiera incident is past history and finished. For Chapter 3, the next chapter, instead of taking us forward chronologically, plunges us into the middle of the events Mitchell had previously recalled; and the narrative, as it proceeds, gradually spirals *back* in time; so that about a hundred pages after the account of Ribiera's downfall, we are told of the circumstances of his first presidential visit to Sulaco at the inauguration of his régime. Not until Chapter 8 are

we shown how his reformist régime has been brought into existence
by means of the money of Gould and Holroyd; and we are told:

> He was more pathetic than promising, this first civilian Chief of
> the State Costaguana had ever known, pronouncing, glass in
> hand, his simple watchwords of honesty, peace, respect for law,
> political good faith abroad and at home – the safeguards of
> national honour.

(p. 119)

Then the narrative slowly spirals forward in time, so that many
pages later, in Chapter 7 of Part II, another character reports as
yesterday's occurrence the very event that Mitchell had described
at the beginning of the book. Decoud writes: 'The missing President,
Ribiera, ... has turned up here . . . . ., riding on a lame mule
into the very midst of the street fighting' (p. 224).

Thus the narrative has reversed the normal sequence and overthrown conventional expectations. What seemed to be preliminary
and peripheral has proved to be a central event; a passing episode
is revealed as a retrospect to a time that had yet to be presented in
detail. What are the purposes of this deviousness?

First, and fairly trivially, this technique gives an unusual plausibility to the fictional historical events. When one character, near
the middle of the novel, reports as yesterday's occurrence an
incident that a different character, early in the novel, had reported
from a different viewpoint and with a different emphasis, the
incident acquires a stereoscopic quality. Secondly, and less trivially,
the method gives a radical and tentacular quality to the ironies. If
normal chronological narration had been used, we would have
learned first about Ribiera's pious hopes at the inaugural banquet
and much later about his ludicrous escape on a lame mule, and
retrospective ironies would have flickered about the original scene.
But the proleptic narration ensures that because we know from the
start about his escape, we become thoroughly sceptical spectators
at that banquet. As President-Dictator Ribiera raises his glass,
our memories superimpose on his hopeful face the features of a
battered fugitive, 'ghastly, livid, one mass of scratches'. The rhetoric
at the dinner has an utterly hollow ring, because the context is a
mocking echo-chamber to the speech – as mocking as the green
parrot which reduces all political rhetoric to a shriek of 'Viva
Costaguana!'

Thirdly, as Baines noted, the sense of history as cyclical and
repetitive plays against the sense that history manifests a steady
evolution. As the narrative impinges on us, Ribiera suffers his
downfall, Ribiera is installed in power, Ribiera suffers his downfall:
a cycle. As we rearrange the impinging events to make orthodox

narrative sense, Ribiera is established by the financial powers in order to protect their interests; he is overthrown; and out of the ensuing turmoil a new independent state emerges which for a time safeguards their interests: a state under President Juste López. In one sense, there is no going back: the modern state cannot be unmade. But in another sense, of which the narrative fluctuations have reminded us, there is a constant recurrence of folly and exploitation, though in varying forms.

Fourthly, and most importantly, the time-shifts and the related dislocations in the narrative have value *as resistances to be overcome*, and in this way they induce a complex moral and political therapy in the reader. Most commentators have failed to notice that there is a curiously close connection between what the novel diagnoses as man's political limitations and what the novel in all its technical richness and deviousness seems designed to do. In the 'Author's Note' to *Nostromo*, Conrad says that the book displays 'the passions of men short-sighted in good and evil'. This preface emphasises the moral short-sightedness of men, and the narrative provides numerous examples of that myopia. There is Gould, unable to foresee the ways in which the mine will corrupt his judgement; Mitchell, complacent about the social changes and insensitive to the agonies entailed and the new strife to come; and Ribiera, failing to foresee the brevity of his régime. There are constant misjudgements of one character by another: some people sacrifice present life on the altar of an imagined future; others are blinded to the future by the immediate present. Conrad's oblique method induces in the reader (however subliminally and fleetingly) the very flexibility that most of the people in the novel lack, and suffer from lacking. While demonstrating the political infancy of men, the novel embodies its political maturity in techniques which entail for the reader an education in that maturity. The basic structure of *Nostromo*, therefore, resembles that of St Paul's paradox: 'One of themselves, *even* a prophet of their own, said, The Cretians *are* alway liars . . . . . This witness is true.' By delaying the decoding of events, Conrad forces us to share the myopia of his characters; and by provoking the decoding, he provides the therapy which helps us to share his own keen vision.

Or so one could argue; but this interpretation would certainly be challenged by some other commentators. Albert Guerard, for instance, has claimed that Conrad maliciously frustrates the reader's attempt to grasp the story:

> The first part of *Nostromo* invites and then frustrates the normal objectives of readers to an astonishing degree . . . . . The common reader's notorious general aim – to enter into the book and

become one of its characters – is carefully and austerely baffled. The novelist . . . . . maliciously chops at his hands.

(*CN*, p. 215)

In practice, however, we can and do decode the scrambled information; we can and do reconstruct the calendar of historical events as a regular sequence. We falsify the novel's meaning if we over-emphasise either the initial chronological flux or the deciphered chronological order; either the contingency or the determinism. The narrative shows and evokes what a semiotician, Michael Riffaterre, has called 'the praxis of the transformation': the very activity of making significant order. A strong patterning of events emerges, but only after we have experienced the recalcitrance of events; a clear historical viewpoint is established, but only after we have been shown the ways in which recorded history may falsify events by smoothing out the knobbly awkwardness of their impact; and a bleak and sombre view of human capacities emerges, but only after we have been given vivid instances of the particular needs, drives and sufferings of a variety of humans. The novel dramatises the ironic disparity between the two senses of 'history', which can mean both 'events which actually occurred' and 'a historian's selective account of events which are believed to have occurred'. Thus, *Nostromo* is a fictional history whose methods cast doubt on the human veracity – the fidelity to the texture of life – of actual historians. Conrad said that in a novel, the 'accumulated verisimilitude of selected episodes puts to shame the pride of documentary history' (*PR*, p. 15); so he would have agreed fully with the spirit of Aristotle's remark, 'Poetry, therefore, is more philosophical and of higher value than history . . . . .' There is a historian in the novel itself – Don José Avellanos, author of *Fifty Years of Misrule* – and the destiny of his work is amply ironic. Martin Decoud says:

> 'Hasn't he seen the sheets of "Fifty Years of Misrule," which we have begun printing on the presses of the *Porvenir*, littering the Plaza, floating in the gutters, fired out as wads for trabucos loaded with handfuls of type, blown in the wind, trampled in the mud? I have seen pages floating upon the very waters of the harbour.'

(p. 235)

Here Decoud sounds like the spokesman of a cynical novelist; so the second example of the time-shifts that I will consider is provided by the treatment of the death of that speaker, Martin Decoud; and this will be a way of testing Albert Guerard's claim that Part III of *Nostromo* is marred by an 'uncertain or uselessly wavering point of view'. There *are* some signs of authorial haste or flagging energies towards the close of the book; but, in this instance, the time-shift is highly functional.

At the end of Chapter 8 of Part II, Nostromo leaves Decoud on the island, the Great Isabel. A boatload of silver is buried there. The island offers a refuge to Decoud, because back in Sulaco the invading forces of Pedrito Montero are seeking to capture him as a political enemy. Decoud isn't marooned, exactly, for he has a rowing-boat with which to intercept some passing ship. However, he is left there, and nobody sees him again. Not until many chapters later, in Chapter 10 of Part III, do we first hear of his death. Years in the future, Captain Mitchell, reminiscing about the history of Sulaco, takes a visitor into the cathedral and shows him a medallion on the wall. The inscription is 'To the memory of Martin Decoud, his betrothed Antonia Avellanos'; and Mitchell explains that it 'commemorates that unfortunate young gentleman who sailed out with Nostromo on that fatal night'. Later in the same chapter, the narrative at last spirals back through the years to give us a close-up, a plangently memorable view of Decoud's isolation on the island.

> Decoud caught himself entertaining a doubt of his own individuality. It had merged into the world of cloud and water, of natural forces and forms of nature. In our activity alone do we find the sustaining illusion of an independent existence as against the whole scheme of things of which we form a helpless part.

Eventually, oppressed and demoralised by exhaustion and solitude, he shoots himself:

> The stiffness of the fingers relaxed, and the lover of Antonia Avellanos rolled overboard without having heard the cord of silence snap in the solitude of the Placid Gulf, whose glittering surface remained untroubled by the fall of his body.
>
> A victim of the disillusioned weariness which is the retribution meted out to intellectual audacity, the brilliant Don Martin Decoud, weighted by the bars of San Tomé silver, disappeared without a trace, swallowed up in the immense indifference of things.

(pp. 497, 501)

One reason for the widely acknowledged power of this sequence is that both Decoud's death and the narratorial comments on it form a thematic nexus: they sum up majestically in image and epigram some of the strongest thematic implications of the work, and those implications have previously been pressing on us, largely subliminally, in a great variety of ways.

When Decoud beholds the universe as 'a succession of incomprehensible images', the possible validity of this view has been hinted by the initial effect of the time-shifts, which have given an impressionistic vividness but also a bewildering dislocation to events. Our plight may well have resembled that of the visitor to Costaguana, who, on listening to Mitchell's reminiscences, was 'stunned and as it were annihilated mentally by a sudden surfeit of sights, sounds, names, facts, and complicated information imperfectly apprehended . . . . .' Eventually, of course, we have sorted the images and given comprehensibility to the initially incomprehensible; the decoding, though often frustrated and delayed, has gradually become less difficult. But that initial sense of confusion has at least invoked the possibility that the world, truly perceived, may be recalcitrant to rational interpretation. Conrad had told Cunninghame Graham: 'Life knows us not and we do not know life – we don't know even our own thoughts.'

Another consequence of the complex narrative techniques has been the prominence gained by the few constant and unambiguous features in the imaginative landscape: throughout the temporal changes, for all the shifts of action in the foreground, the scenic background has remained constant: the Placid Gulf itself, the immense and unchanging snow-capped Cordillera, and the vastly serene and icy Mount Higuerota. So, when the glittering surface of the Placid Gulf remains 'untroubled by the fall' of Decoud's body, this comes as the seemingly inevitable illustration of the narrator's maxim about 'the whole scheme of things of which we form a helpless part'.

As for the *political* implications of that maxim about 'the whole scheme of things', they are not necessarily what they first seem to be. The easy reading is to take them as classically conservative: humans may come and humans may go, but in the long run the Godless non-human environment prevails: in the evolutionary time-scale, man is ephemeral and impotent. If, however, we remember that *Nostromo* first appeared in 1904 (when the European nations were still wrangling about their acquisitions in America, Africa and other parts of the globe, and when advocates of imperialism far outnumbered their opponents), one implication is clearly anti-imperialistic, for it associates imperial activity by nations with the action which is only a sustaining 'illusion' in individuals.

If Conrad had followed orthodox chronological order, the death of Decoud would have been described long *before* Mitchell's résumé of the subsequent events. The time-shift method enables Conrad to reverse the orthodox order, so that the death-scene follows immediately *after* that long complacent account of the ostensibly progressive evolution of Sulaco. In Mitchell's view, history has been progressive: the story of Sulaco has a happy ending; man has mastered nature, and civilised man has mastered society. Almost immediately after these reflections, Conrad deploys the most vivid example of human littleness. Scepticism is validated in a scene which shows the self-destruction of the sceptic.

In the essay 'Autocracy and War', Conrad argued that the governments of states, like individual men, are in moral infancy. Fearing destruction, they react aggressively. 'The idea of ceasing to grow in territory, in strength, in wealth, in influence – in anything but wisdom and self-knowledge – is odious to them as the omen of an end . . . . . Let us act lest we perish – is the cry.' Therefore he commends not aggressive action but 'wisdom and self-knowledge': a phrase which, in the essay, may sound suspiciously vague and cloudy. It begs many questions; it needs many examples. But the novel *Nostromo* had answered some of those questions and provided some of the examples. The wisdom that Conrad had commended in the novel, by implication and through irony, had entailed ample indignation on behalf of the humble, the exploited and the cannon-fodder of history. The wisdom had entailed ample scepticism, about political jargon and rhetoric, about the possibility that a just society could ever be found under conditions of economic imperialism. Yet that wisdom had entailed a hope that can be glimpsed in the challenges afforded by the novel's shifts in time and space, with their therapy for myopia: a hope that some people may work towards maturity by developing and increasing the ability to apply to the present the lessons of the past, to have foresight which does not require the sacrifice of the life of the present, and to test all general doctrines by a mobile responsiveness to individual human experience. As Mrs Gould reflects: 'For life to be large and full, it must contain the care of the past and of the future in every passing moment of the present.' Of course, she remains a lonely and largely-defeated figure. A major source of the ironies of *Nostromo* is Conrad's sense that the values most worth preserving are not those most likely to prevail; but without the sense of those values frustrated (and intermittently rendered absurd by the immensity of the non-human environment), the book would lack its eloquent intensity of pessimistic realism.

When the techniques of *Nostromo* have opened our eyes, therefore, we may finally look upon that novel not as 'a succession of incomprehensible images', but rather as the engineer looked on Mount Higuerota: 'thinking that in this sight, as in a piece of inspired music, there could be found together the utmost delicacy of shaded expression and a stupendous magnificence of effect'.

Critical challenges

Since its first appearance in 1904, *Nostromo* has retained the capacity to outdistance and sometimes to ambush its critics. This capacity can be illustrated by a survey of adverse judgements by influential commentators.

In *Criticism and Ideology* (1976), Terry Eagleton, a Marxist, exploited the 'deconstructive' notion that literary texts are riven with contradictions which are symptomatic of ideological conflicts within strife-torn society. One Conradian contradiction, Eagleton argues, is that between the appeal of organicism (the closed, tightly knit organic community) and Romantic individualism (which gives supremacy to the individual ego). Affirmation is repeatedly undermined by scepticism. Accordingly:

> At the centre of each of Conrad's works is a resonant silence
> . . . . . The absent centre of *Nostromo* is in part Nostromo himself,
> but also the silver of which he is the agent . . . . . As the
> determining structure of which the novel's characters are the
> bearers . . . . ., the silver is the unifying principle of the entire
> action; but since that action has for Conrad no coherent historical
> intelligibility, it is a principle which must of necessity be dramati-
> cally absent . . . . . The need for value, and the recognition of its
> utter vacuity; it is here that the deepest contradiction of Conrad's
> enterprise, one integral to the imperialist ideology he shared,
> stands revealed.

As we have seen, Conrad certainly voiced contradiction, and, as self-proclaimed 'homo duplex', was well aware of the fact. Certainly, Eagleton was right to see in Conrad an extreme tension between affirmation and scepticism. In *Nostromo*, Mrs Gould is sympatheti-cally presented as an affirmer and source of value; yet Decoud is persuasively presented as the voice of a penetrating scepticism. Eagleton's suggestion, however, that Conrad thereby enters into deep complicity with 'imperialist ideology' seems curiously unfair to a writer who raised questions (and voiced the contradictions) which it is supposedly the aim of imperialists to stifle and to conceal. To say that 'the entire action' in Costaguana 'has for Conrad no coherent historical intelligibility' is a rather negative way of sensing that in *Nostromo* Conrad is concerned to challenge the notion of 'historical intelligibility' by depicting rival 'intelligibilities' and questioning their adequacy: Eagleton seems to be trying to teach his grandmother to suck hollow eggs. As a matter of textual accuracy, his assertion that silver is 'dramatically absent' seems quite incorrect. Whether it's filling the lighter in the gulf, weighting the pockets of Decoud as he sinks into the sea, constituting Viola's spectacle-frames or Nostromo's whistle and buttons, silver is ubiqui-tously present, and the process of extracting silver bullion from the rough ore is carefully expounded by the narrator in Part I, Chapter 8. Perhaps misgivings about this matter were in Eagleton's mind when he later described the chapter of *Criticism and Ideology* which discusses Conrad as one marred by 'inexact formulation, metaphorical gesture, partial and reductive reading': nevertheless, his discussion has the provocative verve of bold concision.

In 1981 a popular American critic, Fredric Jameson, claimed in *The Political Unconscious* that *Nostromo* 'accredits the good opinion the industrial West has of itself' by showing that the South American people, being 'lazy' and 'shiftless', need to have order imposed on them from abroad; furthermore, Conrad's conservatism is demonstrated by the fact that 'the Blancos are good, the Monteristas evil'. Jameson overlooks one consistent feature of Conrad's novels and tales: outsiders who seek to impose order on a foreign area usually make matters worse rather than better; and, if Dr Monygham and Mrs Gould are correct, this is true of Sulaco. Certainly, Colonel Sotillo, the Montero brothers and their followers Gamacho and Fuentes are depicted sardonically and satirically; but the Blancos, the aristocratic landowners, are presented variously as anachronistic, naïvely idealistic, vacillating, craven, ineffectual and enfeebled. Consider Decoud's account of Don Juste López, the temporising President of the Provincial Assembly:

> 'Don Juste López had had half his beard singed off at the muzzle of a trabuco loaded with slugs, of which every one missed him, providentially. And as he turned his head from side to side it was exactly as if there had been two men inside his frock-coat, one nobly whiskered and solemn, the other untidy and scared.'

The text then offers a finely ironic and historically astute account of the Provincial Assembly's rationalisation (as hopeful pragmatism) of abject surrender to superior force; and this is only one instance of many ways in which the text's complexity challenges Jameson's schematisation.

Another influential American critic is Edward Said, who, over the years, has given extensive attention to Conrad. In the essay 'Through Gringo Eyes' (*Harper's*, April 1988), Said claims that although Conrad astutely sees imperialism as 'doomed by impossible ambition', he nevertheless 'writes as a man in whom a *Western* view of the non-Western world is so deeply ingrained that it blinds him to other histories, other cultures, other aspirations'. Therefore:

> Conrad was both an anti-imperialist and an imperialist – progressive when it came to rendering the self-confirming, self-deluding corruption of the West's colonial drive; reactionary in his inability to imagine that Costaguana could ever have had a meaningful existence of its own, which the imperialists had violently disturbed. But lest we think patronizingly of Conrad as merely the

creature of his own times, we had better note that we today appear to show no particular advance on his views.

The reader may perceive that, once again, *Nostromo* displays a tenacious capacity to criticise its critics. Far from suggesting that Costaguana could never have had 'a meaningful existence of its own', the novel emphasises that the known history of Costaguana has repeatedly been an *imposed* history: it is the victors, not the victims, who tend to be the historians of any region; the labouring people have known recurrent invasion, conquest and exploitation. Conrad shows that the reign of the new imperialists is just one phase in that long process of imposition. The very first chapter of the novel draws attention to the former era of Spanish rule, and frequent analogies link the old and new *conquistadores*. The novel's rich social panorama does not neglect the indigenous inhabitants: in many detailed descriptive paragraphs their plight is shown. When the first chapter tells us that the poor 'associat[e] by an obscure instinct of consolation the ideas of evil and wealth', it cites a notion that the ensuing narrative will amply support. Edward Said's criticism actually seems to repeat, without due recognition, the case made forcefully at several points in the novel: for instance, by Decoud in Part II, Chapter 5. There Decoud recalls the days when Sir Francis Drake, in the service of English speculators, plundered the town:

'In those days this town was full of wealth. Those men came to take it. Now the whole land is like a treasure-house, and all these people are breaking into it, whilst we are cutting each other's throats. The only thing that keeps them out is mutual jealousy. But they'll come to an agreement some day – and by the time we've settled our quarrels and become decent and honourable, there'll be nothing left for us. It has always been the same. We are a wonderful people, but it has always been our fate to be' – he did not say 'robbed', but added, after a pause – 'exploited!'

(p. 174)

Giorgio Viola makes a similar point when Decoud says: 'We are all for the people – in the end.' He replies: 'Yes . . . . . And meantime they fight for you. Blind. Esclavos! [Slaves!]' Adroitly, the text later satirises a related xenophobia when Gamacho advocates war 'against France, England, Germany, and the United States, who . . . . . aimed at robbing poor people of their lands'.

Edward Said suggests that Conrad ignores the rights of the 'natives'; but *Nostromo* soon makes clear that to define the 'natives' is no easy matter, given that the population is already a 'melting-pot of nations'. The social mixture includes the Indians, who so often serve as the hapless workforce; mulattos; people of European, particularly Spanish, ancestry; many people descended from a mixture of Spanish and Indian forebears (the *mestizos*); and a newer influx of Italians, Britons and North Americans. The very 'patriots' who urge the people to cast out foreign exploiters bear foreign (Spanish) names: Montero, Gamacho, Fuentes, Sotillo. Nor does Conrad sentimentalise the pre-colonial era as a Golden Age: Decoud remarks that in 'old times', 'the persistent barbarism of our native continent did not wear the black coats of politicians, but went about yelling, half-naked, with bows and arrows in its hands'. If the history of Costaguana has been so turbulently unstable as to resemble, at times, a black comedy or savage farce, it is little different in this respect from the history of Argentina, Paraguay, Colombia, Venezuela and other strife-torn republics; and the depredations of the fictional Guzmán Bento were based on, and sometimes exceeded by, those of real-life dictators like José da Francia and Francisco Solano López of Paraguay. As Edward Said notes, the text reminds us that even the great liberator of South America, Simón Bolívar, eventually made the despairing statement: 'America is ungovernable; those who have served her revolution have ploughed in the sea. These countries will inevitably fall into the hands of the unrestrained multitude, to become then the prey of petty tyrants of all grades and races . . . . .'

By a wealth of details, *Nostromo* implies the history which lacks its historian, the story of the common masses. One telling detail comes when Viola is observing the discipline of the new recruits in the army of Barrios: 'One-eyed Barrios and his officers had done wonders with the recruits in a short time. Those Indios, only caught the other day, had gone swinging past in double quick time, like bersaglieri; they looked well fed too, and had whole uniforms. "Uniforms!" he repeated with a half-smile of pity' (p. 167). The telling detail here is the phrase, 'only caught the other day': the Indians may be contented enough, well-fed and in new uniform; but they have effectively been captured, to fight perhaps to the death in order to guard the dividends of investors based in San Francisco and London. The lethal price exacted by material progress is instanced in particulars like this:

> A fire of broken furniture out of the Intendencia saloons, mostly gilt, was burning on the Plaza, in a high flame swaying right upon the statue of Charles IV. The dead body of a man was lying on the steps of the pedestal, his arms thrown wide open, and his sombrero covering his face – the attention of some friend, perhaps.
> (p. 228)

The juxtaposition is typical of Conrad's tirelessly ironic imagination: here, an unknown victim of the revolutionary upheavals lies at the foot of the stony image of the king chronicled by orthodox historians.

In one important respect, declares Edward Said, later writers like Graham Greene and V.S. Naipaul have followed Conrad's unfortunate example: 'When there is something indigenous to be described, it is, following Conrad, unutterably corrupt, degenerate, irredeemable.' To this charge, one answer is provided by the descriptive sequence in Part I, Chapter 8, in which Don Pepe, the overseer of the mine's workforce, is contrasted with Mrs Gould. To her, the miners look all alike; but Pepe prides himself on his individual recognition of them. Whole families, we are told, had travelled from afar to seek the work and security of the mine:

> Father first, in a pointed straw hat, then the mother with the bigger children, generally also a diminutive donkey, all under burdens, except the leader himself, or perhaps some grown girl, the pride of the family, stepping barefooted and straight as an arrow, with braids of raven hair, a thick, haughty profile, and no load to carry but the small guitar of the country and a pair of soft leather sandals tied together on her back.
>
> (p. 101)

It is difficult to see here any evidence of the 'unutterably corrupt, degenerate [and] irredeemable'. In this sequence, one irony is that these people are heading not only to employment, food and apparent security, but also to regimentation: the miners will have to wear uniforms, and these families will be accommodated in identical villages with the utilitarian names 'Village One, Village Two, Village Three'. Pepe's endeavour to know the workers as individuals is in conflict with the institutionalising tendencies of the organisation he serves, an organisation which seeks to render into a regimented and conforming mass so many disparate figures. In such ways, *Nostromo* notes factors that were later to be elaborately postulated and documented by subsequent notable socio-economic analysts (Max Weber, Georg Simmel and R.H. Tawney, among others) and by popular sociologists (like David Riesman and William Whyte).

In short, far from being unable to see life beyond the parameters of imperialism, Conrad has generally anticipated Said by showing very precisely and critically the mechanism whereby imperialism seeks to impose its 'narrative' – its authorship, plots and themes – on Latin America (and elsewhere). Certainly a pessimistic circularity may be seen in the book's explicit political theses. In contrast to 'the development of material interests', we are offered a recommendation of 'the continuity and the force that can be found only in a moral principle'; but, to be effective, that moral principle must become political action; and political action (the novel insists) tends to corrupt the moral ideals: 'There was something inherent in the necessities of successful action which carried with it the moral degradation of the idea.' Certainly, too, Conrad sometimes was unable to resist the convenience of stereotyping, whether in generalisations about the characteristics of 'northern' and 'southern' races, or in depiction of various characters and situations (notably in the predominantly anti-semitic depiction of Hirsch and in the rendering of Nostromo's romantic entanglement with Giselle Viola). Nevertheless, judged in its historical context, *Nostromo* was remarkably progressive in its main historical and political insights.

In recent decades, so many critics have adopted a political approach to literary texts that the hedonistic approach is sometimes neglected. *Nostromo* is not a political manifesto; it is a work of fiction, and therefore belongs to a genre which, first and foremost, succeeds if it entertains. To say this is not to trivialise it, for, though stupid entertainments please stupid people, intelligent entertainments please intelligent people. What gives *Nostromo* its staying-power is largely that its embodied verve and varied insights enable it to sustain multiple readings over long periods of time; its obliquities, ambiguities, ironies and paradoxes provide sophisticated satisfactions, even though many of its features offer graphically immediate rewards: it includes scenes of tragedy, poignancy, absurdity, farce, black comedy, and a stylistic range that offers innumerable pleasures to linguistic sensualists. To condemn the novel because some of its views do not reflect our prejudices (or principles) is short-sighted, for a work which opposes our prejudices may be more effective as literature than a work which flatters them. The genre of satire, which characteristically exaggerates human vices and follies, shows this; and *Nostromo* is a sombre satire on what a great Augustan writer termed 'the vanity of human wishes'.

Chronology and topography

The provision of maps and chronological tables for a fictional Costaguana is mildly absurd but certainly useful. For example, the very disparity between the linear clarity of the table or map and the complex profusion of material deployed by Conrad may help the reader to define for himself or herself the significant features of the text. In *The Matrix of Modernism* (1985), Sanford Schwartz asserts:

At the turn of the century, the human sciences (psychoanalysis, linguistics and ethnology) were undergoing a global shift from the developmental (or 'before-and-after') paradigms of the nineteenth century to the structural (or 'surface-and-depth') paradigms of the twentieth.

Nostromo is the vast terrain on which Conrad has staged a battle between those two contrasting paradigms: repeatedly the linearity of orthodox chronology is challenged by the time-shifts; repeatedly the stability of the regional map is challenged by the perspectival contrasts.

The narrative contains a few chronological anomalies, but most of the time-references in the book cohere satisfactorily. A crucial reference occurs during Gould's meeting with Holroyd in San Francisco, when Holroyd refers to the long war over the Atacama nitrate fields as though it had reached its completion. That war lasted from 1879 to 1884, so this is one of the reasons for giving their meeting the date 1884; which in turn makes 1890 a probable year for the main action of the novel. Again, to a surprisingly large extent the topographical references are consistent and permit reliable maps to be drawn.

When building the imaginary Costaguana, Conrad used writings about many different locations, including Mexico, Colombia, Venezuela, Argentina, Paraguay. He remarked to Edmund Gosse that 'Sulaco is a synthetic product' containing bits of Venezuela, Chile, Mexico and the Golfo de Panamá. Colombia, like Costaguana, has a large town called Santa Marta and a port called Tumaco (which may have suggested Sulaco) – though there is a Sulaco in Honduras. A real Zapiga can be found in Chile, Esmeraldas in Ecuador, and an Azuera and a Punta Mala in Panama. An equestrian statue of King Carlos IV stood in the Plaza Mayor of Mexico City until Mexico gained its independence. In its geographical location, Costaguana resembles Colombia more than any other major South American republic, for, like Colombia, it has not only a prominent Santa Marta, the township of Socorro and a spectacular Cordillera (mountain range), but also both an Atlantic and a Pacific seaboard. On a map of the world for the American edition of *Victory* (1915), Conrad gave Sulaco a location corresponding to Ecuador, which was once part of Greater Colombia.

The name 'Costaguana' has sometimes been misinterpreted as 'Bird-Lime Coast'. But 'guano' means 'palm-tree' (in addition to 'birds' excrement'); and 'Costaguana' should obviously be translated as 'Palm-Tree Coast', for the text specifies the palm-groves of the maritime region, and the national flag displays 'two green palm trees in the middle'.

Conrad emphasised that the history of Costaguana, like its landscape, was 'an achievement in mosaic'; but he added that 'it seems to me much more true than any history I ever learned'.

Table A   General chronology

DATE	EVENT
Sixteenth and seventeenth centuries	Spanish colonialists develop Sulaco, establishing an ecclesiastical court there. Local trade in ox-hides and indigo. Silver-mine worked by slaves.
1821	Charles Gould's grandfather fights for Bolívar in British regiment at Battle of Carabobo.
1830	San Tomé mine reopens after War of Independence.
1832	Holroyd born.
1840	Monygham born.
1842–62	Giogio Viola serves under Garibaldi, first at Montevideo, later in Italy.
1850–56	Epoch of civil war in Costaguana; federalism; Sulaco resists union.
1855	Charles Gould's Uncle Harry, President of Sulaco, defeated; shot by order of General Bento.
1856	Guzmán Bento inaugurates his own 'perpetual presidency'. Twelve years of peace begin.
1860	Charles Gould born; Martin Decoud born.
1864	Antonia Avellanos born.
1866	Nostromo born. Don José Avellanos and Dr Monygham arrested.
1867–68	Monygham tortured by Father Berón.
1868	Don José Avellanos pardoned; Bento dies; Monygham released. During the turmoil following Bento's death, the mine-workers kill their English masters; the mine is closed.
1868–74	Three governments come and go; the fourth obliges Gould's father to accept ownership of the mine.
1876	Linda Viola born.
1878	Giselle Viola born.
1884	Gould's father dies; Gould marries Emilia, and they travel to Sulaco; on the way, Gould talks to Holroyd at San Francisco.
1885	Holroyd visits Goulds; Goulds tour Sulaco seeking labour; mine is reopened.
1888	Holroyd and Gould finance revolution to install a compliant government. During the warfare, General Montero aids the Blanco (Conservative) Party. May: Don Vincente Ribiera elected 'President-Dictator'. November: Ribiera inaugurates National Central Railway at Sulaco.
1889	April: Montero revolts, abetted by his brother Pedrito. May: Decoud arrives in Sulaco with new rifles for Barrios.
1890–91	War of Separation which establishes the Occidental Province of Costaguana as the independent State of Sulaco. (*See Table B.*)
1897	Mitchell takes visitor on tour of Sulaco.

1898	Lighthouse built on Great Isabel.
1899	Mitchell returns to England, having appointed Viola lighthouse-keeper.
1900	Class conflict increasing. Prominent Sulacans (Corbelán, Hernández, Antonia Avellanos) plan war of annexation against Costaguana. Goulds return from European tour. Nostromo killed by Viola. Viola dies.

Table B Chronology of central events

DATE	EVENT
1888, May	Ribiera's 'dictatorship' begins.
November	Railway inaugurated at Sulaco.
1889, April	General Montero revolts.
1890, 21 April	Battle of Socorro: defeated by General Montero, Ribiera flees with Pedrito Montero in pursuit.
27 April	Nostromo negotiates with Hernández on behalf of Blancos.
28 April	General Barrios and his troops embark for Cayta. Decoud learns of Ribiera's defeat. Hernández offers aid.
29 April	5 a.m.: Silver arrives in Sulaco.
1 May	Rioting erupts. Hernández's aid is accepted.
2 May	4 a.m.: Nostromo meets Decoud at *Porvenir* office and promises that the lightermen will support the Europeans. 6 a.m.–noon: Sulacan authorities shelter at OSN offices. Ribiera rides into the mob and is rescued by Nostromo and railwaymen. Decoud joins defenders of the Amarilla Club. Authorities escape in *Minerva*. Nostromo leads lightermen against mob and reaches Casa Viola. Hernández rides to Los Hatos to receive refugees. 4 p.m.–9 p.m.: Gamacho and Fuentes decide to lead the Monterist mob. Barrios reaches Cayta. López and others plan capitulation to Montero. Decoud proposes the secession of Sulaco from Costaguana. Pedrito Montero reaches railhead. Corbelán sets out to join Hernández.
3 May	*c.* 1 a.m.–6 a.m.: Nostromo brings Decoud to Viola's and goes to fetch doctor for Teresa Viola. *c.* 6 a.m.: Pedrito leaves railhead. *c.* 7 a.m.: General Sotillo seizes ship at Esmeralda. *c.* 8 p.m.: Decoud writes to his sister from Casa Viola. *c.* 9 p.m.: Lighter sets out across Golfo Plácido. Refugees from Sulaco make for Los Hatos woods. *c.* 11.30 p.m.: Sotillo's vessel collides with lighter. 11.50: Sotillo enters Sulaco harbour.
4 May	Before dawn, Nostromo and Decoud bury silver on Great Isabel; Nostromo swims ashore as day breaks. Meanwhile Sotillo holds Mitchell and Monygham, releasing Mitchell at dawn. *c.* 7 a.m.: Don Juste asks Gould to welcome Pedrito. 8 a.m.: Pedrito arrives in Sulaco. *c.* 8.30 a.m.: Pedrito orates on the Plaza. *c.* 10–12: Gamacho orates.

4 May (*cont.*)	*c.* 6 p.m: Pedrito's messenger delivers demand to Pepe at mine. Pepe plans march on town. Gould defies Pedrito. *c.* 6.30: Nostromo awakens. Sotillo kills Hirsch. *c.* 7 p.m.: Nostromo and Monygham meet at Custom House: Monygham proposes the ride to Cayta.
5 May	Travelling on the engine to the railhead, Nostromo begins his journey to Cayta to summon Barrios.
14 May	At sunset, Decoud rows westward from the Great Isabel.
15 May	At dawn, Decoud shoots himself.
17 May	Nostromo sees Decoud's boat and rows it to Great Isabel. Barrios reaches Sulaco harbour and attacks Sotillo's ship, saving Monygham; Sotillo is killed. Pepe leads miners into Sulaco via Land Gate, saving Gould. Barrios captures Harbour Gate. Hernández presses from west.
c. 1 June	Don Juste López promulgates new constitution; Barrios pursues Pedrito southwards; Gould prepares to leave for mission to San Francisco and Washington.
1891, *c.* May	Costaguana–Sulaco War ended by international naval demonstration in Sulaco harbour: US cruiser *Powhattan* salutes flag of Sulaco. General (now Emperor) Montero assassinated. The Occidental Province has become the Occidental Republic.

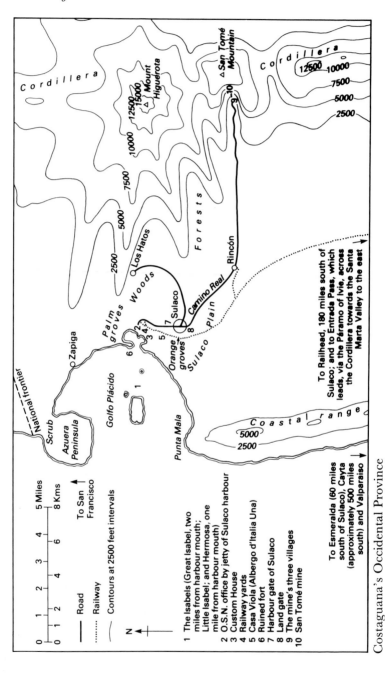

Costaguana's Occidental Province

N

| 0 | 1 | 2 | 3 | 4 | 5 Miles |
| 0 | 1 2 | 3 4 | 5 | 6 | 8 Kms |

—— Road

.... Railway

‾‾‾ Contours at 2500 feet intervals

To San Francisco

1 The Isabels (Great Isabel, two miles from harbour mouth; Little Isabel; and Hermosa, one mile from harbour mouth)
2 O.S.N. office by jetty of Sulaco harbour
3 Custom House
4 Railway yards
5 Casa Viola (Albergo d'Italia Una)
6 Ruined fort
7 Harbour gate of Sulaco
8 Land gate
9 The mine's three villages
10 San Tomé mine

To Esmeralda (60 miles south of Sulaco), Cayta (approximately 500 miles south) and Valparaiso

To Railhead, 180 miles south of Sulaco; and to Entrada Pass, which leads, via the Páramo of Ivie, across the Cordillera towards the Santa Marta Valley to the east

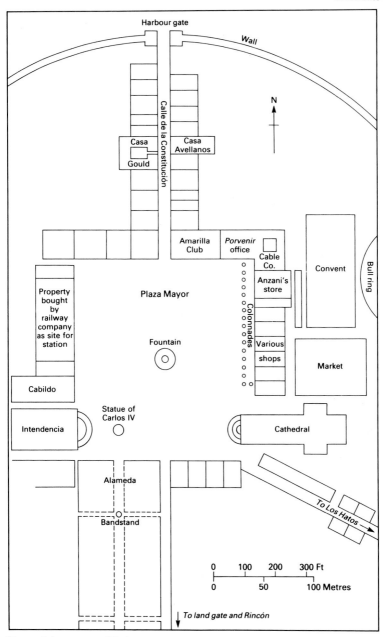

Part of the town of Sulaco

175

8 Heroes, heroines, gender and feminism

The identity of Conrad's fictional world is generated partly by the recurrent character-types and models of conduct. They are discussed in the following sections.

Models of conduct

Conrad's works cumulatively imply a model of admirable masculine conduct: it is chivalric and gentlemanly in its combination of courage, dignity, reticence and respect for traditions of service; it is stoical, too, in the readiness to engage in struggle without confidence in victory; and sceptical in its view of human nature and history. Such an ethical ideal is implicit in the depiction of Marlow and of various anonymous narrators, or is epitomised by such memorable minor characters as the French lieutenant in *Lord Jim*; and it is implicit in the self-image of Conrad as depicted in his various autobiographical writings.

Conrad often likes to work against the grain, however; invoking a convention only to question or complicate or subvert it. If he shows an Achilles, his interest lies in the Achilles' heel. Lord Jim, for instance, looks like a romantic hero – yet he has been partly corrupted by his very dreams of being a romantic hero. The vulnerability of virtue (or its short-sightedness) is one of Conrad's preoccupations; so is his sense of tentacular vice, which sends out a tentacle to grip the seemingly sound and good. Thus, some of his heroes are drawn into complicity with corrupt kindred: Jim with Gentleman Brown, Marlow with Kurtz, Heyst with Jones. Characters may be paired (albeit briefly) in ways which question the initial sense of contrast between them: Gould and Hernández, Decoud and Hirsch. Just as Conrad subverts orthodox principles of plot-structure by 'building holes' (ellipses, elisions, perspectival shifts and chronological jumps) into his plots, so he is sometimes capable of building holes into characterisation by leaving opaque or mysterious those areas which orthodox writers would fill with ample biographical information.

In his major works, the manipulations and fracturings of plot give enhanced importance to thematic connections, and the interlinkages established between characters give enhanced importance to the sense of moral and psychological patterning within events, or to a sense of the ironic workings of history. To compare is to contrast; to contrast is to compare. By the networks of connections between characters, Conrad draws attention not only to individual distinctiveness (and often to human isolation and incomprehension) but also to ironic likeness and common needs.

Conrad can be an acute psychologist, not so much by any profound depiction of an individual's psychology as by his concentration on forces operating variously within particular groupings. *The Nigger of the 'Narcissus'*, for example, dramatises the difficulty of distinguishing a vicarious self-pity (which divides people) from an altruistic co-operation (which unites them): even the wise captain briefly but dangerously confuses the two, as he later recognises. In 'Heart of Darkness', we are invited to realise the full extent of the moral hollowness in 'civilised' men: even the apparently heroic Kurtz proves 'hollow at the core'. In *Nostromo*, we are shown how men habitually idealise the material world in which they are ambushed and are tantalised by their own ideals.

In his treatment of women, as we shall see, Conrad offers a diversity of recurrent types. They variously express male observations, beliefs, hopes, fears and fantasies, and sometimes provide a basis for criticism of masculine limitations. The female counterpart to his recurrent 'gentlemanly' type is, significantly, one in which selfless service (often to a man or men, within a male-dominated world) is a prominent feature. Nevertheless, when Conrad is describing subservient daughters or apparently loyal wives, he frequently notes concealed features which make those females potentially rebellious against their fathers or husbands; as so often, he likes to imply that individuals are largely opaque to each other and that the bonds of solidarity are weaker than people may suppose.

Some of Conrad's women are associated with the jungle, dark and fecund, while others are likened to statues, imposingly beautiful. This dichotomy may be seen as a post-Darwinian version of the traditional literary 'rose and lily' (or 'whore and madonna') pairings which have been assailed by feminists for their apparent denial of an integrated female personality. In addition, Conrad sometimes imagines the symbolic or actual interchangeability of women and wealth. (Here he partly anticipates Claude Lévi-Strauss's notions of females as objects of social exchange.) Thus, in the first novel, *Almayer's Folly*, as Nina turns more and more from her father to Dain, so Dain's wealth flows into Mrs Almayer's hidden coffer; and Almayer's loss of Nina entails the destruction of his hopes of finding treasure in the hinterland. In *Nostromo*, Gould's love for the silver of the mine gradually supersedes his love for his childless wife, who comes to see him as surrounded by 'a circumvallation' of precious metal; he even sleeps at the mine, with the silver. In 'A Smile of Fortune', the hero finds Alice Jacobus so seductive that, to be alone with her, he enters into a distasteful business deal with her father; he loses the young woman but unexpectedly makes a big profit. 'I dreamt of a pile of gold in the form of a grave in which a girl was buried, and woke up callous with greed.' Repeatedly, sexual and emotional relationships are tainted, corrupted or subverted by 'material interests'.

A type-list

Among Conrad's prominent male and female characters, it is easy to discern some recurrent types. Predictably, given the historical context of his writings, females in this list are usually defined in relationship to males, whereas males are usually defined in relationship to work and career-goals.

Males

1. THE HAMLETS (see pp. 72–3). Examples: Decoud (*N*), Heyst (*V*), D'Alcacer (*R*). Civilised, sceptical, reflective, and likely to become immobilised at some point of crisis.

2. THE QUIXOTES (see pp. 67–72). Examples: Lingard of *Almayer's Folly*, *An Outcast* and *The Rescue*, and Captain Anthony in *Chance*. However, all Conrad's active idealists partake of the quixotic: they pursue goals which recede or prove illusory, or they succeed only at the price of a kind of monomania which may result in suffering or destruction for themselves or others. This category includes the men of egoistic imagination, such as Almayer (*AF*), Kurtz (HD) and Gould (*N*): visionaries who may be led to disaster by their vision.

3. THE SYMPATHETIC NARRATORS. None of Conrad's fictional narrators (and possibly not even the narrators of some of his non-fictional writings) should automatically be equated with Conrad. But biographically some of the first-person narrators (particularly some who are anonymous sea-captains) stand very close to the author, having had experiences which relate closely to those of the younger Conrad. Examples are the narrators of *The Shadow-Line*, 'Falk', 'The Secret Sharer' and 'A Smile of Fortune': anonymous yet congruent and continuous (having a consistent common identity), recalling past voyages and encounters; fallible but likeable, curious about life, gentlemanly, but (in important respects) unconventionally tolerant and broad-minded.

A narrator who is carefully individuated and is more distinct from the author than the foregoing figures is, of course, Charles Marlow. The most convincing, intelligent and interesting of Conrad's characters is the Marlow of 'Heart of Darkness', followed closely by the Marlow of *Lord Jim*, at some distance by the Marlow of 'Youth' and at a much greater distance by the Marlow of *Chance*. In 'Heart of Darkness' and *Lord Jim* Marlow is perceptive, sceptical and reflective, but, unlike the Hamlets (our Type 1), he is able to respond bravely to crises – he is a survivor; he has the imagination of Type 2, but also moral stability and (by the standards of his times) a humane liberalism of outlook. He shares the romantic adventurousness of the quixotic type while retaining a critical spirit. As a former *Conway* cadet and ex-captain, he is also a reasonably prosperous English gentleman of the upper middle class who likes the sound of his own voice and can be patronising. The Marlow of 'Youth' is rather sentimental – perhaps slightly the worse for drink; and the Marlow of *Chance* is old, garrulous and at times abrasively male-chauvinistic.

4. THE STALWART WORKERS. Examples: Singleton (*NN*), the boiler-maker (HD), Captain MacWhirr and Solomon Rout ('Typhoon'), Don Pepe (*N*), Jörgensen (*R*), and perhaps Davidson (*V*). Not articulate, bright or imaginative, but industrious and utterly relia-ble: they know their job and stick to it conscientiously even when others fail. They embody the Victorian work-ethic, the seaman's code, and hard primitivism.

5. THE PROFESSIONAL ÉLITE. Examples: the French lieutenant in *Lord Jim* (and possibly Brierly and Stein in the same novel), Captain Allistoun in *The Nigger*, the engineer-in-chief in *Nostromo*, and Captain Giles in *The Shadow-Line*. These are the aristocracy of their professions: men of maturity, courage, integrity and wisdom, though they too may be laconic or gnomic in utterance. (Types blend. Peyrol in *The Rover* is a mixture of Types 4 and 5, with a dash of the quixotic.)

6. THE EXOTIC PRINCE, CHIEFTAIN OR WARRIOR. Examples: Dain Maroola in *Almayer's Folly*, Arsat in 'The Lagoon', Karain in 'Karain', Dain Waris in *Lord Jim* and Hassim in *The Rescue*. Such men are brown, handsome, noble, brave and apparently virile, though susceptible to being unmanned by a woman. They may be helped or brought to disaster by the white friends who patronise them. While their fictional location is the Malay Archipelago of the period 1870–90, they anticipate a stock type in the Hollywood jungle-movies of the period 1920–50.

Females

1. EXOTIC SEDUCTRESSES. Examples: Nina (*AF*), Aissa (*An Outcast*), Kurtz's consort (HD). They are associated with the fecund jungle

179

of which they may seem an emanation; potent and with the effect of weakening or incapacitating the men who embrace them, as though primitive nature were taking its revenge on the civilised or as though the dark and feminine were taking its revenge on the white and masculine.

2. NOBLE IDEALISTS. Examples: Kurtz's Intended (HD), Antonia (*N*), Natalia Haldin (*UWE*). These are radiant romantic idealists who preserve their faith in the men they love but who, to a large extent, are ignorant of those men or of the harsh realities of the world.

3. THE STATUESQUELY BEAUTIFUL OBJECT OF MALE DESIRE. Examples: Hermann's niece ('Falk'), Felicia Moorsom ('The Planter of Malata'), Doña Rita (*Arrow of Gold*), Mrs Travers (*R*). They are associated, in the last three instances, with some of Conrad's most disappointingly conventional writing.

4. THE SEEMINGLY SUBJUGATED. Examples: Mrs Hervey in 'The Return', Winnie Verloc in *The Secret Agent*, Alice Jacobus ('A Smile of Fortune'), Flora Barral in *Chance*, Lena in *Victory*, Arlette of *The Rover*. These are women with unhappy pasts who are or have been so strongly dominated by men that their inner natures seem to have been crushed or suppressed, but who are yet capable of displaying surprising independence: they may strike back.

5. THE LADY ALMONERS. Examples: Mrs Gould in the later stages of *Nostromo* and both Tekla and Natalia Haldin at the end of *Under Western Eyes*. These are idealistic women who have had disillusioning experience of the world but who still, in their limited sphere, do what they can to make the world a better place. (This was a stock type in Victorian literature: George Eliot's Dorothea and Romola are famous instances.)

Feminist criticisms of Conrad

In the decades following the publication of Kate Millett's *Sexual Politics* (1970), feminism burgeoned, transforming cultural history by revealing the appalling extent to which masculist assumptions had hitherto been accepted as generally valid. Eventually feminist literary critics turned their scrutiny upon Conrad. A standard feminist approach is to search literary texts of past eras for evidence of male chauvinism, particularly the stereotyping of female characters in demeaning ways. Predictably, Conrad was usually found guilty; 'predictably', because only a minority of fiction-writers before 1970 (whether male or female) could fulfil the exacting and sometimes anachronistic requirements of latter-day feminists.

There were some extenuating claims. Ruth Nadelhaft, for example (in 'Women as Moral and Political Alternatives', 1982, and in *Joseph Conrad*, 1991), argued that in Conrad's fiction women are centres of intelligent resistance to male vanity and imperialist assumptions: 'Conrad wrote through the critical eyes of women characters.' Other critics were, however, antagonised by 'Heart of Darkness'. Nina Pelikan Straus (in *Novel*, Winter 1987) declared that this novella is 'brutally sexist': male critics have repeatedly become accomplices of Marlow, who 'brings truth to men by virtue of his bringing falsehood to women':

> The woman reader . . . . . is in the position to suggest that Marlow's cowardice consists of his inability to face the dangerous self that is the form of his own masculinist vulnerability: his own complicity in the racist, sexist, imperialist, and finally libidinally satisfying world he has inhabited with Kurtz.

Elaine Showalter (in *Sexual Anarchy*, 1991) said that the tale assumed a distinctively male 'circle of readers'; explicitly and implicitly, it excludes females from knowledge of reality. Johanna M. Smith (in an essay in *Joseph Conrad: 'Heart of Darkness': A Case Study in Contemporary Criticism*, 1991) declared that 'Heart of Darkness' 'reveals the collusion of imperialism and patriarchy: Marlow's narrative aims to "colonize" and "pacify" both savage darkness and women'. This echoed the main point of Bette London's discussion of the same tale (in *The Appropriated Voice / Narrative Authority in Conrad, Forster, and Woolf*, 1990). London argued that Marlow is clearly a male chauvinist:

> Identified with the 'lie' of civilization (imaged as feminine obliviousness), women are denied access to the 'truth' of savagery (imaged as female sexuality) – a truth grounded on the lie it refutes. The novel's competing definitions of the feminine thus uphold a single system of exclusion . . . . . Marlow virulently discredits the world of women, while the life of the natives remains beyond his conceptual reach.

Furthermore, Marlow's narrative 'puts Marlow in the feminine place, literally, the space of Kurtz's Intended', and even 'puts his audience in Marlow's former place: the place of the feminine'.

Within these radical readings, some of the claims seem excessive for want of due historical consideration. By the standards of its own times, 'Heart of Darkness' was a courageously interrogative text; and present-day critics become ideologically narcissistic if they belabour all those past literary works which do not reflect today's ideological preferences or prejudices. Some of the recurrent types discernible in Conrad's depiction of both men and women were recognisable in reality in his time; some remain so in ours. Males as well as females are frequent objects of his ironic and satirical observation; and, not seldom in Conrad's fiction, women are shown to be more perceptive and less self-centred than the men who dominate their world: examples include Nina in *Almayer's Folly*, Emilia in *Nostromo*, Tekla in *Under Western Eyes* and Lena in *Victory*. If women usually occupy subordinate roles in his works, this is partly a reflection of the historical facts of his day. Feminist critics who oppose the principle of stereotyping when it concerns female characters sometimes espouse that very principle when, seeking to stereotype an author as a 'male chauvinist', they envisage in the texts the demeaning features they wish to castigate.

Undoubtedly, Conrad's works often reveal some familiar masculine fears and limitations when women are depicted. As we have seen, the sexually potent woman is often seen as subversive, her male partner as a person unmanned or entrapped by sexual experience. (This was a common literary theme in Conrad's day: the relationship between Gudrun and Gerald in Lawrence's *Women in Love* provides a vivid illustration.) Marital relations more often resemble a trap than a liberation into fulfilment. The sea-captain who takes his wife aboard is rendered unreliable by divided allegiances (as is shown in 'Youth' and 'The Secret Sharer'). Captain Beard in 'Youth' declares: 'A sailor has no business with a wife'; and Captain Mitchell in *Nostromo* concurs: 'I was never married myself. A sailor should exercise self-denial.'

Feminism and the associated controversy figured prominently in *Chance*, and undoubtedly contributed to that novel's popularity. Mrs Fyne, a militant feminist whose sexual ideas reflect Sylvia Pankhurst's, is satirically portrayed as an exploitative lesbian; and the plot has a markedly anti-feminist drift. Flora's neurotic insecurity and her inhibitions about marriage have been caused largely by the malevolence of her governess and by the teachings of the 'emancipated' Mrs Fyne; it is to the chivalrous Captain Anthony and the gallant young Powell that she owes her tardy salvation. In view of the hostility offered by many women to the Pankhursts' campaigns, Marlow's misogynistic pronouncements would not have alienated all *Chance*'s female readers, though today some of his comments seem crudely abrasive:

> 'As to honour – you know – it's a very fine mediaeval inheritance which women never got hold of . . . . . In addition they are devoid of decency . . . . .'
> 'The secret scorn of women for the capacity to consider judiciously and to express profoundly a meditated conclusion is unbounded . . . . . What women's acuteness really respects are

the inept "ideas" and the sheeplike impulses by which our actions are determined in matters of real importance. For if women are not rational they are indeed acute . . . . . I am not a feminist.'

(pp. 63, 145–6)

Marlow does at least (contradicting his opinion in 'Heart of Darkness') claim that whereas men live in a 'fool's paradise', women see 'the whole truth' (p. 144). Another mitigating factor in *Chance* is the portrayal of Carleon Anthony, who is partly based on Coventry Patmore, author of *The Angel in the House*. Carleon is a writer who sentimentalises woman (as domestic angel) in his poetry, but is a tyrant in the home; a partial counterpart to the hypocritical Peter Ivanovitch who, in *Under Western Eyes*, poses as a feminist in his writings but treats his female secretary with ruthless contempt. From 'The Idiots' to *The Secret Agent*, from Willems in *An Outcast* to Schomberg in *Victory*, Conrad critically portrayed the domestic (often sexual) servitude which a husband imposes on his wife. Almost a century before marital rape was made a crime in Britain, Conrad had portayed the woman's ordeal frankly and sympathetically in 'The Idiots'. Even the cumbrously experimental tale, 'The Return', tries to depict the collapse of a chauvinistic husband's delusions as his desperate wife declares: 'I've a right – a right to – to – myself . . .' In *Victory*, Lena (before dying self-sacrificially) suffers in turn the bullying sexual demands of Schomberg, the diffident sexuality of Heyst, an attempted rape by Ricardo and some pathological misogyny from Jones; so the text amply reveals the collusions and contradictions of male dominance. Conrad frequently directed his scepticism against patriarchal authority of various kinds, whether divine or human.

In short, although feminists have substantial grounds for seeking to stereotype Conrad as 'patriarchal', Conrad's works often remind us that a stereotype is a manipulable simplification of a more complex original. Meanwhile, the feminist endeavour to expose the strategies of power may have consequences that Conrad would have applauded. It is now widely recognised that, for centuries, society has inscribed women with submissive characterisation; and, as a result, millions of women have led stunted lives. Similarly, for centuries, society has inscribed men with aggressive characterisation; and, as a result, millions of men have died on battlefields. The study of fiction is increasingly being recognised as the study of social authority. Texts like *Nostromo* offer paradigms – conspicuous models – of social inscription, and they offer warnings about such inscription. Literary studies may obliquely help to liberate individuals from the grip of socially-imposed and inflexible characterisation.

9   Conrad's place in literary history

Conrad's earliest works were distinctive, ambitious and thematically rich, but sometimes cumbrous and inflated in their descriptive modes. There followed, in the years 1897 to 1911, the great period which extends from *The Nigger of the 'Narcissus'* to *Under Western Eyes* and includes Conrad's supreme works, 'Heart of Darkness' and *Nostromo*: he displays a brilliantly exuberant virtuosity in concept and technique which dwarfs the recurrent flaws. From 1911 to 1918 there is a mixed period which includes a great success (*The Shadow-Line*) and some imposing but deeply flawed work: *Chance*, with its gratuitously convoluted narrative procedures, and *Victory*, with its melodramatic allegorising. Then, in the final phase, there are several novels which, for all their lengthy elaboration, resemble old-fashioned tales of love and adventure: these are *The Rescue*, *The Arrow of Gold*, *The Rover*, and the unfinished *Suspense*. The decline in his late years can be explained not only by his age and state of health but also by what has been termed a 'normalisation' in his outlook. As he became an acclaimed and prosperous figure, his writings, which had always been imbued with certain very traditional values (loyalty, heroism, fidelity, justice), gradually became less concerned to submit those values to baptism by the fires of scepticism and cynicism, and the techniques no longer probed and questioned conventional assumptions.

In his major phase, he was 'ahead of his times' in ideas and techniques; and this was because he was more intelligently and perceptively of his times than most writers then were. In his vigilant response to nineteenth-century preoccupations, he anticipated – often critically – many twentieth-century preoccupations. He was a versatile intermediary between the Romantic and Victorian traditions and the innovations of Modernism. He is Romantic in his interest in questing individualism and in his keen responsiveness to the beauty, power and immensity of the natural environment. He is Victorian in his registration of the burdens of thought in an age when science offered bleak vistas; Victorian, too, in his responsiveness to the magnitude of the imperial saga, and in his related understanding of the importance of an ethic of work and duty among its varied participants. Yet his sense of individualism can modulate into the Modernist's intuition of solipsism; and Modernistic, also, are his sense of the absurdity of moral beings in a non-moral universe, his profound scepticism about the value of modern industrial society and its acquisitive imperialisms, and his view of humans as myopic participants in destructive processes. Albert Guerard once remarked that *Nostromo*'s view of history 'is skeptical and disillusioned, which for us today must mean true'. Furthermore, the Modernist's sense of the duplicity, deceptiveness and inadequacy of language is voiced repeatedly by Conrad: 'Words, as is well known, are the great foes of reality'; 'the old, old words, worn thin, defaced'.

In his kaleidoscopic techniques, his mastery of delayed decoding, his reconciliations of realism and symbolism, and his ironic invocation of ancient myths and legends while addressing contemporaneous confusion, Conrad clearly and boldly anticipated the Modernist experimentation which was to burgeon in poetry and the novel a generation after 'Heart of Darkness' first appeared. Even Postmodernism's self-conscious games with fictionality have some precursors in his relays of narrators (particularly in Marlow's self-critical story-telling) and his claim that a major source of *Nostromo* was a history written by a character in that novel.

Predictably, then, Conrad has exerted a rich and varied influence on subsequent writers. The paradox of 'the virtue of evil', so vividly dramatised in 'Heart of Darkness', was developed further by both T.S. Eliot and Graham Greene. This paradox, which stems both from orthodox Roman Catholic theology and from the Romantic emphasis on the value of intensity, is that it is better to be intensely evil than to be mediocre or secularly good. Eliot, for instance, alleged that 'the glory of man . . . . . is his capacity for damnation'. Through the intensity of his corruption, Kurtz gains (intermittently) a stature denied to the mediocre figures around him; perhaps the secular outlook destroys life's significance. In *The Waste Land*, for which this notion provides a theme, Eliot indicated his debt by alluding to the tale's opening and, more significantly, by initially choosing as the poem's epigraph a passage from 'Heart of Darkness' culminating in Kurtz's words 'The horror!' The same theme is pursued in *The Hollow Men* (1925), which not only bears a Conradian title and epigraph but also holds echoes of Marlow's plight when, close to death, he experienced 'some inconceivable world that had no hope in it and no desire'.

Graham Greene's *Brighton Rock* (1938) exploits again the paradox of the virtue of evil, but Greene's greatest Conradian debt is probably to *The Secret Agent*: for Greeneland, that seedy, vulgar, tawdry urban territory, has clear affinities with the base, murky, slimy London of Conrad's novel. There are minor but significant debts: Greene's *It's a Battlefield* has an Assistant Commissioner borrowed from *The Secret Agent*, and its hero, Conrad Drover, owes his first name to 'a seaman, a merchant officer' who had once lodged in his parents' home.

The Conradian theme that loyalty may entail treachery was extensively developed by Greene, as we are reminded by the epigraph, from *Victory*, which heads his novel *The Human Factor*: 'I only know that he who forms a tie is lost. The germ of corruption has entered into his soul.' This theme was present in his early works (for example, *The Man Within* and *The Name of Action*); and, later, in *A Sort of Life*, he said that at that period Conrad's influence on him had been 'too great and too disastrous':

> Never again, I swore, would I read a novel of Conrad's – a vow I kept for more than a quarter of a century, until I found myself with *Heart of Darkness* in a small paddle boat travelling up a Congo tributary in 1959 . . . . .

One of the subtlest examples of a cinematic debt to Conrad may be the brilliant film *The Third Man* (1949), directed by Carol Reed and based on a story and script by Greene. In some ways, it is a transposition to post-war Vienna of motifs and situations in 'Heart of Darkness': Martins is a weak descendant of Marlow; Harry Lime (played by Orson Welles) is a powerful descendant of Kurtz; and Anna shares the mournful fidelity of the Intended. (The 'river of darkness' is transmogrified as the vast sewer beneath the city.) Once again, Greene incorporated sly homage: one of Lime's loyal henchmen is known as 'Mr Kurtz'.

Before appearing briefly in *It's a Battlefield*, Conrad had appeared in H.G. Wells' *Tono-Bungay* (1909), satirically transformed into a haughty Romanian sea-captain, proud of being 'a gentleman of good family', who, though now a naturalised Englishman, expresses anti-British views in a markedly foreign accent. In 1985 Conrad entered Gabriel García Márquez's novel, *Love in a Time of Cholera*, as a seaman from the ship *Saint-Antoine* who sells arms to a corrupt agent of the Colombian government. Joseph Conrad, like some of his own characters, here shimmers on the borderline between fact and fiction.

Conrad's range is emphasised by the fact that writers as diverse as Virginia Woolf, Malcolm Lowry, John le Carré and V.S. Naipaul have acknowledged his potent presence. As his works dealt with exotic locations and urban squalor, economic imperialism and duplicitous espionage, and as he was both sage and entertainer (published in *T.P.'s Weekly* and the *Daily Mail* as well as *Blackwood's* and *The New Review*), Conrad provided the bases of many subsequent developments. Woolf's essay 'Modern Fiction' asserted that Conrad's 'Youth' was superior to Joyce's *Ulysses*; and parts of the 'Time Passes' section of *To the Lighthouse* pay the tribute of imitation (and near-pastiche) to the lyrical-philosophical rhetoric of 'Youth' and lyrical weatherscapes of *The Mirror of the Sea*. Malcolm Lowry's tribute took the form of a sonnet, 'Joseph Conrad'; and commentators have suggested that Lowry's greatest novel, *Under the Volcano* (1947), is indebted in some of its stylistic, descriptive and thematic modes to 'Heart of Darkness', *Nostromo* and particularly *Lord Jim*. John le Carré's narratives of espionage distantly recall *The Secret Agent* and *Under Western Eyes*, and they are sprinkled with Conradian allusions: Westerby in *The Honourable Schoolboy* diligently reads Conrad; Charlie, Kurtz and Joseph in *The Little Drummer Girl* are named after the two main characters and the author of 'Heart of Darkness'; and Smiley in *Smiley's People* seeks the face 'that, like a secret sharer, seemed to have swum out . . . . . to board his faltering consciousness'. V.S. Naipaul's *The Bend in the River* (1979), as its reviewers noted, holds various echoes of 'Heart of Darkness'. The narrator of J.L. Carr's *A Month in the Country* (1980) initially declares: 'If I'd been Josef Conrad I'd have gone into a peroration about the lost land of youth'; and the outcome of his narrative is indeed a peroration about that lost land. Howard Brenton's televised play of political assassination and betrayal, *The Saliva Milkshake* (1977), borrowed its plot largely from the Razumov–Haldin encounter in *Under Western Eyes*.

A recent British writer with whom Conrad might have felt greatest affinity, and who is of comparable stature, is undoubtedly William Golding: another naval officer who later became a novelist. In *Lord of the Flies* (1954), Ralph weeps for 'the darkness of man's heart', at the conclusion of a novel whose main thesis, about the capacity for corruption within supposedly civilised beings, extends that of 'Heart of Darkness'. The Conradian techniques of covert plotting and delayed decoding were exploited with new intensity in *The Inheritors*, *Pincher Martin* and *The Spire*. Conrad's treatment of voyages as locations of moral ordeal and endeavour are inevitably recalled by Golding's maritime trilogy, *Rites of Passage*, *Close Quarters* and *Fire Down Below*. The trilogy's period, like that of several Conradian novels and tales, is the Napoleonic era; the plot concerns the perils and dissensions of a voyage under sail; and the main source of irony (comic and tragic) is the disparity between different characters' interpretations of the same events. In descriptive verve and depth of vision, in his imagination that kindles with enthusiasm for the task of 'making you see' the life of the ship and the ocean, and even in his rather patrician public stance as a reserved but weathered sage, Golding might be a younger brother of Conrad.

Continental writers who have admired Conrad include Thomas Mann and André Gide. Mann's enthusiasm for *The Secret Agent* in particular and Conrad's outlook in general was published in *Past Masters and Other Papers* (1933), in which he concluded:

> Conrad's objectivity may seem cool; but it is a passion – a passion for freedom . . . . . His intellectual message will be for those among us who believe – in opposition to the views of the large majority – that the idea of freedom has a rôle to play in Europe that is not yet played out.

André Gide visited and corresponded with the ageing Conrad, and later claimed: 'He was the only one of my elders that I loved and knew.' Gide supervised the translation into French of various works of Conrad, and himself was responsible for the translation of *Typhoon*; while his *Voyage au Congo* is dedicated to Conrad and discusses 'Heart of Darkness'. The journals show that Gide was particularly fascinated by *Lord Jim* and its demonstration that a momentary and apparently involuntary act can engage the whole subsequent lifetime: Gide's idea of the 'motiveless' or wilfully immoral act (*l'acte gratuit*) offers a contrast (which is emphasised by the epigraph from *Lord Jim* in Book V of *Les Caves du Vatican*). Gide's obituary tribute to Conrad declares: 'Nobody had lived more savagely than Conrad; nobody had then submitted life to so patient, sensitive, and wise a transmutation into art.'

In the United States, three major twentieth-century novelists, Ernest Hemingway, Scott Fitzgerald and William Faulkner, all admired and were influenced by Conrad. Hemingway, asserting that 'from nothing else that I have ever read have I gotten what every book of Conrad has given me', deplored the notion that in 1924 T.S. Eliot might now be more fashionable than Conrad:

> If I knew that by grinding Mr Eliot into a fine dry powder and sprinkling that powder over Mr Conrad's grave Mr Conrad would shortly appear, looking very annoyed at the forced return and commence writing, I would leave for London early tomorrow morning with a sausage-grinder.

There is a kinship between Conrad's Singleton and Hemingway's Santiago (in *The Old Man and the Sea*): an ethic of stoic endurance in facing an environment which may be serenely neutral or ruthlessly hostile. Both writers look with sympathy on the reticent courage of simple men, battered by life, who persevere without illusions; both are fascinated by the moral support afforded in testing circumstances by a code of masculine conduct which may be appreciated only by initiates.

Scott Fitzgerald, who repeatedly extolled Conrad's art, claimed that the Preface to *The Nigger of the 'Narcissus'* provided 'the greatest "credo" in my life'; and his intensive study of Conrad's themes and techniques bore fruit in *The Great Gatsby*. Nick Carraway, the partly critical, largely fascinated observer of Gatsby, owes much to Marlow and his ambivalent relationships to Jim and Kurtz. Both writers were fascinated by dreamers and over-reachers, and both saw youth as a time of promise and illusion which dims with experience.

Commentators on William Faulkner have frequently noted affinities with Conrad: the fondness for multiple narrators, chronological dislocations and the adducing of evidence through imagery as well as event; the interest in absurdity and cruel irony; the interplay of meditative comment and impressionistic starkness; and an ambivalence in treating racial matters. When Faulkner was awarded the Nobel Prize, his speech of acceptance was based upon (and vainly attempted to surpass) the humanism of Conrad's essay 'Henry James'.

Conrad is reported to have said that Eugene O'Neill had 'no sense of style', but critics have repeatedly detected debts to Conrad in the plays of that American who, like Conrad, voyaged the seas before becoming an author. O'Neill had actually considered giving *Bound East for Cardiff* the title *Children of the Sea* (the American title of *The Nigger of the 'Narcissus'*); and *The Emperor Jones* inevitably evoked comparisons with 'Heart of Darkness'. Among lesser American writers, Jack London (rather to Conrad's embarrassment) regarded himself as a disciple of the author of *The Nigger of the 'Narcissus'*. Critics have postulated correspondences between 'Heart of Darkness' and London's *The Sea Wolf*. Robert Penn Warren, too, said that he was 'under the spell' of Conrad, and Conradian echoes have been detected in Warren's *Night Rider* and *All the King's Men*. Herman Wouk acknowledged Conrad's influence on his *The Caine Mutiny*. In addition, B. Traven, the reclusive German-American author of *The Treasure of the Sierra Madre*, wrote partly in reaction against Conrad and partly in emulation; and that harsh novel may bring to mind the story of the doomed treasure-seeking gringos which opens *Nostromo*.

Several 'Third World' critics, among them Peter Nazareth, D.C. Goonetilleke and C.P. Sarvan, have paid tribute to Conrad's pioneering work as an anti-colonialist author; and his writings have continued to provide both guidance and challenges abroad. Nazareth, who drew on *Nostromo* in his novel *The General Is Up*, has declared that 'influence' is 'too mild a word for the impact Conrad has had upon the Third World'. Tayeb Salih, of Sudan, has acknowledged some Conradian contribution to his *Season of Migration to the North*. Most strikingly, the acclaimed novel by Ngugi wa Thiong'o, *A Grain of Wheat* (1967), boldly adapts to Kenyan locations and Kenyan politics various themes and conflicts in *Under Western Eyes*. Victor Haldin, the assassin betrayed by Razumov, has thus fulfilled his own prophecy by continuing to haunt the earth: he reappears as Ngugi's Kihika, betrayed by the guilt-ridden Mugo. Conrad's Heyst and Lena, of *Victory*, are among the literary ancestors of Munira and Wanja in *Petals of Blood* (1977). Conrad had asserted that a Russian revolution would merely restore old tyranny under a new name; Ngugi (who was imprisoned for his views) made a similar judgement of black rule in post-imperial Kenya. Above all, Ngugi valued Conrad as an interrogative author: 'With Conrad, I have felt I have come into contact with another whose questioning to me is much more important than the answers which he gives.'

In his themes and techniques, Conrad was a liberator: he eloquently questioned what other people took for granted. His innovations have been diversely developed, and his linguistic beauty and audacity have challenged emulation. Certainly, his outlook, though complex, was unbalanced: generally it inclined towards pessimism. In domestic matters, he often made drastic and limiting exclusions: there are many fulfilments that his works neglect. His depiction of women has inevitably provoked feminist strictures. In various large-scale political matters, however, his outlook has proved predominantly wise. Perhaps the most telling vindication of Conrad's genius has been provided by the follies and brutalities of subsequent history.

Part Three
Reference Section

A list of symbolic or allegoric names in Conrad's fiction

The prevailing mode of Conrad's fiction is a realistic one in which the vast majority of proper nouns have the arbitrariness and inconsequentiality of real life. However, just as Conrad's fiction sometimes generates the allusiveness of symbolism or allegory, so, among the names, we sometimes encounter one which has special significance. The fictional context usually confirms this significance: indeed, on several occasions Conrad makes punning jokes for the purpose.

ALMA/MAGDALEN/LENA (*V*). That the heroine of *Victory* should have not one name but three, and all of them allusive, is a sign of a major fault in this novel: it is heavy-handedly allegoric. *Alma* is both a Spanish and an Italian noun meaning 'soul'; it is a Latin adjective meaning 'kind or nourishing'. These connotations are vaguely appropriate to her role as would-be helper to Heyst and as a force of love and life in the world assailed by the force of hate and death represented by Jones. *Magdalen* is the name of the biblical 'fallen woman', and is appropriate to a heroine whose working life has threatened her with possible prostitution and who now feels intermittently sinful in living with Heyst as his devoted mistress. *Lena* is the name bestowed by Heyst: perhaps as a diminutive of Magdalen; more likely as an abbreviation of Helena, for the plot of the novel has occasional parodic resemblances not only to *The Tempest* but also to the story of Helen of Troy, who, abducted by Paris to be his mistress, occasioned the siege of Troy and the burning of its 'topless towers'. The abduction of Alma by Heyst results in the invasion of his island, a battle, and the conflagration in which Heyst perishes. (The legend of Helen of Troy had been discussed by Lingard and Shaw at the beginning of *The Rescue*, which itself has parodic echoes of the Homeric saga.)

GENTLEMAN BROWN (*Lord Jim*) and GENTLEMAN JONES (*V*). Edgar's remark in *King Lear*, 'The Prince of Darkness is a gentleman', partly explains the sobriquet of these rather melodramatic villains. (Gentleman Brown also owes a little to Marlowe's *Tamburlaine*, 'the scourge of God'.) Jones, who has 'devilish eyebrows', is described as 'an insolent spectre on leave from Hades'; and, in the following passage (which makes a joke of the point), we are clearly invited to identify him with the fallen Lucifer:

> 'Having been ejected, he said, from his proper social sphere because he had refused to conform to certain usual conventions, he was a rebel now, and was coming and going up and down the earth . . . . . I told him that I had heard that sort of story about somebody else before. His grin is really ghastly . . . . .'

KURTZ (HD). In the Congo, Conrad had met a dying trader with the Germanic name Klein, which means 'small'. *Kurz* is German for 'short', and Marlow emphasises the ironic appropriateness of the name in its adaptation as a surname for a man who is a living lie: '"Kurtz – that means 'short' in German – don't it? Well, the name was as true as everything else in his life – and death. He looked at least seven feet long."'

LEGGATT ('The Secret Sharer'). The name is homophonous with 'legate', meaning an envoy from some foreign power. As an intermittent sub-text, the tale invokes the possibility that he is a supernatural visitant. At his first appearance, he resembles 'A headless corpse'; he is repeatedly likened to a ghost, and, when he remarks 'It would never do for me to come to life again', the captain observes 'It was something that a ghost might have said.' Eventually, he departs by swimming for the looming mass which has been compared several times to the gate of Erebus, the entrance to Hades.

NARCISSUS (*NN*). Conrad had actually served on a ship with this name; but his decision to preserve the name in the novel makes excellent thematic sense. Narcissus, in classical mythology, fell in love with a beautiful form, not recognising that it was his own reflection: his apparent love for another was unwitting self-love. The central theme of *The Nigger of the 'Narcissus'* is the distinction between (a) unsentimental solidarity, which binds men to each other and to the ship in bonds of co-operative labour (the ethic of the captain and Singleton), and (b) sentimental pseudo-solidarity, the apparent altruism which actually divides the crew, leads to near-mutiny and imperils the ship. (The latter ethic is generated and fostered by Jimmy, abetted by Donkin.) The narrator emphasises that the sympathy expressed by some of the men for Wait is in reality a vicarious self-pity. The spectacle of a dying man reminds them that they too must die; they comfort him because they secretly wish to be comforted themselves. 'The latent egoism of tenderness to suffering appeared in the developing anxiety not to see him die.' 'Latent egoism': they are sliding towards ethical narcissism. Even

Captain Allistoun is briefly tainted when, feeling pity for Jimmy, he brusquely orders him back to his cabin: and this act precipitates the near-mutiny. (Ethically, *The Nigger* is one of Conrad's most ruthless works, bringing to mind Nietzsche's claim: 'Pity . . . . . preserves what is ripe for destruction; it defends life's disinherited and condemned . . . . . [;] in every *noble* morality it counts as a weakness.')

NIKITA/NECATOR (*UWE*). *Necator*, Latin for 'killer', is an appropriate pun on the Russian name Nikita (Nick), given the character's sadistic nature. In the tale 'Because of the Dollars' (*Within the Tides*), a similarly vicious character has the name Fector, which derives from the Latin *interfector*, meaning 'slayer'.

NOSTROMO. *Nostromo* is Italian for 'bosun', and this character was indeed a bosun on his arrival in Saluco. The main ironies surrounding his name depend, however, on the more obvious fact that 'Nostromo' is an abbreviation of the Italian phrase *nostro uomo*: 'our man'. The text says that the name derived from 'Captain Mitchell's mispronunciation' – presumably of the phrase. Linda complains that it is no true Christian name: 'no name either for man or beast'; and Teresa says: 'People . . . . . have given you a silly name – and nothing besides – in exchange for your soul and body.' Clearly, it emphasises his identity as one who prides himself on his public utility as a general factotum, though it becomes increasingly ironic as his egotism becomes more rebellious; and there is heavy irony when, having betrayed his trust, he assumes the new name, Captain Fidanza; for *fidanza* is Italian for 'trust'.

Nostromo's Christian name, Gian' Battista (John-the-Baptist), holds an irony which the text underlines. John the Baptist prepared the way for Jesus Christ and was thus the inaugurator of the Christian era; Nostromo prepares the way for the control of Sulaco by the economic imperialists and is thus an inaugurator of its capitalist era. Decoud calls him 'this active usher-in of the material implements for our progress'.

RANSOME (*SL*). His uncanny 'grace', both of movement and of nature, is stressed; self-sacrificingly, he helps the guilty captain to bring the apparently accursed ship safely to harbour. As the name is homophonous with 'ransom', it is a mnemonic of Jesus Christ, whom the Bible several times calls the ransom of mankind; and, in the context provided by the tale's hints of supernatural evil, there is aptness in the occasional fleeting suggestions of a Christ-like aura about Ransome. The narrator makes a joke of the homophone when he remarks of Ransome: 'He was a priceless man altogether.'

RAZUMOV (*UWE*). The name derives from the Russian noun *pazym*, pronounced '*rahzoom*', which has the same root as the English word 'reason' and means 'mind' or 'intellect'. 'Razumov' may thus be translated as 'Son of Reason' and is a name appropriate to a dedicated student whose parentage is unknown to the public. 'The word Razumov was the mere label of a solitary individuality.' *Under Western Eyes* is variously indebted to Dostoyevsky's *Crime and Punishment* (notwithstanding Conrad's avowed hostility to its author), and the name may have been suggested by that of Raskolnikov's friend, Razumikhin – a surname, Dostoyevsky remarks, 'deriving . . . . . from the word "reason"'.

SINGLETON (*NN*). This character was based on a seaman called Sullivan, and Sullivan was the name Conrad used in the manuscript; but he changed it to Singleton, probably because he preferred a name with connotations of 'uniqueness', 'simplicity' and 'integrity'. (In the novel, Singleton is the lone survivor of the older generation of simple, reliable seamen; and, in a letter to Cunninghame Graham, Conrad remarks that he is 'simple and great like an elemental force'.) In his 'singleness' of character he contrasts with the duplicity of the ambiguous James Wait.

SOFALA ('The End of the Tether'). This is the vessel commanded by Captain Whalley. Sir James Frazer's *The Golden Bough* says that the kings of Sofala in Africa would kill themselves if they suffered physical disability. In the tale, Whalley attempts to conceal his blindness but commits suicide when he realises tardily that it has been detected.

WAIT (*NN*). The narrative exploits various connotations of this name. When shouted, the name is ambiguous, for it sounds like a command: the imperative form of the verb meaning 'halt' or 'pause'. Thus, at his first utterance in the tale, Wait brings confusion – and a challenge, for the mate initially infers that a stranger is daring to tell him to interrupt the roll-call. ('Mr Baker advanced intrepidly. "Who are you? How dare you . . .?" he began.') This makes a finely symbolic opening to *The Nigger of the 'Narcissus'*, portending the bewilderment and near-mutiny that Jimmy will engender during the voyage. The word 'wait' can be a noun meaning 'a delay', and the ship appropriately makes increasingly slow progress until his death, upon which the vessel spurts for home. 'Wait' is, in addition, homophonous with 'weight' – a burden; and the novel clearly exploits this sense, too. When the ship is blown over on its side during the storm, the side which is downwards is that on which

Wait is trapped in his cabin, as though the vessel were weighed down by him; and when his corpse, after waiting, lingering even in death on the plank, at last slides into the sea, the ship rolls 'as if relieved of an unfair burden'.

Gazetteer

Si monumentum requiris, circumspice: if you seek his gazetteer, read
Conrad. In his odysseys he traversed far more of the earth's surface
than did the majority of writers, and in his works he rendered
vividly – and charged with his own distinctive patterns of significance – locations as far apart as South America and Bangkok,
Kraków and Stanley Falls, Geneva and Sydney, Borneo and the
South Downs. The more effectively the location, when taken over
into a work of art, is invested with significance, the more defiantly
neutral the original area may seem when we visit it; and some
Conradian locations have been devastated by modern developments, as foreseen in *Nostromo*.

POLAND. A visit to Poland may nevertheless do more to illuminate
Conrad than may the reading of numerous commentaries. It is in
any case good to be reminded at first hand of the patriotism,
sufferings and heroism of the Polish people, in a land which, by its
solidarity in resistance to the Marxist régime, eventually helped to
bring about the dissolution of the USSR's empire in Eastern Europe.
For those who seek localities with strong Conradian associations,
Kraków is poignantly rich: there is St Mary's Church with its
'unequal massive towers', busy Florian Street where Conrad stayed,
the Florian Gate ('thick and squat under its pointed roof'), and the
Rakowicki Cemetery, where the grave of his father declares Apollo
Korzeniowski 'the victim of Muscovite tyranny'. (See 'Poland
Revisited' in *NLL*.)

ENGLAND. In England, most of Conrad's former dwellings survive,
though they remain in private hands; there is as yet no 'Conrad
home' converted to a museum. If you walk through the dingy streets
to the rear of Victoria Station, you can soon come to 17 Gillingham
Street, where Conrad had lodgings and wrote *An Outcast of the
Islands*. (Further down towards the Thames, the house in Bessborough Gardens where he began his first novel has recently been
demolished.) Admirers of *The Secret Agent* can test their abilities as
literary detectives by retracing Verloc's route to the Russian
Embassy: Gustav Morf's *The Polish Shades and Ghosts of Joseph Conrad*
offers an itinerary; and the visitor who retraces Stevie's fatal
progress across Greenwich Park uphill towards the former Observ-

atory will be rewarded with extensive vistas and close proximity to the National Maritime Museum. At Hammersmith, the Polish Social and Cultural Centre (POSK) has a library dedicated to Conradiana.

The coast-line of south-east Kent, around Dymchurch, with its Martello towers, coastguard stations and long beaches of shingle, still resembles the landscape of the tale 'Amy Foster', though to the south a nuclear power-station dominates the shore at Dungeness.

Pent Farm (at Postling, near Hythe) survives. This is the most famous of Conrad's dwellings, where he lived from 1898 to 1907. At Bishopsbourne, near Canterbury, stands Oswalds, the large house in which Conrad resided from 1919 until his death. These and other homes are described in Borys Conrad's *My Father: Joseph Conrad*. Conrad's grave at Canterbury is in the public cemetery on Westgate Court Avenue.

THE VOYAGES. For discussions of the voyages to the West Indies (which contributed to *Nostromo*), of the Congo journey (the background to 'Heart of Darkness'), and of the Eastern voyages to Bombay, Bangkok, Singapore, the Sunda Strait, Borneo, etc. (which contributed to the South-East Asian novels and to many of the sea tales), see variously: Jocelyn Baines: *Joseph Conrad*; Norman Sherry: *Conrad's Eastern World* and *Conrad's Western World*; and Zdzisław Najder: *Joseph Conrad: A Chronicle*. The best introductory survey is probably Norman Sherry's well-illustrated *Conrad and His World*.

Short biographies

MAX BEERBOHM (1872–1956). Essayist, novelist, parodist and caricaturist, knighted in 1939. His parody of Conrad in *A Christmas Garland* constitutes the most incisive criticism of the early (pre-1897) Conradian style and outlook. Conrad wrote (*TU*, p. vi): 'I have lived long enough to see ["The Lagoon"] most agreeably guyed by Mr. Max Beerbohm in a volume of parodies entitled *A Christmas Garland*, where I found myself in very good company. I was immensely gratified. I began to believe in my public existence.'

TADEUSZ BOBROWSKI (1829–94). The rich uncle who became Conrad's guardian after the early deaths of Conrad's parents. Pompous but shrewd, responsible and fair-minded. To his records, letters and reminiscences we owe much of our knowledge of Conrad's family and upbringing. The tale 'Prince Roman' (*TH*) is indebted to his *Memoirs*.

THOMAS CARLYLE (1795–1881). Scottish-born historian and social–political polemicist whose works include *Sartor Resartus*, *The French Revolution* and *Heroes and Hero-Worship*. Conrad knew some of his writings and may have been influenced by their emphasis on salvation by work rather than reflection.

FRÉDÉRIC CHOPIN (1810–49). The Polish composer and pianist. Conrad in late years would invite John Powell to play compositions by Chopin to him – compositions which often, in their romantic virtuosity and plangent melancholy, have affinities with the relatively lyrical parts of Conrad's writings.

JESSIE CONRAD (1873–1936), née Jessie George, a typist, who married Conrad at a Register Office in 1896 and subsequently bore him two sons, Borys and John. He wrote a preface to her *Handbook of Cookery for a Small House* (1923). After his death she published *Personal Recollections of Joseph Conrad, Joseph Conrad as I Knew Him* and *Joseph Conrad and His Circle*. These emphasise the stresses and strains of marriage to a temperamental genius.

STEPHEN CRANE (1871–1900). The American reporter and author whose most celebrated work, *The Red Badge of Courage*, appeared in

1895. He was introduced to Conrad in 1897 and the two became good friends. Conrad was interested in his vivid descriptive techniques ('He is *the only* impressionist and *only* an impressionist'), and *The Red Badge* may perhaps have influenced *The Nigger of the 'Narcissus'*. Conrad wrote (*LE*, p. 95):

> Crane dealt in his book with the psychology of the mass – the army; while I – in mine – had been dealing with the same subject on a much smaller scale and in more specialized conditions – the crew of a merchant ship, brought to the test of what I may venture to call the moral problem of conduct.

Discussing a projected play, Conrad remarked (*LE*, p. 116) that 'Crane and I must have been unconsciously penetrated by a prophetic sense of the technique and of the very spirit of film-plays, of which even the name was then unknown to the world.'

R.B. CUNNINGHAME GRAHAM (1852–1936). Scottish aristocrat, traveller, adventurer, pioneer socialist, public orator, turbulent MP, and prolific author of tales, essays, biographies and histories. In 1888 he founded Britain's first Labour Party. A close friend of Conrad's for many years, he supplied material for *Nostromo*. He appears as Saranoff in Shaw's *Arms and the Man*, as Mr Courtier in Galsworthy's *The Patrician*, and as Mr X in Conrad's 'The Informer' (*A Set of Six*).

CHARLES DARWIN (1808–92). The naturalist whose *The Origin of Species* (1859) gave the stamp of scientific authority to the widespread Victorian belief in ruthless competition as a means to progress. The sense of nature as wastefully predatory is particularly important in Conrad's earlier novels and tales.

ALPHONSE DAUDET (1840–97). Author of tales and novels; probably best remembered for *Lettres de mon moulin* (*Letters from My Windmill*). Rather surprisingly, in view of its sentimentality, Conrad had an early enthusiasm for his work; but in 'Alphonse Daudet' (*NLL*) the enthusiasm was firmly qualified: 'Daudet, a man as naïvely clear, honest, and vibrating as the sunshine of his native land; that regrettably undiscriminating sunshine . . . . .'

CHARLES DICKENS (1812–70). From childhood onwards, Conrad was familiar with Dickens' novels; and the grotesque characterisations and nightmarish depictions of urban squalor in such works as *Bleak House* anticipate effects in *The Secret Agent*. Conrad may also have learnt from Dickens' bold command of leitmotifs and symbolic detail.

FYODOR DOSTOYEVSKY (1822–81). Conrad purported to regard this great Russian novelist as a mad barbarian ('the grimacing haunted creature' who offers 'fierce mouthings from prehistoric ages'), but *Under Western Eyes* is variously indebted to Dostoyevsky's masterpiece, *Crime and Punishment*.

JACOB EPSTEIN (1880–1959). The creator of stark, powerful and often controversial works of sculpture. His bust of Conrad and his reminiscences of the sittings (in *Let There Be Sculpture*) form a sombre record of the aged writer.

GUSTAVE FLAUBERT (1821–80). French novelist and story-writer of priestly dedication who, in *L'Education sentimentale*, *Madame Bovary* and *Trois contes* (which Conrad admired), strove for a coolly objective portrayal of life's ironies and human fallibilities. 'An Outpost of Progress' derives details from Flaubert's *Bouvard et Pécuchet*.

ANATOLE FRANCE: pen-name of Jacques Anatole Thibault (1844–1924). A cool, drily ironic writer whose most successful work was the anti-clerical satire, *L'Ile des pengouins* (*Penguin Island*). His essay on Prosper Mérimée was one of the sources of *Nostromo*. Conrad praised him in two reviews (republished in *NLL*).

SIGMUND FREUD (1856–1939). The father of modern psychoanalysis, whose theories have prompted various approaches to Conrad – part of Albert Guerard's *Conrad the Novelist* and much of Bernard Meyer's *Joseph Conrad: A Psychoanalytic Biography*. Conrad spoke scornfully of Freud, no doubt foreseeing that psychoanalytic approaches to literature can be reductive.

EDWARD GARNETT (1868–1939). The publisher's reader and literary critic who encouraged and publicised Conrad (and Cunninghame Graham, W.H. Hudson, D.H. Lawrence and others). A sceptical romantic, politically left-wing, he valued vividly heterodox writings. His wife Constance, by her labours as a lucid translator, brought the works of Chekhov, Turgenev and Dostoyevsky before the British public.

ANDRÉ GIDE (1869–1951). French novelist and critic who corresponded with the ageing Conrad and undertook the translation of *Typhoon* into French. His tribute to Conrad was published in *La Nouvelle Revue Française* in December 1924.

FORD MADOX HUEFFER, subsequently Ford Madox Ford (1873–1939). Novelist, critic, editor and raconteur. His best novel is *The Good Soldier* (1915). He collaborated with Conrad between 1898 and 1910 (*The Inheritors, Romance, The Mirror of the Sea* and 'The Nature of a Crime'), and left lively if unreliable reminiscences of him in *Return to Yesterday* and *Joseph Conrad: A Personal Remembrance*.

HENRIK IBSEN (1828–1906). Norwegian dramatist whose notion of the 'life-lie' or 'sustaining illusion' reverberates in Conrad's works. His play *Vildanden* (*The Wild Duck*) seems to have influenced the depiction of Verloc's household in *The Secret Agent*.

HENRY JAMES (1843–1916). Prolific American-born novelist who settled in England and took British nationality in 1915: a writer capable of great subtlety who, in his later work, became vapidly prolix. In its slow pace and elaborate narratorial deviousness, *Chance* is probably the most Jamesian of Conrad's novels. Ironically, it was in an essay so vapid as to be obscure that James criticised *Chance* for prolixity: 'It places Mr. Conrad absolutely alone as a votary of the way to do a thing that shall make it undergo most doing.' ('The New Novel', 1914.) Conrad's tribute to James, whom he terms 'the historian of fine consciences', is in *NLL*.

LORD KELVIN, formerly William Thompson (1824–1907). British physicist and inventor. His second law of thermodynamics, the law of entropy, propagated a pervasive nightmare in the imaginations of writers of the late nineteenth century: the nightmare in which the sun cools and dies, so that all life becomes extinct on a dark earth. Numerous passages in Conrad's letters, essays and fiction express this idea.

RUDYARD KIPLING (1865–1936). The prolific and highly successful writer of short stories, novels and poems: a patriot who celebrated the British Empire, amplifying the imperialistic fervour around the turn of the century, and who commended the 'work ethic' and martial virility. He corresponded briefly with Conrad, who respected his techniques but distrusted his outlook. Conrad's 'An Outpost of Progress' can be seen as a riposte to such tales by Kipling as 'At the End of the Passage'.

APOLLO KORZENIOWSKI (1820–63). Polish writer, translator, patriot, and father of Joseph Conrad.

D.H. LAWRENCE (1885–1930). The greatest novelist of the generation after Conrad's. The characterisation of Gerald Crich in *Women in*

Love seems indebted to that of Charles Gould in *Nostromo*; but the two authors were antagonistic. Whereas Conrad sensed the universe to be essentially dead, Lawrence believed it to be essentially alive. Hence Lawrence jeered at Conrad as one of the 'Writers among the Ruins': 'Snivel in a wet hanky like Lord Jim.' In Conrad's opinion (as recalled by Epstein), 'Lawrence had started well, but had gone wrong. "Filth. Nothing but obscenities." '

DR JOHN MACINTYRE (1857–1928). The pioneer radiologist who in 1898, as a party entertainment, demonstrated his X-ray machine to Conrad, thus prompting *The Inheritors*. (See *LCG*, pp. 107–8.)

FREDERICK MARRYAT (1792–1848). Naval commander who, on retirement, wrote popular novels of the sea, firmly establishing this genre. The young Conrad avidly read these maritime works which seemed 'the beginning and the embodiment of an inspiring tradition' (*NLL*, p. 55).

GUY DE MAUPASSANT (1850–93). Author of numerous sceptical, realistic and ironic tales and novels. Conrad greatly admired his works, and was influenced particularly by the novel *Bel-Ami*, the tale 'Les Sœurs Rondoli' and the Preface to *Pierre et Jean*.

ADAM MICKIEWICZ (1798–1855). The greatest of Polish poets, author of the epic *Pan Tadeusz* and of the verse-dramas *Konrad Wallenrod* and *Dziady*. All of these are fervently patriotic; the last two feature heroic Konrads. In *Pan Tadeusz*, Jacek Soplica (like Lord Jim later) atones by subsequent heroism for former disgrace. The ballad 'Czaty' was a source of 'Karain' (*TU*).

J.B. PINKER (1863–1922). Conrad's literary agent from 1900 onwards. He loyally enabled Conrad to survive as a writer by courageously advancing huge sums of money to him; eventually, after 1914, Conrad became profitable, and Pinker's faith was rewarded. They collaborated on a film-script (*The Strong Man*) based on 'Gaspar Ruiz'.

MARGUERITE PORADOWSKA (1848–1937). A Frenchwoman who married a distant cousin of Conrad's and who, widowed in 1890, maintained an intense correspondence with Conrad during the 1890s. That she was a prize-winning writer of tales and novels (though today they are little read) doubtless encouraged him to persevere with *Almayer's Folly*. She was evidently a model for the Intended in 'Heart of Darkness'.

BERTRAND RUSSELL, Third Earl (1872–1970). The philosopher, logician and polemicist. He met Conrad in 1912 and entered a memorable friendship with him, vividly described in Russell's *Portraits from Memory* and *Autobiography*, Vol. I. Russell named his eldest son John Conrad (the name of his friend's younger son) and his youngest son Conrad.

ARTHUR SCHOPENHAUER (1788–1860). German philosopher whose works are bleakly pessimistic: 'On the whole, life is a disappointment, nay, a cheat.' In *Victory*, the outlook of Heyst and his father is largely Schopenhauerian.

IVAN TURGENEV (1818–83). Russian fiction-writer and essayist, to whom Conrad pays tribute in *NLL*. Conrad particularly liked *A Sportsman's Sketches* (originally intending *The Mirror of the Sea* to be in the spirit of that work); the essay 'Hamlet and Don Quixote' provides a proleptic commentary on Conrad's ideas of character; and *Rudin* and 'Enough' may have contributed some ideas to *Lord Jim*. Conrad saw Turgenev as a civilised, liberal and humane contrast to Dostoyevsky.

RICHARD WAGNER (1813–83). The German composer whose innovatory operas and music-dramas were a potent cultural influence in the late nineteenth and early twentieth centuries. Conrad remarked that *Almayer's Folly* 'ends with a long *solo* for Almayer which is almost as long as Tristan's in Wagner'; and the heroine of 'Freya of the Seven Isles' likes to 'play fierce Wagner music in the flicker of blinding flashes'. It may be coincidental that both Wagner's *Ring* cycle and *Nostromo* have the theme that treasure confers both power and a curse, causing dissension and treachery while destroying love.

ALFRED RUSSEL WALLACE (1823–1913). The British naturalist, traveller and evolutionist. Richard Curle once wrote that Conrad 'loved old memoirs and travels – and I think Wallace's *Malay Archipelago* was his favourite bedside book'. Details from *Malay Archipelago* helped to provide local colour for *Lord Jim* and *The Rescue*.

H.G. WELLS (1866–1946). Writer of novels, tales, essays and histories, whose virtuosity in science fiction brought him great popular success. His unstable, initially warm, friendship with Conrad began when he reviewed *An Outcast of the Islands* in 1896: 'Only greatness could make books of which the detailed workmanship was so copiously bad, so well worth reading, so convincing, and so stimulating.' Wells's *The Time Machine* and *The War of the Worlds* may have had some influence on 'Heart of Darkness' and *The Inheritors*.

Eventually, the two writers disagreed strongly. Conrad said: 'The difference between us, Wells, is fundamental. You don't care for humanity but think they are to be improved. I love humanity but know they are not.' In *Boon*, Wells jeered at 'the florid mental gestures of a Conrad': 'Conrad "writes". And it shows.'

BRUNO WINAWER (1883–1944). Polish author of short stories and comedies; Conrad helped him by translating his play *Księga Hioba* into English as *The Book of Job* (1921). This was Conrad's sole translation of a literary text.

Further reading

Bibliographies

K.A. LOHF and E.P. SHEEHY, *Joseph Conrad at Mid-Century* (Minneapolis: University of Minnesota Press, 1957).

T.G. EHRSAM, *A Bibliography of Joseph Conrad* (Metuchen, New Jersey: Scarecrow Press, 1969).

B.E. TEETS and H.E. GERBER, *Joseph Conrad: An Annotated Bibliography of Writings about Him* (De Kalb, Illinois: Illinois University Press, 1971).

Conradiana magazine frequently publishes bibliographical supplements.

Editions of Conrad's works

The 'Collected Edition' which was published by J.M. Dent between 1946 and 1955 became, through accessibility and frequent citation, a 'standard' British edition; it was incomplete, however. Cambridge University Press is producing a scholarly edition of the whole canon. Most of Conrad's works are inexpensively available in Penguin and Oxford paperbacks. The Norton edition of 'Heart of Darkness' has abundant paraphernalia.

Editions of Conrad's letters

G. JEAN-AUBRY, *Joseph Conrad: Life & Letters* (two volumes; London: Heinemann, 1927).

Letters from Conrad 1895 to 1924, ed. Edward Garnett (London: Nonesuch, 1928).

Conrad's Polish Background, ed. Z. Najder (London: Oxford University Press, 1964).

Joseph Conrad's Letters to R. B. Cunninghame Graham, ed. C. Watts (London: Cambridge University Press, 1969).

The Collected Letters of Joseph Conrad, ed. Frederick R. Karl and Laurence Davies (Cambridge: Cambridge University Press; Vol. I, 1983; Vol. II, 1986; Vol. III, 1988; Vol. IV, 1990).

Biographies

JOCELYN BAINES, *Joseph Conrad: A Critical Biography* (London: Weidenfeld and Nicolson, 1960; Harmondsworth: Penguin, 1971).

JERRY ALLEN, *The Sea Years of Joseph Conrad* (N.Y.: Doubleday, 1965; London: Methuen, 1967).

BERNARD C. MEYER, *Joseph Conrad: A Psychoanalytic Biography* (Princeton, N.J.: Princeton University Press, 1967).

NORMAN SHERRY, *Conrad and His World* (London: Thames & Hudson, 1972).

FREDERICK R. KARL, *Joseph Conrad: The Three Lives* (N.Y.: Farrar, Straus & Giroux; London: Faber & Faber, 1979).

IAN WATT, *Conrad in the Nineteenth Century* (Berkeley: California University Press, 1979; London: Chatto & Windus, 1980).

ZDZISŁAW NAJDER, *Joseph Conrad: A Chronicle* (Cambridge: Cambridge University Press, 1983).

CEDRIC WATTS, *Joseph Conrad: A Literary Life* (London: Macmillan, 1989).

OWEN KNOWLES, *A Conrad Chronology* (Boston, Mass.: Hall, 1990).

Reminiscences

FORD MADOX FORD, *Joseph Conrad: A Personal Remembrance* (London: Duckworth, 1924).

JESSIE CONRAD, *Joseph Conrad as I Knew Him* (London: Heinemann, 1926).

BORYS CONRAD, *My Father: Joseph Conrad* (London: Calder & Boyars, 1970).

JOHN CONRAD, *Joseph Conrad: Times Remembered* (London: Cambridge University Press, 1981).

Joseph Conrad: Interviews and Recollections, ed. Martin Ray (London: Macmillan, 1990).

Criticism

Early reviews of Conrad: *Conrad: The Critical Heritage*, ed. Norman Sherry (London: Routledge & Kegan Paul, 1973).

MAX BEERBOHM, ' "The Feast" by J-s-ph C-nr-d' in *A Christmas Garland* (London: Heinemann, 1912).

F.R. LEAVIS, *The Great Tradition* (London: Chatto & Windus, 1948).

DOUGLAS HEWITT, *Conrad: A Reassessment* (Cambridge: Bowes & Bowes, 1952).

THOMAS MOSER, *Joseph Conrad: Achievement and Decline* (Cambridge, Mass.: Harvard University Press, 1957).

ALBERT GUERARD, *Conrad the Novelist* (Cambridge, Mass.: Harvard University Press, 1958).

The Art of Joseph Conrad: A Critical Symposium, ed. R.W. Stallman (East Lansing: Michigan State University Press, 1960).

ELOISE KNAPP HAY, *The Political Novels of Joseph Conrad* (Chicago and London: Chicago University Press, 1963).

ANDRZEJ BUSZA, 'Conrad's Polish Literary Background . . . . .': *Antemurale* X (Rome: Institutum Historicum Polonicum, 1966).

AVROM FLEISHMAN, *Conrad's Politics* (Baltimore: Johns Hopkins, 1967).

PAUL KIRSCHNER, *Conrad: The Psychologist as Artist* (Edinburgh: Oliver & Boyd, 1968).

TERRY EAGLETON, *Criticism and Ideology* (London: NLB, 1976).

ADAM GILLON, 'Conrad's Reception in Poland for the Last Sixty Years': *Joseph Conrad: A Commemoration*, ed. Norman Sherry (London: Macmillan, 1976).

CEDRIC WATTS, *Conrad's 'Heart of Darkness': A Critical and Contextual Discussion* (Milan: Mursia International, 1977).

CHINUA ACHEBE, 'An Image of Africa': *The Chancellor Lecture Series 1974–75* (Amherst: University of Massachussets, 1976); reprinted in *Massachusetts Review*, 18 (Autumn 1977); revised and reprinted in *Heart of Darkness*, ed. Robert Kimbrough (3rd edn: N.Y.: Norton, 1988), with responses by Wilson Harris, Frances B. Singh and C.P. Sarvan.

J.A. VERLEUN, *The Stone Horse* (Groningen: Boema's Boekhuis, 1978).

FREDRIC JAMESON, *The Political Unconscious: Narrative as a Socially Symbolic Act* (London: Methuen, 1981).

CEDRIC WATTS, *The Deceptive Text: An Introduction to Covert Plots* (Brighton: Harvester, 1984).

ROBERT SECOR and DEBRA MODDELMOG: *Joseph Conrad and American Writers* (Westport, Conn.; London: Greenwood Press, 1985).

NINA PELIKAN STRAUS, 'The Exclusion of the Intended': *Novel*, 20 (Winter, 1987).

EDWARD SAID, 'Through Gringo Eyes': *Harper's Magazine*, 276 (April, 1988).

JAKOB LOTHE, *Conrad's Narrative Method* (Oxford: Oxford University Press, 1989).

JOHANNA M. SMITH, ' "Too Beautiful Altogether": Patriarchal Ideology in *Heart of Darkness': Joseph Conrad: 'Heart of Darkness': A Case Study in Contemporary Criticism*, ed. Ross C. Murfin (N.Y.: St Martin's Press, 1989).

CEDRIC WATTS, *Joseph Conrad: 'Nostromo'* (London: Penguin, 1990).

BETTE LONDON, *The Appropriated Voice: Narrative Authority in Conrad, Forster, and Woolf* (Ann Arbor: Michigan University Press, 1990).

DAPHNA ERDINAST-VULCAN, *Joseph Conrad and the Modern Temper* (Oxford: Oxford University Press, 1991).

ELAINE SHOWALTER, *Sexual Anarchy* (London: Bloomsbury, 1991).

RUTH NADELHAFT, *Joseph Conrad* (Hemel Hempstead: Harvester Wheatsheaf, 1991).

Conrad's Cities: Essays for Hans van Marle, ed. Gene M. Moore (Amsterdam and Atlanta: Rodopi, 1992).

Recommended films based on Conrad's works

The Shadow-Line, directed by Andrzej Wajda, 1976.
The Duellists, dir. Ridley Scott, 1977.
Apocalypse Now, dir. Francis Coppola, 1979.

Periodicals devoted to Conrad

Conradiana: A Journal of Joseph Conrad Studies (published by Texas Tech University at Lubbock).
Joseph Conrad Today (Philadelphia).
The Conradian: Journal of the Joseph Conrad Society (UK) (London).
JCS (Italy) Newsletter (Pisa).
L'Epoque Conradienne (Limoges).
The Conrad News: Polish Conradian Club (Gdańsk).

General Index

Index

Warsaw, 9, 11
Warsaw Uprising, 11
Watt, Ian, 102, 115
Weber, Max, 168
Welles, Orson, 186
Wells, H.G., 32, 112, 205–6;
 The Island of Doctor Moreau, 90–1;
 quoted, 91;
 The Time Machine, 83; quoted, 83;
 Tono-Bungay, 186
Whistler, J.M., 112
Whyte, William, 168
Wilde, Oscar, 95;
 Preface to *Dorian Gray*, quoted,
 93–4

Williams, A.P., 24
Williams, Gordon,
 The Duellists, 41
Winawer, Bruno, 206
Winchell, Alexander, quoted, 83
Wittgenstein, Ludwig, 129
Woolf, Leonard, 40
Woolf, Virginia, 186–7
World War I, 37
Wouk, Herman, 189

Yeats, W.B., 94

Żeromski, Stefan, 100

Index to Conrad's Works